52-5385

9/10/72

RUSSIAN RESEARCH CENTER STUDIES

* Publications of the Harvard Project on the Soviet Social System.

RUSSIAN RESEARCH CENTER STUDIES 7

THE NEW MAN IN
SOVIET PSYCHOLOGY

The Russian Research Center of Harvard University is supported by a grant from the Carnegie Corporation. The Center carries out interdisciplinary study of Russian institutions and behavior and related subjects.

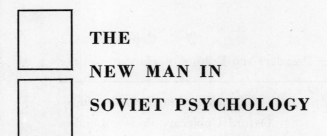

THE
NEW MAN IN
SOVIET PSYCHOLOGY

Raymond A. Bauer

HARVARD UNIVERSITY PRESS · CAMBRIDGE

1959

This volume was prepared under a grant
from the Carnegie Corporation of New
York. That Corporation is not, however,
the author, owner, publisher, or pro-
prietor of this publication and is not to
be understood as approving by virtue of
its grant any of the statements made or
views expressed therein.

Library of Congress Catalog Card Number 52–5385

Printed in the United States of America

TO
Alice and Linda

PREFACE

It is axiomatic in the field of Soviet studies that one is never right; he is only wrong with varying degrees of vulnerability. In this area more than in most the writer must make the choice between avoiding risks and eliciting the maximum of meaning from the material. Obviously no one person can hope to command adequately all the skills and knowledge that a work such as this demands. Relying on the charity and forbearance of the community of scholars, I have chosen to run risks rather than sacrifice meaning.

This book is essentially an essay in the history of ideas. It is partially a history of the science of psychology in the Soviet Union, partially a study of the pattern of social change in that country, largely an analysis of changing conceptions of human nature under conditions of social change, to a certain extent an inquiry in the relation of ideology to action, somewhat a study of the relationship of psychology to society. Being so many things, it is not satisfactorily any one of them. I have tried particularly to avoid excessive documentation, so that the general reader might not be diverted from the main argument of the book. The specialist will find a more detailed treatment of the work of psychologists, and a vastly greater source of bibliographical references in my doctoral thesis "The Conception of Man in Soviet Psychology," on deposit at the Harvard College Library, Cambridge, Massachusetts.

There are certain topics with which it would have been tempting to deal, but which I have deliberately not touched on. I have not discussed the assumptions about human nature which are found in pre-Revolutionary Marxist writings. I have not done this because I feel that the question of the orthodoxy of the position taken by Soviet Marxists at any subsequent period is peripheral to the question of why a particular interpretation was put on Marxist doctrine. There was in Marxist writings a sufficient store of ideological weapons to arm both sides of the controversy. What was important was the reason for selecting one rather than another view. The writings of Marx and Engels on human nature are treated in Vernon Venable's book, *Human Nature: The Marxian View* (New York: Alfred Knopf, 1945).

The problems and material of Soviet psychiatry are sufficiently different from those of psychology, so that an adequate treatment of these topics would have demanded a separate book. Because of the inherent interest which Soviet psychiatry has for the American reading public, I would have attempted some coverage of this topic if it had not been for the publication of Dr. Joseph Wortis' *Soviet Psychiatry* (Baltimore: Williams and Wilkins, 1950). There are some rather basic points of disagreement between Dr. Wortis' interpretation of the political and social context in which Soviet sciences operate and the interpretation presented here, but this does not detract from the value of the psychiatric material he has gathered. I wish also to take the opportunity to thank Dr. Wortis for his generous sharing of materials with me during the period in which we were both doing research, and for the many stimulating conversations we have had on this topic.

In recent years there has been a spate of books and articles about political interference with science in the Soviet Union. They have been devoted almost exclusively to demonstrating the fact of political intervention, a matter about which there was some need for educating the citizens of Western countries. The effect of these writings has been to illustrate that the Soviet system operates according to an entirely different set of values than ours does—which is worth restating—and to generate in Western readers feelings of righteous indignation, certainly one of the most comforting of human sentiments. This book attempts to take one step beyond this and to inquire into the rationale behind interference in one science, psychology, and thereby to get further insight into the nature of the system.

Leninists are fond of insisting that the scholar who studies a phenomenon and demonstrates the causal relationships that account for its existence tends to become an apologist for that phenomenon. This is a point which Leninists have in common with other critics. While everyone grants that the Soviet Union is a potent political and military threat to the West, somehow it must be insisted simultaneously that the system does not work. It is my belief that the Soviet system is based on a set of values to which we in the West are antipathetic, but it is a system which has both strengths and weaknesses. The fact that in this book we are dealing with one of its areas of greatest weakness should not lead us to overconfidence. To deal with this system effectively we must understand it in its own terms. For this purpose we need to scrutinize it with cold objectivity, particularly avoiding the temptation to easy self-delusion about its internal weaknesses.

In the Soviet field one works always from small islands of information, and he is compelled often to infer what lies between these islands. I have tried at all points to indicate the degree of certainty or uncertainty with which I feel my statements are established.

Some comment is also in order about the sources I have used. This book is based primarily on official Soviet sources, and these sources pose some problems of interpretation. In using these sources, I have drawn on the accumulated experience of Western scholars working with Soviet materials, and on my own background of research in the Soviet field. In addition, I have been able to check occasional points against the testimony of Westerners who have observed some of the events dealt with in this book, and also have had the opportunity to talk to Soviet émigrés who had been involved in many of these events.

The procurement of sources was in itself a major problem. Utilizing the combined resources of the major libraries of the country, and of a few private individuals who had rare materials in their possession, I was able to assemble an almost complete collection of the Soviet psychological journals for all periods, copies of almost all major textbooks published since the Revolution, and a fair representation of other works.

The major psychological journals ceased publication in the period 1932–1934, and after these years, publication facilities for psychological research were very sparse until 1946, when the serial publications of the Academy of Pedagogical Sciences were inaugurated. In the intervening period, large quantities of psychological research went unpublished. At all times, and in this period in particular, the publication of psychological research has been so widely distributed through such a variety of publication media that a systematic treatment of the empirical work of Soviet psychologists has seemed to me to be unfeasible. Accordingly, I have more or less limited the discussion to theoretical positions which have been accepted as officially correct at various periods of time, and I have concentrated on the reasons for the adoption of a particular point of view at a particular point in time.

Especially after 1930, there has been virtually no opportunity for the expression of "noncorrect" views in print. This makes it more difficult to establish whether or not such "incorrect" views are held in private (as indeed they must be) or what covert role such ideas play in the development of the science. At the same time, this enforced homogeneity of expression simplifies enormously the problem of sampling printed sources. Recognizing the limitations of the material available to me, I have tried to trim my analysis accordingly. The reader himself will have to be the final judge of the adequacy of the precautions I have taken.

The problem of how to render Russian names in English can never be solved without some residual complications. A consistent system of transliteration often compels one to render in an unfamiliar form names with which American readers are familiar. (Thus, Blonsky becomes Blonskii.) My practice has been to follow the Library of Congress system of transliteration for all names and titles, even when occasionally a given author may be familiar to American readers in another form. (Thus, Vigotsky, or Vygotsky, becomes Vygotskii.) An exception has been made for a few persons of prominence where a change of the accepted English usage would be a needless pedanticism. (Thus, Trotsky does not become Trotskii.)

Having been a person who viewed the acknowledgments which other writers appended to their works as *pro forma* gracious gestures, I have become increasingly impressed with the extent to which one is concretely in debt to so many people for the effective completion of any sizable piece of research. My first debts are to my wife Alice and my daughter Linda, who have been extremely patient in the face of an extended disruption of our home life. To Alice I owe additional thanks for editorial assistance in preparing the manuscript, and to Linda for promising to read the book as soon as she thinks she is up to it. Jerome S. Bruner not only gave me patient tutelage during my several years of graduate work, but most careful guidance in the execution of this project. The Russian Research Center; its sponsor, the Carnegie Corporation; and the Center's Director, Clyde Kluckhohn, are to be thanked for very generous financial assistance. Professor Kluckhohn must be doubly thanked for many kind and helpful suggestions. Talcott Parsons, of the Department of Social Relations at Harvard, has sharpened my understanding of the working of society, and has given much time and attention to advising me on this present study. Gordon W. Allport suggested the problem to me, and impressed me with its importance when I could see only its difficulty.

My colleague, Ivan D. London, has been exceedingly generous in sharing with me his materials and experience. It has been my good fortune to have had close contact with him, during the final revision of this manuscript, when I could benefit from his own detailed studies of present trends in Soviet psychology. To Alex Inkeles I owe more apologies than thanks for the extent to which I have intruded unsparingly in his busy schedule for assistance only he could give. John Zawadsky not only was patient in checking the references of the manuscript, but tolerant in untangling my handling of philosophical concepts. Many of my colleagues of the Russian Research Center have been helpful in a variety of ways, and except for each of them the present work would be poorer. The following have each helped substantially in improving the content of this work or in preparing the manuscript: Harold Berman, Sally Cheney, Robert Daniels, Ada Dziewanowski, Miriam Haskell, Irene Hay, Donald Hunt, Rose Kelly, Alfred Meyer, Catherine Prince, Joan Silverman, Richard Suter, and Mary Wyle.

As a member of the Harvard Interview Project in Germany in 1950–51, I had the opportunity to talk to scores of ex-Soviet citizens, scholars, psychologists, historians, teachers, people from all walks of life. Many of them were persons who themselves had experienced the events dealt with in this book. With their help I have been able to understand better the life situation of the Soviet citizen, and particularly of the Soviet scholar. Furthermore, their testimony has been a very rewarding record against which to check generalizations arrived at from printed sources.

While a draft of the present book existed before my participation in the Harvard Refugee Interview Project, sponsored by Air Force Contract 33 (038)–12909, my participation in this project added very substantially to my comprehension of many of the issues involved and contributed much to the final version of the book. My gratitude is therefore expressed to the Human Resources Research Institute of the Air University for its support of this Project.

It would indeed be an omission not to realize the degree of dependence on early teachers. John C. Eberhart and Melville J. Herskovits have both been kinder and more helpful than I could hope for over the years since I first began my studies under them at Northwestern University. My only regret is that I have not been able to express my gratitude to them sooner.

R. A. B.

Cambridge, Massachusetts
September, 1951

CONTENTS

FOREWORD

One can find no better key to the internal logic of a society than its conception of man and his place in nature. Perhaps it is a paradox that we sense most vividly the conception of man in our own or in another society when that conception is changing. Western man's image of himself has undergone so many and so profound changes in the past six centuries—and particularly in the last one—that he has become acutely sensitized to the problem of defining what he is.

There is a more profound basis for this sensitivity. For the centuries behind us were marked not only by change but by a devaluation of man's place in nature. From a place at the center of the pre-Copernican universe man has been pushed outward to a position in an impersonal solar system. Man in the image of God has been replaced by man as a phase in the phylogenetic series. Locke's formulation of infinite perfectibility, culminating a steady development in the idea of inevitable progress, has given way to a new despair in man's irrationality. In every period since the Renaissance there has been a goad to self-awareness contained in the never-resolved conflict between the Hellenic conception of "man the measure" and the Judaic query: "What is man that thou art mindful of him?"

Indeed, one can argue that it was a change in the conception of man—a change growing out of the rational-scientific revolution of the eighteenth and nineteenth centuries—that created the basis for modern scientific psychology. For the doctrine that man is a suitable topic for objective study is neither ancient nor universal. By whatever change in circumstances it came about, psychology has grown into the privileged but precarious position of defining with primary if not exclusive authority what the nature of man is.

Why precarious? Dostoevsky's Grand Inquisitor berates Christ, returned miraculously to Toledo, for giving to man an image of himself that complicates infinitely the task of the Church in guarding the True Faith. John Dewey in one vein and Vernon Parrington in another speak of the need for a psychology that may support democracy. For man's image of the nature of man is not only a matter for objective inquiry; it is and has always been a prime instrument of social and political control. He who molds that image does so with enormous consequences for the society in which he lives.

In an open society, committed to the universality of reason, an unfettered psychology takes its place in the debate on man. What we have learned in our own time is that when the open society moves toward the conception that both power and rationality must be exercised by the few, psychology can no longer remain an unfettered party to the debate on man. The first shock was Nazi psychology, whose foundations were crudely warped to conform to barbaric conceptions of race. The crudeness and stupidity of Nazi psychological perversions are, as Mr. Bauer remarks, a reflection of the intellectual poverty of the leaders of National Socialism—a leadership committed to anti-intellectualism and a mystic romanticism about Aryan man. However crude the efforts of National Socialism, what we must not overlook is that for the first time on a large and conspicuous scale psychology was officially exploited as an instrument of national policy.

Soviet psychology is no such simple case of crude perversion in the interest of maintaining power for a ruling group. Mr. Bauer presents in this book the subtle interplay of social and intellectual forces that have molded the official Soviet conception of man culminating in what he has called the New Soviet Man. Those who wish to understand the logic of Soviet society must understand the curious blend of intellectualism and political activism that goes into the Communist science of man. And those who would fully appreciate the place of psychology in any society may well study this painstaking case study in intellectual history. For, as Mr. Bauer points out with an admirable directness, Soviet psychology is considerably more than an *ad hoc* reflex to compelling political circumstances.

It has grown not only from Marxist and Leninist sources but also from the prevailing materialistic mechanism of pre-Revolutionary Russian psychology. More than that, it has been washed by the changing currents of psychology outside the Soviet Union—at various times and under various circumstances by Freud, by *Gestalttheorie*, by American behaviorism, and by less well-known currents as well. But, as Mr. Bauer remarks, the extent to which and the way in which the psychologies of the times have been incorporated in Soviet thinking has been markedly affected by two sets of requirements faced by the regime: the one ideological, the other circumstantial. Early in the regime, for example, it became necessary to jettison the environmentalism of some of Marx's thinking: it became increasingly difficult to account for the ills of man by referring to an environment now under the control of the proletariat, even by invoking "capitalist vestiges." But revision to a more suitable point of view had to fulfill two and perhaps three requirements. First, it had to be reconciled with Leninism as interpreted by the newly ascendant Stalin. Second, it had to be reconciled with the educational, political, and social requirements facing the new State. And third, perhaps, it had to be represented to Russian psychologists and intellectuals in such a way that it not only escaped the taint of opportunism but also seemed a just and important step to be taken "in the public interest." And throughout, the discussion must maintain a ring of scientific verisimilitude.

Over the years, as circumstances have changed, Soviet psychology has undergone one or perhaps several revolutions. From a view of man as a creature of the forces of the environment and therefore of the historical process, there has evolved a new image of man capable of self-initiation, responsible for his actions, neither controlled by the environment nor by heredity—a picture of man capable of being an activist and at the same time capable of being the source of his own error and evil. His freedom rests not in indeterminacy but in his capacity for recognizing necessity. The early excoriations of consciousness as a concept smacking of bourgeois idealism has come full round: consciousness is now a central process in making man capable of forging his own destinies—or even of committing punishable crimes against the state. The reward of Stakhanovism and the punishment of treason are both justified. The intent has surely not all been fully conscious, nor have all the aims been narrowly political. The outcome has been a subtle and changing tapestry of controversy, directive, and reformulation which Professor Bauer sets forth with incisiveness and perspective.

Whether the Soviet regime has managed to keep the creative loyalties of its psychologists while directing their activity from above and whether the psychologists have been successful in convincing their countrymen of their changing views—these things we do not know. It is quite clear that Russian scientists are still doing creative work in psychology, sometimes in areas where the rules are not too fully prescribed, sometimes in areas where the rules do not conflict with the pursuit of interesting problems. This book, in any case, is not

an assessment of the success or failure of psychology in the
Soviet Union or of the effectiveness of the controls placed
upon it by the regime. It is, rather, an attempt to see the
changing conception of man in Soviet psychology as a reflection of the changing ideological, political, and practical pressures that have formed and transformed the Soviet Union.

Mr. Bauer has performed a service not only to his psychological colleagues but also to the general reader interested in
Soviet affairs. For this book is at once an essay in psychological
history and a study in political control. If we are to understand the sources of Soviet action, to respond to Russia as
something more than a screen upon which we project our
fears or aspirations, we shall have to depend increasingly upon
the kind of broad scholarship, humane sensibility, and lively
intelligence that informs this book. Mr. Bauer has succeeded
in bringing to bear on his subject a mature knowledge both of
psychology and of Soviet history and ideology, along with
an appreciation of the place of ideas in the realm of action.

Jerome S. Bruner

Institute for Advanced Study
December 26, 1951

THE NEW MAN IN
SOVIET PSYCHOLOGY

"*Every organized society is built upon a concept of the nature of man and of his function and place in society. Whatever its truth as a picture of human nature, this concept always gives a true picture of the nature of the society which recognizes and identifies itself with it.*"—Peter F. Drucker, *The End of Economic Man in Europe* (New York: John Day, 1939), p. 45.

1 THE RELATIONSHIP OF PSYCHOLOGY TO SOCIETY

Every society has in its institutions broad assumptions about human nature: Man is naturally good, or he is naturally bad. He is primarily rational, or he is primarily emotional. Human nature can be changed, or it cannot be changed. Man's personality and behavior are determined by external forces, or he himself has control over and is responsible for his behavior. He is motivated primarily by hedonism, altruism, desire for material goods, patriotism, or any one of the variety of motives that have been found in man. The adoption of any of these propositions has broad implications for the society involved. It indicates whether the society is oriented toward change or stability, whether individuals in the society will be treated "kindly" or "strictly," whether social mobility will be encouraged or discouraged, whether close controls over human behavior will be enforced, or whether man will be left pretty much to go his own way. Such assumptions are reflected in the legal system, the system of education, in literature and art, in the economic system of the society. In fact, it can be said without qualification that, although there is some variation in the consistency of such assumptions from situation to situation in various societies, even for the most heterogeneous of societies it is possible to identify a dominant set of such assumptions, and that they are an essential element in understanding the nature of that society.

When one can describe the basic conception of human nature which is held in a given society he has come a long way toward understanding the nature of that society. When, as in the case of the Soviet Union, he can see this conception in formation—when, in fact he can see one set of assumptions tried and rejected, and replaced by a contrasting set of assumptions—the insight which can be gained into the essence of the system is enhanced. Even though focusing primarily on assumptions about human nature as they are expressed in the personality theories of Soviet psychologists, this book has also the broader goal of understanding the conception of man that underlines the Soviet system, and thereby contributing to the understanding of the system itself.

The science of psychology occupies an anomalous position with respect to the conception of man held in society. It is the discipline explicitly concerned with arriving at a scientifically formulated, empirically tested definition of the nature of man, and might, therefore, be expected to be the source to which social and political theorists would turn in formulating their ideas about human nature. To an extent this is true. But, on the other hand, there is no denying the fact that many of the basic assumptions of the psychologist are themselves not empirically derived but are taken from the values and ideas prevalent in a given society at a given time, or from the methodological fads prevalent in the scientific ethos of the time. Ironically, this is particularly true of the more general propositions about human nature that underlie psychological theories. John Dewey marked this at the turn of the century and said that "in this sense, psychology is a political science." [1] Even though the progress of psychological research since that time has broadened the body of empirically established propositions, the influence of the culture and of prevailing practical circumstances on the science of psychology has not been entirely abolished. During the thirties American psychologists affirmed the superiority of democratic leadership and stressed the possibility for equalizing differences between races by training, while German psychologists supported the doctrines of racism and authoritarianism by empirical research.[2]

The theories of psychologists and prevailing political and social ideas act upon each other. The findings of psychological research carry political and social implications and influence social and political ideas, just as social and political ideas influence the areas of interest of the psychologist and often condition his basic assumptions. Only by studying each instance in its own terms can we establish the direction and extent of influence of psychological theories on society and vice versa. There can be no doubt, however, that the psychologist's theories of personality and the assumptions about human nature prevalent in society are related. As Bertrand Russell observed facetiously, even the experimental animals used by psychologists seem to reflect the national character of the experimenters: "Animals studied by Americans rush about frantically, with an incredible hustle and pep, and at last achieve the desired result by chance. Animals observed by Germans sit still and think, and at last evolve the solution out of their inner consciousness."[3]

Beyond the inherent interest which the study of any aspect of the Soviet system has because of the role of the USSR in the world today, the study of the development of psychological theory in the Soviet Union has certain additional attractions. One is the magnitude of the social change, much of it controlled and directed, that has taken place since the time of the Revolution—thus offering an approximation of a laboratory situation. Another is the fact that Marxism is associated in the popular mind with a particular conception of human nature, one which we shall see has been largely

discarded in the Soviet Union. A third is the fact that Soviet
leaders have continually and strenuously proclaimed that their
social and political theories are "the only truly scientific theories" in the world, and if one were to take these statements at
face value, he would expect the empirical research of psychologists to have a great deal of influence on the theories of politicians. Finally, and seemingly paradoxical in the light of the
third point, the Soviet leaders subject Soviet science to active
and explicitly political interference to an extent unheard of in
any other modern state. Because the theoretical formulations
and the practical work of psychologists have such important
political and social implications, the study of Soviet psychology is particularly adapted to an understanding of this paradox of science's being simultaneously highly valued and subject to political control. Further, we shall find that tracing the
relationship between the social changes which have taken
place in the USSR and the changes which have taken place
in the science of psychology throws very considerable light
on the essential nature of these social changes themselves.

From the early days of the Bolshevik regime to the present
the discipline of psychology in the USSR has undergone a
number of fundamental changes—one might even refer to
them as revolutions—which cannot be understood except as a
function of social and political conditions in the Soviet Union.
Psychology has changed from an empirical, relatively independent science, which strove to arrive by investigation at
general laws that could be applied to social living, to a relatively unempirical, applied science which is enjoined to make
theory follow practice. In range of activity, Soviet psychology has narrowed from an extremely broad discipline which
studied animal and human, normal and abnormal, child and
adult subjects, to one which focuses most of its attention on
the study of normal, human children.

In the earlier period the range of application of psychology extended to the full breadth of industrial psychology, medical and abnormal psychology, criminology and delinquency, the study of social attitudes, child and educational psychology, and testing and guidance in the schools. In addition, a wide range of theoretical work was done and a variety of theoretical positions tolerated. Today, virtually all of applied psychology is confined to developing techniques of education and to training the New Soviet Man. A limited amount of work is done in such areas of application as medical psychology, vast fields of applications are forbidden, and there is, for practical purposes, only one theoretical position allowed.

Viewed in the light of psychological theories of the twenties, man was a machine, an adaptive machine which did not initiate action but merely *re*-acted to stimuli from its environment. Concepts like "consciousness" and "will" were suspect; they smacked of subjectivism, voluntarism, idealism. After all, man and his behavior were determined by antecedent social and biological conditions. Man as depicted in present day Soviet psychology is not passive in the face of his environment. He takes the initiative away from his environment. Rather than being determined by his environment, he determines it. Furthermore, he shapes his own character by training and by "self-training." Whereas the proper subject of psychological behavior in the twenties was objective behavior—the correlation of external stimuli with externally observable responses—today psychology is the study of consciousness, "the highest form of organized matter" and the instrument whereby man shapes himself and his environment.

The problem is: what do these changes in psychology mean in terms of political events and social and economic developments in the USSR? Briefly, one may say that developments in psychology have reflected the resolution of the conflict between two doctrinal trends in Marxism. One corresponds to the popular conception of Marxism, but has been referred to by the Bolsheviks, particularly in the last twenty years, as "vulgar Marxism." It is materialist, mechanist, and deterministic—materialist in that it holds for the reality of matter independent of the perceiver, and stresses the importance of material factors over ideas in life; mechanist in that the basic model for all theories is that of a machine which is essentially a system of levers and is moved by the application of external force; deterministic in that it considers all events of the universe to be subject to rigid causality, but most especially in that it places a strong emphasis on the inevitability and predictability of future events. The other trend, the one which currently reigns in the Soviet Union, is materialist insofar as it holds for the reality of matter independent of the perceiver, but it accords a far more important role to ideas and consciousness in the affairs of man than does the first trend. It is non-mechanist in that the basic model for all theories is closer to that of an organism than to that of a machine, and it sees movement as generated from within rather than as a result of the application of external force. Finally, it is deterministic only in a special and restricted sense. Without denying the basic principle of determinism it provides for the occurrence of accident, and specifically opposes a rigid conception of the inevitability of future events.

The conflict between these two doctrinal schools was far more than an academic controversy. The importance of the differences between these points of view was that the question under debate was that of man's role in history and, by immediate implication, the nature of man and the nature of society. The controversy came to a head in concrete problems of economic planning, and it was expressed in developments in law, education, literature, art. In fact, the entire pattern of social change which has been called the Stalinist Revolution—the violent change in direction that took place after 1928—is bound to this doctrinal conflict.

The issue was usually phrased as one of "spontaneity" versus "intervention," of "genetics" versus "teleology." What these phrases meant in practice was whether in the development of Soviet society one was to place preëminent emphasis on the tendencies immanent in the situation (a deterministic and semi-quietistic attitude) or whether emphasis should be placed on the goals for which one was striving (a voluntaristic attitude).

The term "spontaneity" in this context has a broader meaning than is ordinarily ascribed to it. "Spontaneous" usually refers to the free, uninhibited action of a person. Obviously the root meaning is that of any action which is self-generated and not influenced from outside. Thus, the Marxist use of the term refers to those elements in a situation which are following their own course. A "reliance on spontaneity" means sitting passively and letting the operation of automatic laws do the work.

The conflict over "spontaneity" and "intervention" was essentially resolved in 1930 in favor of the latter point of view. During the next several years—between 1930 and 1938—partially as a result of this shift in orientation toward man's role in society, and partially as a result of the concrete problems of industrialization and of the collectivization of agriculture, the institutions of Soviet society were more closely coördinated with the over-all goals of the state: there was more intervention and less reliance on spontaneous processes. The dominant conception of man became that of an increasingly purposeful being, who was more and more the master of his own fate, and less and less the creature of his environment. It is to these changes in society that we shall relate the changes in the theories and activities of Soviet psychologists.

The specific questions of psychology with which we shall be concerned are: (1) What assumptions have been made in the various periods of Soviet history about the determinateness or the voluntary nature of human behavior? (2) What has been assumed about human motivation in each period? (3) What assumptions have been made about the plasticity of human nature? These questions have traditionally been the questions in psychology which were most controversial from a political viewpoint. They have in fact been the pivotal questions around which development in psychology in the Soviet Union turned.

The influence of social and political factors on the discipline on psychology can be assumed only when concretely demonstrated. Psychology as a science is an empirical discipline which seeks for general laws of human nature by investigation. It is also an applied discipline which serves certain functions in society. Finally, it has ideological importance in that the content of its general propositions have social and political meaning. The extent to which each of these aspects of psychology is stressed varies from society to society, and from time to time in each society. The extent to which one or the other of these aspects of the discipline is given preëminence will affect the degree, direction, and nature of social influence. Since psychology is an empirical discipline, the bulk of propositions generated are a function of developments within the science. Furthermore, all psychologists in Western civilization —and Soviet psychologists are part of the Western cultural community—are affected by the work of psychologists in other societies. Hence, the influence of a particular society on psychology may be assumed only under two conditions. (1) When a development runs counter to or cannot be explained in terms of trends in the field of international psychology, but is in conformity with existing social trends in the society in question, this development may be assumed to be socially determined. (2) Or if a development is in accordance with trends internal to the discipline, it may be considered in-fluenced (partly determined) by social factors if there is *con-*

crete evidence of social facilitation of the particular trend or of the repression of another and competing trend. The mere fact of points of consistency between a given school of psychology and a given social system may be a coincidence, and social influence must be concretely demonstrated.

In the case of developments in Soviet psychology we shall find no essential discontinuity between these trends and trends in America and Western Europe. Soviet society is a system which picks and chooses from the available supply of psychological concepts in the world. One must focus his attention on the specific reasons why certain trends were facilitated and others discouraged, and not be content with the mere discovery of uniformities. He must insist on understanding the reasons behind them. The reintroduction of an idea that was originally prevalent in pre-Revolutionary Russian psychology, for example, cannot be interpreted as "the Russian character reasserting itself." Interpretations must be made on the basis of the concrete conditions under which decisions were made.

In making such interpretations one must take care to include the full range of factors which might affect psychology. Specifically, there should be no a priori commitment that either cultural factors (the influence of Marxist ideology or of Russian idea and values systems) or material factors (the conditions of social living, economic considerations, et cetera) are more important or are the determining elements. As we shall see, there is an extraordinarily close relationship between ideology and practical problems in the Soviet Union, and it is impossible to say categorically which is in general more important. Which of these factors, culture or socioeconomic considerations, will be dominant in a given situation will be determined by the relative urgency assessed to each, the relative case of manipulating each at a given time, and of the time perspective employed by the persons acting in the situation.

There remains the question of how the relationship between psychology and society is effected. The mechanisms of the mediation may be either spontaneous or directed. In most societies they are spontaneous; they are not deliberately controlled by an over-all agency according to a unified scheme. The psychologist—usually unconsciously—adopts the assumptions of his culture as "natural" or "self-evident" truths. The values of the culture facilitate or discourage the investigation of certain problems such as religion, politics, or sex. The institutions of the society stimulate the development of certain applications of psychology—industrial psychology, psychology of propaganda, the psychology of esthetic experience. In such a system individuals acting within a relatively limited frame of reference take actions whose ramifications extend beyond that frame of reference. The student of such a system sets up a scheme of analysis which systematizes these "unintended consequences." A classic example of this kind of analysis is *laissez-faire* economics, in which anarchy is raised to the level of an unseen guiding hand.

In a totalitarian state such mechanisms ideally are directed according to some over-all scheme, from some central point. To the extent that such relations are deliberately structured by persons acting with either an explicit or implicit theory, they may be said to be controlled. It must be stressed that inasmuch as these relationships in the Soviet Union are mediated by persons who have a very explicit theory of what they *should* be, we are dealing with a phenomenon qualitatively distinct from what we would find in a liberal society.

The fact that the relationship of science to society in the Soviet Union is a controlled relationship is in itself an aid in meeting the criteria outlined above for demonstrating the existence of social influence. The disadvantages of working with Soviet sources are well known. The suppression of certain types of information in Soviet publications is known, as is the absence of adequate sources of Soviet published material in the libraries of the United States. However, these handicaps are compensated for by the extent to which major policy decisions are preceded and/or followed by extensive controversies and discussions in which the issues involved and the attitudes of the parties to the controversy are made clear. It is true that at times the defeated opposition has no opportunity to state its case after a decision is made, but it is usually possible to piece out the position of the opposition from the arguments which are brought to bear against it. In any event, it is always obvious what the official position is and how the situation was viewed by the proponents of the official position, and it is with this that we are mainly concerned.

Any study of the Soviet Union has political implications, if only because people read them in. This book is not an attempt to establish the fact of political intervention in psychology. It would be naïve indeed to "discover" that which is so overtly proclaimed. This is a study of changes in the policy of control, in the reasons which were behind changes in policy, and of their effect on psychology. The Stalinist who reads this work will see in it a testimony to the wisdom of the Bolshevik Party—although it will be obvious to him that the author is himself too dull to realize it. The anti-Stalinist Marxist will consider it a documentation of the betrayal of the Revolution. The apolitical psychologist will be dismayed at the extent to which psychology is controlled. This study is concerned with what happens within the political framework, and would suffer a major set-back if the reader were to approach it primarily as an attempt to demonstrate political interference in the work of psychologists. Where efforts are made to establish the fact of such intervention it is for the purpose of building a firm foundation for the interpretations which follow.

In summary, psychology is a discipline which is strongly affected by the political and social climate in which it develops, and likewise one whose theories and applications have profound political and social implications. The theories of psychology are related, to a greater or lesser degree, to the conceptions of human nature current in a society. The study of the conception of human nature in the personality theories of Soviet psychologists, considered in the context of the historical factors affecting the development of this particular theoretical orientation, affords us an opportunity both to understand better the relationship of psychology to society and to further our comprehension of the essence of the Soviet system.

2 | TWO KINDS OF MARXISM

Soviet society was distinguished from the beginning by the facts that it was associated with an explicit body of theory and that its development was to be directed according to that body of theory toward the achievement of a specific type of social order. This society is now just as much distinguished by the extent to which that body of theory has been modified under the impact of concrete historical conditions, and by the extent to which the social order has moved in a direction quite opposite to that which had generally been anticipated.[1] When the Bolsheviks came to power, Marxist-Leninist theory was a combination of empirical sociological analysis, historical prophecy, revolutionary doctrine, and nineteenth-century rational-humanitarian values. Each element had its historical reason for being, not all were compatible with each other, and the entire corpus did not furnish an adequate guide for running the new state. In the course of approximately two decades of trial and error, consideration and reconsideration, and a considerable amount of political struggle, a new body of social theory and practice has evolved which may legitimately be called Stalinism. The changes which have taken place in Soviet psychology are but a particular manifestation of this broader pattern of social, economic, political, and ideological change. Accordingly, the discussion of the essentials of the "Stalinist revolution" in this and the following chapter are a necessary preface to the study of Soviet psychology.

The development of Stalinism involved essentially the conflict between two alternate sets of assumptions embedded in Marxism, one focused on the understanding of causal relationships, the other focused on the achievement for some purpose. The first corresponds to what has come to be known as "mechanistic Marxism," the latter as "dialectical Marxism." Setting these positions in direct opposition to each other is an unwarrantedly abstract and schematic distinction. These systems of thought were not the exclusive property of any individual or group of individuals; they were alternate assumptions which any person might use in a given situation. Every Russian Marxist used both to some extent and in some situations, but there were individual differences in the degree to which persons from situation to situation, and from time to time, tended to favor one over the other. It is equally incorrect to think that these assumptions were neatly parcelled out in any physical sense in the writings of Marx and Engels. They must both be present in some mixture in any body of writing which employs analysis as a tool to action. Once such an analysis has been made, those persons who approach this body of writing at a later date will vary in the extent to which they focus on the elements of sociological analysis and the elements of revolutionary practice.[2]

A considerable proportion of Marx's and Engels' own writings was devoted to an analysis of the institutions of capitalism and to a generalized sociological approach to history. There were two main trends to this analysis. The first was the study of the functional interrelationship of the institutions of capitalism, and the second was the study of the dynamics of capitalism, which were projected into the future to predict the fall of the capitalist system. This analysis of the functional interrelationship of the institutions of capitalism argued that the state, the law, the family, religion, and various other social institutions were essentially reflections of the economic base of the society in that they were shaped to serve the interests of the dominant class of the society. This led to the conclusion that with a change in the economic base of society these institutions would wither away—become useless and atrophy. Further, since many of these institutions were inhumane, or had inhumane aspects, there was a tendency to attribute the evils of society and the perversions of human nature to the capitalist order, and thereby to posit, by implication, the innate goodness of man. Finally, since the function of the institutions of capitalism in the service of the bourgeois class had been demonstrated, there arose the tendency for "vulgar" Marxists to regard a wide range of institutions as "bourgeois" and therefore undesirable, even though there was no other basis for objection to them. The result of this functional analysis of the institutions of capitalism was to create in many minds an anarchistic attitude toward the institutions of society, a feeling that they had no positive function in a proper society and should be dispensed with as soon as possible.

The second aspect of the Marxist analysis, stressing the inherent contradictions of capitalism and projecting them into the future, tended to give Marxist thinking a fatalistic cast. The emphasis on prediction combined with the materialist philosophy to produce a strongly deterministic orientation. There was even a tendency for some "revolutionaries" to predict but not implement revolution.

There were other things in Marxism, however, besides social analysis. Marxism was intended to be a tool of revolution, and the social analysis and predictions of Marx and Engels was made with this in mind. To a large extent this action-oriented trend in Marxism is most clearly reflected in those works devoted to the fusion of Hegel's dialectics to philosophical materialism. These were mainly early works, and often fragments published some time after the original writing. It was this corpus of thought which came in later years to be fused with the revolutionary theory and the tradition of activism that characterized Lenin's thinking.

It would be a mistake to divorce Lenin's thinking from the body of sociological analysis in traditional Marxism, or to hold that he did not at one time or another accept anarchistic assumptions which were involved in this way of thinking. However, Lenin, much more than many other Marxists, believed that one can and should intervene in the course of events. From the beginning of the century he fought with the moderates in socialism, splitting off from the Mensheviks in 1903 and developing the point of view that the Party should be composed of a small group of highly disciplined revolutionaries who would lead rather than follow the trend of social movements. He thus introduced a paradoxical element of elitism into a movement that was based on and supposedly served the interests of the masses. In fighting for the principle that the Party should take the leading role in the direction of the masses, in espousing activism in general, Lenin exploited the revolutionary potentialities of Marxism. Lenin, more than anyone else, is responsible for the development of the militant activism that characterizes present-day Bolshevism.

In contrasting the interpretations which Lenin and his one-time mentor Plekhanov gave to Marxism, Sir John Maynard says:

George Plekhanov does not appear to me to emphasize the freedom of man, so much as he emphasizes the inevitability of history. In this his interpretation was at one with the general interpretation given in Germany, where it was probably the cause of the final defeat of the Marxist party. It passed into the Menshevik doctrine, where it threw a pallor over the native hue of resolution. The Bolsheviks on the other hand transferred the emphasis to the freedom of man. They interpreted Marx as meaning, not that Communism is fated to be realized, but that, if society is to survive, Communism is the only way of escape from Capitalism's inability to provide a good life for its wage-

earners. Marxism in this form, or thus coloured, is a call to man
to make his own history.[3]

Since it is the Stalinist interpretation of Leninism with
which we are dealing in our study of social change in the
USSR, Stalin's view of Lenin's relation to the previous body
of Marxist theory is of particular interest. Stalin has stressed
the activist element in Leninism. He cited, for example, Lenin's
opposition to the theory of "spontaneity" on the ground that
reliance on the elemental forces in the social process undermined the active role of the Party. Stalin has said that if the
interpretation of social processes held by some groups at the
beginning of the century had been accepted there would have
been no need "for an independent working class party." He
suggests a mock conversation with a person who overempha-
sizes the importance of relying on spontaneous forces. Suppose, he queries, you were to ask such a person what the role
of the Party should be.

"What are you talking about?" comes the ready answer.

"Can the Party do anything to affect the working of so
decisive a factor as 'the level of the forces of production'?" [4]

Thus, the Party, in the eyes of such a person can have no
effective role in shaping history.

Lenin, says Stalin, revived the revolutionary aspects of
Marxism, which had been played down by the moderate so-
cialists, and in addition adapted Marxism to the demands of
modern conditions: "It is a fact that Lenin brought to light
once more the revolutionary social content of Marxism, which
had been glossed over by the opportunists of the Second International, but that is only a fragment of the truth. The
whole truth is that Leninism is a development of Marxism
adapting it to the new conditions of capitalism and to the class
struggle of the proletariat." [5] Thus Stalin places himself and
Lenin firmly on the side of those who favor action rather than
rely on the determinate course of events.

For particular historical reasons the question of determinism and freedom has been a central problem in the development of Marxist-Leninist thought and action. All social action—and implicitly all social theory—involves some compromise between determinacy and indeterminacy, some judgment of the extent to which one is free to act and the extent to which one is constrained by circumstance. As practical experience has made the limitations of circumstances more explicit, an ever greater emphasis has had to be placed on the power of the individual to act in such a way as to overcome these limitations. This condition evolved because early predictions based on assumed determinate relationships gave a sanguine picture of the trend of social developments—thus minimizing the emphasis which had to be placed on the role of the individual—whereas later predictions forecast conditions which could not be accepted—therefore necessitating reliance on individual action to negate the trend of determined (that is, predicted) events. An optimism based on predicted immanent developments became replaced with an "optimism" based on man's ability to make his own fate. It is not true that in every instance early predictions were optimistic and later predictions were pessimistic. It is true, however, that a particular set of early "optimistic" predictions about the withering away of the state and about the nature of socialist institutions were not realized, and it is also true that the relative weight to be assigned to "spontaneous," or determinate and noncontrolled, forces in a situation was a recurrent question in problem after problem.

The social postulates of extreme mechanistic Marxism, certainly include the following: (1) Man is a product of his inheritance and his environment; therefore society is responsible for man's character and behavior, rather than man's being responsible for society. (2) All social events are determinately related; therefore the trend of future events can be predicted.

(3) Essentially, the course of events is determined by abstract forces external to man himself, and there is little that he could or should do to direct them. (4) Since all oppressive and repressive institutions are a function of conflict in class society, a classless society will speedily do away with repression. (5) Class society is a result of a particular form of economic relations, and a change in the economic base of society will eliminate class divisions, which in turn will result in the withering away of the state and bring about ideal social conditions. (6) Man is inherently rational and inherently good; and once he is freed from the institutions of a class society, he will revert spontaneously to rationality and goodness. In addition to these premises, mechanistic Marxism posits the desirability of a freely developed and fully expressed personality, of freeing man from excessive burdens and of respecting his dignity.

Many of the premises involved in this type of thinking, and in fact some of the specific postulates outlined above, could be found in the work of virtually every Bolshevik at one time or another, and they found expression briefly in most of the Soviet social institutions. However, as the history of the Soviet Union unfolded, it became evident that these postulates were untenable in various areas of society, and factions began to develop on the basis of whether they gave predominant emphasis to the determinate trend of events or to the shaping of these events to a given goal. What had been a conflict in the minds of men became a conflict between men of different minds.

The conflicts between these two sets of postulates was resolved in two critical events. The first was a crisis in economic planning in connection with the First Five Year Plan, and the second, a controversy between the mechanists and the dialecticians in philosophy. Beginning independently, these two events converged in the late twenties to precipitate a series of parallel crises in other areas of Soviet life.

During the very early twenties the socialist goals of the Soviet state were temporarily abandoned and the New Economic Plan, a system of limited capitalism, was introduced. However, during this period of limited capitalism the Gosplan (State Planning Board, established in 1921) began work on the problem of transition to a complete socialist economy. From 1926 to the spring of 1929 the Gosplan developed two drafts of a five-year plan for economic expansion, each of which was rejected as being too conservative, and a third plan which was finally accepted. While this was happening, a torrid discussion involving very fundamental questions of economic planning was in process.

The Party found itself in a dilemma over the relationship of the industrial and agricultural sectors of the economy. Most economists agreed that these two sectors place conflicting demands on the economy. The Left wing of the Party, identified politically with Leon Trotsky, then Stalin's main political rival, argued that industrialization should be pushed at the expense of the peasantry. The Right wing, identified with Bukharin, who after Trotsky was Stalin's most important rival, argued that industrialization must be slowed down and concessions made to the peasants. Neither program seemed to offer a solution. If the program of the Left were followed, the expansion of heavy industry would involve curtailing consumer goods (already at a "famine" level) and consumer goods were needed to keep the economy running. The concessions to the peasants which the Right advocated, however, seemed to involve a dangerous, perhaps fatal, step back toward capitalism. In any event, it would certainly have meant slowing up the pace of industrialization in the Soviet Union to an extent that was incompatible with the goals of the Party.

In retrospect, the Left appears to have been correct in antic-

ipating many of the difficulties into which the economy was
drifting. The Stalinists and the Right, however, combined to
drive the Left out of the Party by 1927, leaving only the
Right and the Stalinists as effective groups in the Party. The
main theoretical controversy of the last stages of developing
the Five Year Plan took place between these two groups.

Bukharin, leader of the Right opposition, argued that the
real cause of the existing crisis was the fact that industrial expansion was proceeding too rapidly for the conditions of agricultural production. For him, the maintenance of "equilibrium" in the system was essential. The primary task of
economic planning, he said, was to determine "the conditions
of the correct co-ordination of the various spheres of production, or in other words the conditions of *dynamic economic
equilibrium.*" He went on to say that "crisis-like factors disturbing the process of production . . . can only rise from a
failure to observe the conditions of economic equilibrium." [7]
Thus he took a conservative view of the problem.

Bukharin's position was parallel to that of the "geneticists,"
a group of economists who were in opposition to a second
group, identified with the Stalinists, called the "teleologists."
Like Bukharin, the geneticists argued that the equilibrium
relations in the economy must be respected, that one could
proceed with industrialization only at a certain pace which
could be determined by analyzing the existing tendencies in
the economy. Then, given certain other data, such as the
probable increase of the population and the consumption
needs of the urban population, most of the other values in any
plan of economic development would be determined within
fairly narrow limits. Thus, they posited relatively narrow
limits within which the economic planner was free to make
decisions. Outside these limits he could merely study, extrapo-
late, and predict.

Until 1928, the Stalinist Center had played only a negative

role in the theoretical controversies. Initially, as mentioned above, they had united with the Bukharinites in opposing the Left proposals as too extreme. Now, however, they stepped forward as champions of essentially the former Left position. The Center rejected the "genetic" approach of the Right. Its economists advocated the teleological or "purposive" approach, and rejoined that "the primacy of teleology * was determined for us as far back as the days of the October revolution when we acted contrary to the 'eternal laws' of capitalist development." They added, "Our task is not to study economics but to change it. We are bound by no laws. There are no fortresses which Bolsheviks cannot storm. The question of tempos is subject to decision by human beings." [8]

The basic error of the "Right opportunists" lay in their miscomprehension of the dynamics of social development, it was said. This originated in their mechanistic approach to change. For example, Bukharin held that the Kulaks would gradually be absorbed into the socialist structure, whereas the "dialecticians" argued that the trend of events would intensify rather than ameliorate the class struggle.[9] Further, while the Right "proved" by their projections that the Five Year Plan was not possible, the Center maintained that the lawful relationships on which the Right based their predictions would not obtain in the new system of social relationships which would result from the changes that would result from the plans for industrialization and agricultural collectivization. The Center rejected not only the principle of "equilibrium," as stated by Bukharin, but also the theory of "spontaneity," the complement of the theory of equilibrium.[10] The theory of "spontaneity" said that forces active in the

---

* The frank use of the term "teleology" during this period must be regarded as an impulsive indiscretion. The reader will see in later chapters that present-day theorists are careful to point out the difference between their conception of will and teleology.

system bring about the desired change "spontaneously" if not disturbed by ill-advised action.

Two broad methodological issues were at stake. The first of which, as Bukharin himself put it in the early thirties, after accepting the defeat of his position, was between two orders of lawfulness: the lawfulness of events impinging on each other and working out their own resolution, and the lawfulness of events consciously organized and directed by man. The second issue involved the nature of evolution in general. The mechanistic conception of evolution or development sees events as proceeding linearly and sees the future as a direct projection of the past. The other point of view sees evolution as a discontinuous course of development involving periods of crisis and revolution producing sudden basic reorganizations of the elements in the system. This results in a new form of organization, subject to different laws—the dialectical law of quantity changing into quality. According to the dialectical point of view an accelerated program of industrialization and collectivization would produce such a "leap" in development and would result in restructuring of social relationships that would negate the predictions of the mechanists.

Further, the supporters of Stalin said that mechanists had no place for chance (accident) in their scheme of thinking. "They undertook a mystical view that everything was defined by preceding events. For this, we inevitably slip down to fatalism in practice, to an excuse for abandoning the revolutionary fight, for reaction and all subjective errors. This mechanistic necessity forces us to dig in the past, seeking there the causes of the actual event, to look—not forward, but—backward." [11] In other words, the Right opportunist has used scientific analysis to make man the slave rather than the master of events.

The victory of the Stalinist position had a number of important consequences for the future of Soviet society. (1) The primacy of "teleological" over "genetic" considerations was established in economic and social planning. There was, in effect, a basic redefinition—or clarification—of man's relation to his environment. It made official the view that man is the master of his own fate. (2) The controversy in planning crystallized the controversy in philosophy by underscoring the practical implications of the contesting philosophical positions. Under the pressure of the fight over the Five Year Plan, the "dialectical" position became clarified, and was established as the "correct" Marxist (Stalinist) philosophy. This, in turn, meant that dialectical materialism (as opposed to mechanistic materialism) became the accepted methodology of science. (3) The scope of the Plan itself precipitated a series of social crises, social needs, and problems which set their own chain of causation working. Social institutions (some soon, some late) became more tightly integrated, more explicitly directed toward the service of specific functions. Demands on and opportunities for the individual increased. At the same time the government actually had to be stricter in its control of the individual because of the large number of persons—kulaks, nepmen, and so on—against whom it had taken action. It also had to demand more of the individual in the service of the rapidly expanding economy.

THE VICTORY OF THE DIALECTICAL POINT OF VIEW IN PHILOSOPHY [12]

The period of the twenties in Soviet Russia was marked by an extended controversy in science and philosophy over the relative merits of dialectical and mechanistic materialism. There were actually two prongs to the discussion. One issue was whether or not the principles of dialectics, part of the official Marxist philosophy, were applicable to the natural sciences. The other issue was the actual definition of the principles of dialectics.

The initiative in this controversy was taken by a group of natural scientists who maintained that natural science discovers its laws by empirical research, and should not be subject to the imposition of preëxisting philosophical laws. Their early spokesman, S. Minin, said that philosophy had to be thrown overboard together with religion. The slogan, "overboard with philosophy; science is all-sufficient," was regarded by many mechanists as the fighting slogan of revolutionary Marxism. In addition, they favored the models of mechanics as the basis for scientific explanation, and many of the scientists believed that the principles of dialectics could actually be expressed in terms of mechanics.[13] In this contention they found support from Bukharin in his *Historical Materialism*, which, when published in 1922, was generally regarded as the most advanced statement of Marxist theory.[14] A victory on the first point would have made empirical science independent of the official philosophy. A victory on the second point would have substituted the laws of mechanics for the laws of dialectics in the official philosophy.

Resistance to this attack was organized among a group of philosophers led by A. M. Deborin at the Communist Academy, an organ of the Central Committee of the Party. A Society of Militant Materialist Dialecticians was organized, and support was gained from philosophers at the Lenin Institute, the Marx-Engels Institute, and the Institute of Red Professors. The dialecticians, who originally were almost exclusively philosophers, trained their own scientists, who then carried the fight to the mechanist scientists, offering the theories of Einstein and Heisenberg as a support for their position.[15] The position of the dialecticians was given further valuable support in 1925 by the Marx-Engels Institute's publication of two important fragmentary works, Engels' *Dialectics of Nature* and portions of Lenin's philosophical notebooks.

The victory of the dialecticians was announced in April 1929, the same month in which Bukharin and other members of the Right opposition were stripped of much of their political power. The Second All-Union Conference of Marxist-Leninist Scientific Institutions passed a resolution labeling the view of the mechanists "a clear departure from the Marxist-Leninist philosophical position" and stating that "the theoretical discussion with the mechanists is really finished." [16] Shortly after this the Central Committee of the Party issued a decree instructing the Communist Academy to implement the introduction of the dialectical point of view in the natural sciences.[17] Psychologists at the academy began immediate preparations for the First All-Union Congress on Human Behavior, at which the dialectical point of view was introduced in January of the following year.

The victory of the Deborinites in philosophy was quickly followed by a second controversy. Since it will be discussed in detail in a later chapter, it is sufficient to note here that this controversy was introduced by a group of militant young philosophers under the direction of M. B. Mitin, and that they pressed for a closer subordination of philosophy to practical political needs.

THE ISSUES BETWEEN DIALECTICS AND MECHANICS

The main theoretical issues which separated the dialecticians and the mechanists were their approaches to the concepts of force, system, and causality.

1. *The Concept of Force.* To the mechanist the concept of force is the means of explaining causal relationships in the world. Since his theoretical model is that of a machine which responds or adjusts to external force, there would be no initial motion in the system without the application of external force. The mechanist sees the world as consisting of rigid, isolated elements, so that if force is applied at one point it is trans-

mitted by these rigid elements to other elements and so on. If forces equal in magnitude but opposite in direction are effective on the same point, no motion results but an equilibrium is established.

This type of conception of the way in which the universe operates brings into use the terms "response," "adaptation," "adjustment," "equilibrium." Bukharin's conception of equilibrium was a good example of this approach. To him society was a system which adjusted to the natural environment. The internal structure—the state of equilibrium within the system—is a function of the system's external equilibrium. In such a scheme, the initiative always rests in external factors. This is illustrated by Bukharin's statement: "We may say of a system that it is in equilibrium if that system of itself, without the application of external energy, cannot change its condition." [18]

The dialecticians argued that motion is an inherent property of matter, while the mechanists considered motion to be a property that is imparted to matter from without. The dialecticians contended that the mechanists' position involved the positing of a prime mover to set matter in motion, and thus led to such concepts as God. The mechanists, on their part, labeled the stand of the dialecticians as vitalism.

This difference in interpretation of the nature of force is a key to understanding how certain Marxists who considered themselves to be dialecticians were criticized as being mechanists. The problem hinges on the dialectical law of the unity (or interpenetration) of opposites. This principle of dialectics was broadly interpreted as referring to the processes whereby opposing forces resolved themselves and produced some sort of resultant phenomenon (thesis, antithesis, and synthesis). However, in the controversy it became established that the "correct" view was that these forces ("contradictions") were internal to the system; that is, that the dynamics of the system were derived from forces within it and not from forces impinging on it. A. Martinov, for example, in criticizing Bukharin, cites as the basic law of dialectics Engels' statement: "The dialectical is that which embraces contradictions *in their unity*." [19] The standard critique of these "unconscious mechanists" was that they could conceive of the unity of contradictions only as that of forces external to the system.

For psychology this changed conception of motion meant the end of the conception of man as an adjustive mechanism that tended to maintain itself in a state of equilibrium with its environment, and the inauguration of the concept of "autogenetic movement," thus giving to man the initiative in the disturbance of the equilibrium between himself and the environment.

2. *The Concept of System*. Much of what has been said about the contrasting ideas of force overlaps, necessarily, with the ideas of systems. The mechanistic world-image is that the original state of universe was one of disintegration. Material points are connected temporarily by an equilibrium of forces, but a real synthesis cannot be achieved. The whole is equal to the sum of its parts, and nothing more. The laws of the whole are reducible to the laws of the parts. Dialectics, on the other hand, maintains that the whole is a phenomenon of organization; that its laws cannot be reduced to the laws of its parts.

This position is closely related to the dialectical law of quantity changing into quality, inasmuch as a process of quantitative change may go on to the point where a "new synthesis" is effected, at which point a qualitatively new system which operates on a new set of laws comes into being. The political implications of this orientation have already been stated in relation to the crisis in economic planning, when the teleologists argued that the reorganization of Soviet society resulting from the Five Year Plan would establish a different order of lawful relationships in society. Therefore, it was argued, policy need not and should not be based on the pro-

jection of past trends. The same premise—that each qualitatively distinct system has its own order of lawfulness—was
used also to bolster Stalin's contention that socialism could be
developed in the USSR without the necessity of creating a
world-wide revolution. A writer argued in opposition to
Trotsky that the USSR is a qualitatively distinct unit which
has its own laws of development, and can, therefore, follow
an independent course of development.[20] This is a point at
which an observer to such a dispute finds it difficult to distinguish between sophistication and sophistry. All that is relevant, for our purposes, is that the doctrine that each organized
system has its own distinctive lawfulness was used consistently
as a device for refuting the determinate relations which the
Right and the Left oppositions posited.

The implication for the sciences is also profound in that it
meant the end of reductionistic theorizing. The laws of phenomena on one level did not have to be expressed in terms of
phenomena on some simpler level.

The dialectical conception of the nature of a system provided the rationale for a whole series of fundamental changes
in psychology which had, to then, been operating on essentially mechanistic principles. (1) The "psyche" was represented as a qualitatively new synthesis of matter, the laws of
which were not reducible to those of physiology. (2) Since
consciousness was an attribute of the psyche, a qualitatively
distinct form of highly organized matter, and could not be
reduced to the laws of physiology, conscious processes have
therefore a relative independence from their material substratum. Therefore, consciousness was restored to an important
role in the direction of human affairs. (3) By similar reasoning
the discontinuities between animal psychology and human
psychology were stressed, and the attention of psychologists
was shifted to the study of that which was characteristically
human in man, as opposed to those characteristics which man

and animals have in common. (4) The generalized conception of development as a process was changed to include the ideas of qualitatively distinct "levels." Development was seen as a discontinuous rather than a continuous process. The child was conceived of as passing through qualitatively distinct stages in which the "laws" of his behavior were transformed. (5) Similarly, the psychological laws which apply to man in different historical eras and different societies were affirmed to be qualitatively distinct.

3. *The Concept of Causality.* The mechanists were criticized for being rigid determinists. They argued that change or accident were merely the products of our ignorance: ". . . in reality they think that only necessity exists. Accident is a product of our ignorance, and therefore exclusively a subjective phenomenon." [21] To the extent that the dialectic view of accident can be disentangled from Hegelian terminology it is this: Certain elements in a situation are more relevant than others for the problem at hand. The analyst concentrates on these elements, and factors external to his scheme of analysis, but which may impinge on the events with which he is dealing, he calls "accidents." "Hence the accidental may be defined as a cause which is not directly related to the lawful inner development of a given phenomenon. It appears as something external in relation to it. That is to say there may be two or more quite independent series of causes and effects which may intersect, and this intersection is accidental." [22]

The mechanists, in holding to the view that chance is incompatible with causality, are accused of failing to distinguish between the relevant and the irrelevant. Thus Rudas is frequently quoted as saying that if the hero fighting behind a barricade should scratch his ear, he is nevertheless a hero, and his scratching is accidental to that fact. [23] The essence of the difference is that to the person looking into the past, "complete" determinism makes sense since the relevance of events can be judged on the basis of the effect they have produced. The person looking into the future does not have such wisdom of hindsight, and he must make some decision before the fact of the relevance of the factors involved since he cannot take all conceivable variables into consideration. Hence, "when accident and necessity are pushed together and all phenomena considered necessity, the way is opened for the perversion of dialectical materialism . . . Such theoretical *kasha* [a type of porridge] is fertile ground for opportunism."[24]

The implications of this revised concept of causality for psychology are almost too broad to comment on. The idea that determinism is not a "prison" was a key postulate necessary for shifting the attention of psychologists from the ultimate causes of man's behavior to more proximal causes, such as his immediate motives and his conscious processes.

In summarizing and interpreting any complicated theoretical position there is always great danger of overstatement and distortion, particularly when one attempts to translate Hegelian and Marxian terms into ordinary language. Therefore, it is necessary to concentrate only on the minimum essentials of this discussion. (1) The dialectical position sees forces (dynamics) as internal to the system. The system has autogenetic movement. (2) The various stages of development of any system (or the various stages of the organization of matter) have each their own laws which are not reducible to the laws of any other stage. (3) Determinism is not rigid. There is room for accident.

Each one of these three points involves rather arbitrary decision of broad theoretical and practical importance. One may assume that the natural state of matter is either motion or rest. He may focus on the relationships between various levels of phenomena, or concentrate his attention on the elements that are distinctive to each level. He may assume complete determinism for purposes of explanation, or construct a scheme of analysis based on a limited number of essential variables, assuming that within the limitations of their determinate relationships he is free to cause changes in the system in pursuit of a goal. What is significant in this philosophical discussion is that in each instance the dialecticians chose the point of view that left the Party free to act in reconstructing society and provided a rationale for holding the individual responsible for his behavior.

Fighting out the battles of everyday practical politics and economics in so scholarly an arena as philosophy may seem somewhat out of place to anyone not versed in the history of Bolshevism, but it was standard procedure in the Bolshevik manual of tactics to use every weapon available, from the most prosaic to the most esoteric.[25]

Consider the situation in which the philosophical controversy reached its peak. Stalin was coming into ascendancy as the leader of the Party. While by no means handicapped by an inferior intellect, he had neither stature nor experience as a theorist. But he is and was a man of far more than average shrewdness and common sense, who realized that the Soviet Union had reached a crisis. At the same time he was maneuvering for position with contending factions in the Party. It seems to have become obvious to Stalin about 1928 that the program of the Left, which had been rejected two years before, was originally correct, or that the situation had changed so that the Leftist program either had to be or could be put into effect. In any event, he espoused essentially the program of industrial expansion that the Left had originally proposed, and then found himself opposed by the "learned arguments" of the newly developed Right opposition. Without considering the merits of the two positions, we know that there were substantial temperamental differences between men like Nikolai Bukharin and Michael Tomsky, on the one hand, and Stalin and his supporters, on the other. The latter group were primarily men of direct action, men who favored active intervention to passive waiting. They were, further, men who were used to bending philosophy to the service of action. The position of the dialecticians offered a way out of the dilemma of determinism, of escaping from a fatalistically determined course of history. Also, the arguments of the dialecticians were a powerful weapon against the theories of Stalin's chief remaining competition, the Party's leading thinker, Bukharin. Thus, by force of circumstance, the least theoretically minded of Bolshevik leaders seems to have become the sponsor of one of the most sophisticated and possibly the most sophistic of theories.

3 | THE PATTERN OF SOCIAL CHANGE

The controversy in economic planning that preceded the First Five Year Plan was the most important event in precipitating a fundamental ideological revolution in the late twenties. But the same problems of spontaneity versus intervention; of determinism versus freedom and/or responsibility were encountered in various other areas of Soviet society.

The order in which events are presented generally tends to imply an order of casual relationship—that which is presented later seems to be a result or expression of that which was presented earlier. But, the relationship of developments in the Soviet economy to developments in other institutional areas was one of interaction. It is true that economic developments played a leading role, since the development of the economy was the single goal pushed most vigorously during the period from 1928 to 1936, and the results of industrialization and collectivization had a powerful impact on other institutions. Nevertheless, most of the problems that arose in areas like law and education would most likely have arisen in the same form, although less acutely, if forced industrialization had not taken place. In reviewing the changes which took place in Soviet society in general in the decade between 1928 and 1938, we must consider them simultaneously as manifestations of the general conflict between mechanistic and dialectical Marxism and as a result of the impact of industrialization and collectivization.

THE REVOLUTION IN LAW[1]

Perhaps the most characteristic premise of mechanistic Marxism was that many of the institutions of society, including the state itself, would wither away. Perhaps nowhere was this premise more sharply expressed, and nowhere did it create greater problems, than in law. From the beginning Bolshevik theorists argued that since law is an instrument of class domination the advent of a classless society would mean the withering away of law, and that any law which existed in a socialist society existed only to facilitate transition to a classless society. As a matter of fact, in the earliest period of the Revolution, Bolshevik leaders did not even perceive this temporary function of law in a transitional society. As they themselves admitted, they had little idea of what the status of law should be under their rule.[2] The first decrees were not intended seriously to be enforced. Trotsky said they were "the program of the Party uttered in the language of power"[3] primarily for propaganda purposes. It was not until Lenin had had some experience in government that he stated, in 1919, that it was necessary to set up regular legal codes which must be obeyed by all.[4]

The acceptance of the utility of law did not include an acknowledgment of its permanency. The "Leading Principles of the Criminal Law of the RSFSR," published by the People's Commissariat of Justice in 1919, specifies that law is an attempt on the part of the proletariat to work out rules for repressing its class enemies. The successful repression of these class enemies would bring about the liquidation of the state and of law itself. "Only with the final smashing of the opposing overthrown bourgeois and intermediate classes and with the realization of the communist social order will the proletariat annihilate both the state as an organization of coercion and law as a function of the state." [5]

Despite the acknowledgment of the short-run necessity of having a legal code, Soviet jurists of the twenties continued to regard law as an institution of a class society, antipathetic to their notions of socialism. "We refuse to see in law an idea useful for the working class . . . Religion and law are ideologies of the exploiting classes . . . we have to combat the juridical ideology even more than the religious." [6]

The leading theorist of the early period of Soviet law was Eugene Pashukanis.[7] Two aspects of his theories are of importance here. First, he was a leading proponent of the theory of the "withering away of law." Second, he shared with other jurists of the twenties the attitude that guilt and punishment were "un-Marxist" concepts, inconsistent with a determinist philosophy. Pashukanis' influence over the legal profession as a whole was great, and he is credited with the abandonment of courses in civil law and their replacement with courses in administrative planning—which Pashukanis called "economic law." Textbooks in civil law were replaced with texts in economic law; and in anticipation of the disappearance of criminal law, general principles for the guidance of judges were substituted for precise formulations of crimes and penalties.

In 1929 the Marxist theory of the withering away of the state—and the withering away of law—began to be revised drastically. In 1930 Stalin announced:

We are for the withering away of the state. But at the same time we stand for strengthening of the proletarian dictatorship, which constituted the most powerful, the mightiest of all governing powers that have ever existed. The highest development of governmental power, this is the Marxian formula. Is this "contradictory"? Yes, it is. But this contradiction is life, and it reflects completely the Marxian dialectic.[8]

Under the pressure of changing circumstances and changing dogma Pashukanis made several revisions in his theories.[9] When Stalin announced in 1934 that "We need the stability of laws more than ever," [10] it is noteworthy that Pashukanis agreed that the theory of the withering away of law was "opportunistic nonsense." [11]

However, the Soviet authorities were not content to let the matter rest with an acceptance of Pashukanis' denunciation of his own theories. In 1937 a full-scale attack was launched against him and his students. The attack was led by Andrei Vyshinsky, who had been Assistant Attorney General during the period of Pashukanis' dominance and who apparently had agreed with these theories at the time.[12] Characteristically Pashukanis' deviation was not labeled a mere error, but a deliberate attempt to wreck the state. Vyshinsky said,

They [Pashukanis and his followers] preached anti-Marxist subversive "theories" of the withering away of the State and law. To disarm the working class in front of its enemies, to undermine the might of socialism—that was the aim of these attempts. To the students, the growing cadres, a nihilistic attitude toward Soviet law was suggested.[13]

Since 1936 law has been accepted as an integral part of the socialist state, and neither the state nor the law are to wither away in the foreseeable future. Earlier theories are denounced by present-day legal commentators as anti-Marxist.[14] Thus another of the premises of mechanistic Marxism was rejected.

THE INDIVIDUAL BEFORE THE LAW

The treatment which society affords the social deviant is one of the best sources of insight one can have into the assumptions about human nature prevailing in a given social order. The deviant is one who has not responded to the ordinary means of social control and raises the problem of invoking extraordinary controls. His behavior poses the task of explaining deviation, of fixing responsibility for it, of taking corrective action (and of justifying the action), and, finally, of considering the effects of the deviant's behavior and the corrective measures on other members of the society. Just as the relationship of law to the state illustrated the mechanist premise of the withering away of the state, the attitude of Soviet legal theorists of the twenties toward the individual deviant illustrates still another mechanist premise: that man is innately good, and his faults are the result of the social order in which he lives.

The first Soviet criminal code (1919) states that crime in a class society is a result of the latter's social structure, not of the "guilt" of the criminal. Punishment ought not to "redeem the guilt." It should not exceed the demands of expediency or inflict upon the criminal injurious and needless sufferings.[15] The very term "crime" was considered unacceptable because it was linked with the concept of guilt, which, in its turn, was considered incompatible with a determinist philosophy. For "crime," the term "socially dangerous act" was substituted. In place of "punishment"—a concept tainted with bourgeois notions of morality—the term "measure of social defense" was introduced in the code of 1924.[16]

The substitution of "socially dangerous act" for "crime" and "measure of social defense" for "punishment," and the abolition of the concept of "guilt," brought about a series of interesting deductions. A "socially dangerous act" was evaluated on the basis of the danger of that act to the state. An article of the criminal code of 1926 states, "An act which, although formally falling within one of the articles of the special section of the present code, is free from socially dangerous characteristics, owing to its obvious insignificance or absence of harmful consequence, is not a crime." [17] Also, legal theorists argued that an act varied in seriousness depending on the social class of the person who committed it. Hence, workers, Party members, non-Party persons, rich and poor peasants, and so forth might each receive different treatment for the same act. Furthermore, the length of sentence was dependent on the rate at which the criminal reformed, since the intent of the "measure of social protection" was largely to restore him as soon as possible to useful standing in society.

It would be incorrect to claim that because of the humanitarian premises of this attitude toward the social deviant—excluding of course the differential treatment of members of different social classes—the treatment of criminals, especially of those guilty of political crime, was entirely lenient. Yet, in the light of later policies the lot of the criminal of the early period was a good one. There was a tremendous amount of enthusiasm for experimentation on the rehabilitation of criminals by humane means.

Pashukanis, naturally, was one of the main spokesmen for the abolition of the concept of guilt, and his role in promoting this approach was attacked sharply in 1937 by Party spokesmen. Part of the attack charged, ironically, that Pashukanis, among other things, had stood the originally humane premises of this position on their head by advocating penalties for dangerous acts whether or not the person had been at fault in committing the act. His critics maintained that this extremely deterministic position overlooks the role of the individual in society and history. Eugene Pashukanis was accused of having fallen under the influence of such "vulgar Marxists" as the historian N. N. Pokrovskii, an early hero of Soviet historiography who was also repudiated, and thereby was led to overestimate the influence of economic factors on the course of history. Pashukanis' critics cited Lenin to the effect that although the basic question in evaluating a person's social activity is undoubtedly the conditions which make that activity possible, the fact is that man can reason and has a conscience, and this fact must be taken into consideration. Class interests,

the critics said, direct human activity, but people make their
own history and consequently must be held responsible for
their acts.[18]

As is to be expected in these revisions of doctrine, the
criticism did not stop at pointing out the error of the older
position but also posited specific bad intent. Soviet judicial
psychiatry, for example, had followed a trend similar to that
of criminal law. Soviet psychiatrists had accepted the idea that
antisocial acts were the result of objective social and biological
conditions, and had rejected the concept of guilt.[19] In a relatively recent review of this period of Soviet judicial psychiatry, a leading authority, Ts. M. Feinberg, refers to attempts to do away with the concepts of guilt and responsibility
as "wrecking." [20]

Since 1937 Soviet criminal law has stressed condemnation
and disapproval of the crime and the criminal. Earlier jurists
have been reprimanded for failing to understand the educative
value of punishment. These earlier theorists "erred" in drawing a distinction between punishment and education, since
punishment itself is one of the most effective means of education.[21]

The mark of punishment which distinguishes it from other
measures of political compulsion is that it inevitably causes the
criminal *a definite suffering* which is painful to him. Punishment
should correspond in its severity, i.e., in the measure of suffering
it causes the criminal, to the degree of his guilt. [It is by punishment that the state expresses its] negative evaluation of the crime
and the criminal . . . Condemnation, disapproval, as a component
of punishment acquires special significance in the Socialist state.[22]

This revision in the status of the individual before the law
involved a drastic change in attitude toward the social deviant.
It was symptomatic of a general trend in Soviet society of
tightening controls on the individual, of shifting responsibility
from the system to the individual. Nowhere is this change of

attitude more sharply expressed—and the reasons for it more clearly revealed—than in the treatment of juvenile delinquents, known as *bespirizorni*, which means "those who are not looked after."

Writers who could find nothing else to praise in the USSR in the twenties could say fine things about the treatment of juvenile delinquents. In the treatment of delinquents there was a slight trend toward increased strictness up to 1935 and then a sudden change, which marked a complete reversal of attitude. Under the criminal code of 1919 children under fourteen years old were not to be held responsible before the law, and children from fourteen to eighteen years old were responsible only if they acted consciously.[23] This code went through several changes until in 1929 it was amended to bring all children up to sixteen before a commission for medical and pedagogical measures of correction, and children over sixteen were to be treated as adults. On April 7, 1935, a decree was passed under the title "Concerning Measures for Combating Crime among Minors." It provided that all children over twelve years of age were to be responsible under the regular provisions of the criminal code. This decree, according to an article celebrating its fifth anniversary, corrected the fallacious notion that punishment is not an educational measure.[24] As a writer in *Pravda* said, at the time of the decree, children with criminal tendencies "must be made aware that they will not be fed on lollipops." [25]

Behind all the talk of "false doctrines" there is every indication that a fundamental reversal of policy in the treatment of juvenile delinquents was forced on the Soviet Union by problems generated within the Soviet system itself. Refugees from the USSR who lived there during the early thirties tell with monotonous regularity in a variety of contexts of the enormous social unrest that accompanied the period of industrialization and collectivization; of the large number of children who were made homeless; of the general inability of parents to maintain effective control over their children in a situation of unparalleled disorganization; and of material want and collapsed moral standards.[26] During the period, they say, more and more mothers had to leave their children untended while they worked. Soviet writers themselves admit that in these years a new type of delinquent arose. One of them wrote in 1940:

> But in this period, when we conquered the problem of homeless children in the streets, a new cadre of delinquent children began to present a serious problem. Their social ties were not disrupted by such elemental phenomena as war, flight, or famine. These children came from broken homes and from families which were not able to maintain effective discipline.[27]

In Moscow, for example, delinquency increased 100 per cent between 1931 and 1934.[28] In 1935 extensive statistics were cited to show the necessity for the reform of family and criminal law in order to improve the situation with respect to juvenile delinquency.[29]

As in the case of the adult criminal, the social system could be blamed for the antisocial behavior of children only when the Communist Party itself was not clearly responsible for the system as it existed. If crime is a product of the contradictions of a class society, then the elimination of the contradictions by the liquidation of classes should eliminate the social basis of crime. Soviet theorists were quick to point out that Stalin's declaration of the achievement of socialism in 1936 meant that the social basis for crime had been eliminated, and that any subsequent deviations from the moral norm are an evidence of "capitalist remnants in the consciousness of man" and must be eliminated.[30] Thus, when the system had generated more problems than could conveniently be explained away, the responsibility for them was shifted by blaming them on a previous system. Since that system no longer obtained, the individual carrier of the influence of that system was himself held responsible.

THE CHILD IN THE SCHOOL [31]

Soviet education has changed from a highly experimental, extremely permissive system, in which the basic assumption was an idealized conception of the child, to a traditionalistic approach which places a high emphasis on discipline and obedience. The techniques of instruction have shifted from "learning through doing" to "the method of conscious understanding" which places a predominant emphasis on explanation and rational comprehension. The goal of education has changed from "the bringing up of a creative personality developed on many sides" [32] to that of creating a person fulfilling the explicitly defined demands of the social and political order. This includes not only mastery of certain skills and holding certain points of view, but the possession of a specified character structure.

The early period of Soviet education was permeated with most of the assumptions which dominated the legal profession and other aspects of Soviet society—the general reliance on spontaneous processes, but especially the belief in the innate goodness of the child. External discipline was considered not only unnecessary but undesirable; the child would develop in desirable directions if that which was natural to him were only permitted to unfold freely. Even though the extreme emphasis on student self-government which prevailed in the early years (1917–1921) was quickly modified, it was still possible in 1929 for Samuel N. Harper to refer to self-government as "one of the bases of the internal organization of all Soviet schools, from the lowest to the highest." [33] The editor of a recent volume of assembled decrees on education, for example, called attention to several "serious errors" of the early period, among which was "the idealization of the 'nature' of the child." [34] Despite some tendency for this early policy to be modified throughout the twenties, the really drastic shift of attitude toward the child in the school did not take place until after 1931.

As is to be expected, there was a doctrine of "the withering away of the school." The main proponent of this point of view was V. N. Shul'gin, director of the Marx-Engels Institute of Pedagogy until it was dissolved in 1931, and a leading educational theoretician of the period. To Shul'gin, organized education was no more than the complement of "spontaneous education." "The masses learn from their own experience," he quoted Lenin as saying. In a socialist state the school would wither away, and the socialist environment would take the place of the school.

In my opinion, there will be no school in the future communist society. The child will go immediately into social work. There he will find no pedagogues, but a work director, who will be a sufficiently cultured person, and one who knows how to handle children. More correctly, we will all be pedagogues. The child will go directly from social work to industrial work, and from there to the library, where he will find answers to all the questions which interest him. We are approaching closer and closer to this all the time. [35]

Despite the opposition of a number of prominent educators, who held that the state is a "purposive organization" which organizes education for its maximum effectiveness, [36] Shul'gin's position remained the officially dominant one until 1931.

The principles of didactics in vogue before 1931 were quite in harmony with Shul'gin's emphasis on "spontaneous" education. The basis of early Marxian theories of education was that the child should learn by doing socially useful work. Despite several modifications in this doctrine between 1917 and 1932, it remained essentially a project approach similar to that of American progressive education. In fact, it was largely an imitation of the most progressive techniques of American education. The teacher organized the child's school work around a given theme and the content and skills of the three R's were presumed to be acquired in the course of working out the project.

But, as in other areas of Soviet society, after 1930 reliance on spontaneous processes gave way to active, purposeful intervention. By 1931 steps began to be taken to "restore the teacher to his rightful place in the school." In 1932 the project method was dropped and instruction in the three R's was introduced. In July of 1936 the final and most decisive step in reversing the early trend of Soviet education was taken when the Central Committee of the Party issued a memorable decree "Concerning Pedological Perversions in the System of the People's Commissariat of Education." With the implementation of this decree primary reliance on spontaneous processes in education disappeared. "Training," the deliberately directed process of education, took the place of the "environment." Responsibility for the development of the child was placed on the teacher and the family, rather than on a general faith in the innate qualities of the child and the favorable influence of the environment. Ultimately the category of "self-training" was added, thus fixing much of the responsibility on the child himself.

CONSOLIDATION OF THE NEW SOCIAL ORDER

There were two critical periods in the course of social change in the Soviet Union: 1928–1931, when the First Five Year Plan got under way and many policy decisions were made, and 1935–1937, when the new social order was consolidated. The changes of the latter period were a logical and virtually inevitable result of the policy decisions of the early period. They were in essence the process of putting back together what the first changes had torn apart.

The period of rapid industrialization and collectivization accentuated old problems and created many new ones. From 1931 on it became gradually apparent that the urgency of human problems was becoming greater than the urgency of problems of material and technique. Beginning with this year one finds in the speeches of Stalin and other leaders an increasing preoccupation with the question of individual responsibility and initiative, and of social control. To some extent this was a result of the demands which the new industry placed on manpower. In 1933, for example, Molotov announced that the chief task of the Second Five Year Plan would not be industrial expansion, but the consolidation of the organization of the new enterprises and the mastering of techniques.[37] The climax in the recognition of this problem came in Stalin's speech of 1935 when he said, "Having emerged from the period of dearth of technique, we have entered a new period, I would say, of a dearth of people, of cadres . . . the old slogan, 'Technique decides everything' . . . must now be replaced by a new slogan, 'Cadres decide everything.' "[38] As we shall see in subsequent chapters, this marked an upsurge in the importance of training in Soviet society, and produced important changes in psychology, psychotechnics, and education.

In addition to the demands of industry there were other developments accentuating problems of social control and creating the need for tighter controls over the individual. Soviet refugees are emphatic in their contention that although the rapid industrialization of the country created new enthusiasts in some quarters, there was a general decline in the over-all level of enthusiasm among the older supporters of the regime —some because they belonged to defeated factions, others because they disapproved of the human costs involved in liquidating various social groups and the general sacrifices involved in forced industrial expansion and agricultural collectivization.

The speeches of Soviet leaders in the period after the First Five Year Plan show a recurrent theme, the difficulty of social control. One point is made repeatedly, the success of collectivization had created a vast new class of malcontents, the displaced kulak and his family, relatives, and friends. (Interviews with ex-peasants indicate that in the minds of the peasants the Bolshevik regime began only with collectivization.) As speaker after speaker pointed out, those new malcontents presented special problems since the kulaks and nepmen (profiteers of the NEP) were now destroyed as a group and dispersed throughout the social order.[39] They were no longer identifiable as kulaks or nepmen, but they were the "two hundred per centers" and the "yes-but-ers" who did not oppose the regime openly, but sabotaged it by calculated over- or under-enthusiasm, by well meaning "mistakes." Thus attention had to be focused on the individual rather than on the social group. Not only did antisocial behavior have to be forestalled by explicit external sanctions, but the enlistment of support for the regime had to be stimulated by the creation of positive rewards in the form of increased wage incentives.

The same trends we have noted in law and education were manifested in other sections of Soviet society. In literature, the rise of the importance of the individual was reflected by a shift from featuring the broad anonymous mass as a hero to the depiction of the individual Soviet man as the leading figure.[40] In 1934, Soviet writers were urged to create a literature of "revolutionary romanticism," and to avoid the tendencies of bourgeois literature, "which depicts the small deeds of small people." [41]

In 1935, the Stakhanovite movement which involved enlisting the support of the workers themselves in reorganizing the work process and stimulating increase in production was initiated to spur industrial production. In the early and middle thirties, the school of the historian Pokrovskii, previously the official historical school, was attacked for underestimating the role of the individual in history. In 1938, the new "Short History of the Communist Party" was issued along with a special decree warning against the "vulgarized" conception of the individual in history; [42] that is to say, against underestimating the importance of the individual in history, and the importance of the Party in shaping Soviet history.

Two phases are apparent in the development of the new conception of the role of the individual in society. The first phase, reflected in the controversies in economic planning and philosophy, was designed to liberate the leaders from the bonds of determinism so that they might be free to act in changing social institutions. The second, exemplified by increasingly tight controls on the individual, was designed to place on the ordinary Soviet citizen responsibility for his own behavior and to remove from the social system the blame for many of the social problems which arose. The individual Soviet citizen, according to the new formulation, is a conscious, purposeful actor. But he is free to act only within the limits circumscribed by the regime, free to act only in the pursuit of socially accepted goals.

4 | THE BEHAVIORAL PSYCHOLOGIES OF THE TWENTIES

Let us consider briefly the scientific ethos of the Soviet Union in the years immediately following the Revolution. There was above all a tremendous faith in the powers of natural science—the expression "science is the religion of the Soviet Union" was frequently used to describe the atmosphere of the twenties. It was this belief in the ability of man to create miracles by the free play of rational intellect that almost carried the day for the mechanistic scientists in the philosophical battle with the dialectical philosophers. Along with this enthusiasm for natural science went a strong emphasis on materialism, on objective methods, on determinism, and on quantitative as opposed to qualitative methods of investigation. A further concomitant of the high prestige of the natural sciences was the acceptance of the scientific models of physics and mechanics as the prototype of scientific theorizing, with the assumption that the laws of all phenomena were potentially reducible to the laws of physics and chemistry.

These beliefs stemmed to a great extent from the tenets of nineteenth-century science, and enthusiasm for them was high because it was felt by many that the new order would permit the full use of man's rational powers to the benefit of humanity. To a large extent these beliefs were supported directly by the Marxian doctrine. There was much in Marxist sociology about the stultifying effect of the capitalist order on the development and application of science. Further, Marxian philosophy is militantly materialistic, and the leaders of the Party made it a matter of immediate policy to support materialist scientists in their opposition to "idealism" and "subjectivism."

The reigning principles of science were: materialism, objectivism, determinism, quantification, and (implicitly) reductionism. To some extent these principles were to conflict with the rising trends in official doctrine in the twenties. Conflicts arose, as we have seen, over the introduction of the principles of dialectics, over the nature of determinism, and over the question of reductionism in science. But despite the rising trend of opposition, this set of principles was dominant in the years immediately after the Revolution, the period from which the first attempts to formulate a Marxist psychology date.

An over-all characteristic of this period, and one which distinguishes it markedly from the era after 1930, is a fundamental faith in free scientific debate. This meant that a far wider variety of psychological views were expressable in the twenties than was permitted later. After 1930 the "schools" began to dwindle rapidly. After 1936 there was, for practical purposes, one school of Soviet psychology. It is important to keep this characteristic of the era in mind because the influence of the Party on psychology was much less direct and detailed than it was to be later.

During the course of Soviet history, psychology has tended to become increasingly an applied science and less a science looking for general laws. Yet, paradoxically, the attitude toward the application of psychology to social problems was freer and more optimistic during the twenties than it was to be after 1936. This attitude arose from the belief that psychologists in their laboratories would arrive at general principles of human behavior which could then be applied to social living.

As the possible implications of some of psychology's findings were seen to be in conflict with the social program of the Party, and as inappropriate attempts to apply rather abstract concepts were not successful, this attitude was reversed, and the dictum that practice leads theory was introduced, with the area of practice circumscribed. Until the end of the twenties, however, enthusiasm for the application of psychology was undiminished. Such high Party leaders as Trotsky, Bukharin, Krupskaia, and Lunacharsky displayed an active interest in both the application and the theory of psychology. M. A. Reisner, one of the founders of the Communist Academy, became an enthusiast for the development of a social psychology based partially on Pavlov and partially on Freud.[1]

THE BEGINNINGS OF MARXIST PSYCHOLOGY

Some of the trends developing in Russia and world psychology, particularly in American behaviorism, fitted in well with the general scientific ethos of the early Revolutionary period. Pre-Revolutionary Russian psychology had exhibited a strong materialist and objectivist trend in the work of Ivan Pavlov and V. M. Bekhterev. But there were also many exponents of subjectivist and introspective psychologies. Experimental psychology was developed by Georgii Chelpanov, N. Lossky, A. P. Nechaev, N. Lange, and others. Most of these men were either philosophical idealists or professed philosophical neutrality, and this soon became a point of difficulty for them. The most extreme idealists, such as Frank and Lossky, lost their positions shortly after the Revolution,[2] and the tide began to turn very strongly to the objectivists and materialists in psychology. In fact, the tide turned so strongly in their favor that for a time, psychology per se was virtually annihilated and replaced by physiology and biology.

The first strong wave of opposition to the old subjectivist psychology of such men as Lange, Nechaev, N. Ia. Grot, L. M.

Lopatin, and Chelpanov came in the years 1921–1923. Within this period, Bekhterev and Pavlov each published important works—Pavlov making available in book form for the first time the results of twenty years of research on conditioned reflexes. P. P. Blonskii, a former pupil of Chelpanov, published *Ocherki Nauchnoi Psikhologii* (Essays in Scientific Psychology), which showed the influence of American behaviorism. K. N. Kornilov, another of Chelpanov's former pupils, published *Uchenie o Reaktsiiakh Cheloveka* (The Study of Human Reactions), still another attempt at an objective study of behavior. V. Struminskii's *Psikhologiia* (Psychology) and Yenchman's *Vosemnadtsat' Tezisov k Teorii Novoi Biologii* (Eighteen Theses on the Theory of the New Biology) were avowedly anti-psychological approaches to human behavior. Yenchman's "new biology" produced a "Yenchmanist" cult of anti-psychological enthusiasts.[3]

About this same time active steps began to be taken to develop a "Marxist" psychology, and further moves were made to restrict the influence of subjectivist psychologists. In 1922 the Institute of Communist Education was formed under the initiative of the Agit-Prop Bureau of the Central Committee of the Party and serious discussion of the problems of Marxist psychology was begun in the psychophysiological section of the Institute.[4] In January 1923 the First All-Russian Psychoneurological Congress convened in Moscow. The feature of the Congress was a speech by Kornilov which for the first time set forth as an active program the necessity of establishing psychology on a dialectical materialist basis.[5] As a result of Kornilov's speech and the support he received from his younger colleagues (and presumably from the Party), Kornilov took over Chelpanov's position as director of the Moscow State Institute of Experimental Psychology,[6] a position which Chelpanov had held since the founding of the Institute in 1911.[7] The following year, 1924, the Second All-Union Psychoneurological Congress was held. Here, for the first time, there was a broad presentation of various views and an obvious conflict between the reflexologists—already well established in official favor—and the psychologists, a conflict that was to continue for many years and that was to be focal in the development of Soviet psychology up to 1930.

In the years 1923–1924 the struggle of psychology for the right to exist began. This struggle was waged largely in terms of Marxist methodology, but rested also on broad scientific concepts. The high prestige of the natural sciences, coupled with the enthusiasm for Pavlov's work on conditioned reflexes, made psychology very suspect. Suspicion of psychology was fostered by the practice of the Pavlovians and Bekhterevians of grouping the new behavioral psychologists with the old subjectivists. The task of the "Marxist" psychologists, then, was one of demonstrating their right to exist on the basis of general principles of science, and also on the basis of the writings of the Marxist authorities. Since the chapters which follow are concerned in part with the details of this struggle, this section will give only a broad description of the various psychological schools which were active during the twenties.

THE STUDY OF REFLEXES

"Behaviorism" or "objective psychology" originated independently in America and in pre-Revolutionary Russia. In both countries one of the sources was animal research. In Russia this source was Pavlov's work on the conditioned salivary reflexes of dogs. Equally important perhaps was Bekhterev's early plea for an objective psychology which originated in human psychology. The work of both of these men began at the very start of the twentieth century, and their views were well established at the time of the Revolution. Even though each rejected the label of psychology, Pavlov calling himself a physiologist and Bekhterev referring to his school as reflexology, both addressed themselves to the same range of problems as did the psychologists, and they considered psychologists to be their scientific competitors.

Pavlov's studies of conditioned reflexes were carried out initially on dogs, and he employed the salivary reflex as his unit of study.[8] By training animals to salivate to new stimuli under a variety of conditions he hoped to work out laws of the operation of what he called "the highest nervous activity." Since he considered himself a physiologist rather than a psychologist, he couched his laws in physiological terms—such as the excitation, generalization, inhibition, and so forth, of the nervous processes. Pavlov was not inclined toward the direct usurpation of the field of study of psychology, but preferred to build from below, extending his knowledge of the processes of the brain in the direction of the explanation of psychological phenomena. For this reason, and because of the difficulty of working on salivary reflexes with human subjects until the invention of Lashley's funnel, Pavlov's own work did not encroach directly on the grounds of psychology.

Some of Pavlov's students went further than their master, however, and attempted to extend his teachings to wide areas of human behavior. N. I. Krasnogorskii did rather rudimentary work with children as early as 1907, counting the number of times a child swallowed in response to a conditioned stimulus as an index of the conditioning of the salivary reflex. In 1926 systematic work on salivary conditioning in humans began on a rather large scale.[9] G. P. Frolov proposed about the same time that psychology be replaced by physiology in the field of education. He attempted to ground education on the doctrine of conditioned reflexes.[10] In general, the Pavlovians made less of a direct assault on psychology than did Bekhterev and his students, but Pavlov's work captured the fancy of many prominent persons and contributed to the enthusiasm for reflexology that was to make the position of psychology so precarious. After the Second Psychoneurological Congress, *Pravda*, the central organ of the Party, said that the doctrine of conditioned reflexes was one of the foundations of materialism in biology, and *Izvestiia*, the government organ, devoted a special laudatory article to Pavlov's work.[11] Lenin's widow, Krupskaia, wrote in 1928 that the study of reflexes would make possible the understanding of the relationship of material and psychic phenomena.[12] Trotsky favored a fusion of Freudian theory and Pavlovian method for a correct materialist model of human behavior.[13]

The term "reflexology" is properly applied only to the work of Bekhterev and his students, although Soviet writers had a tendency to group the work of both Bekhterev and Pavlov under this term. Bekhterev became interested in reflexes from an initial interest in human psychology, rather than from a desire to understand the functioning of the nervous system.[14] In 1904 he published an article, "Objective Psychology and Its Subject," in which he submitted a plan for replacing the old subjective psychology with a study of the objective correlations existing between the person and the inorganic, the organic, and the social environment. He insistently pointed out that reflexology must not be confused with physiology, "which is the science of the functions and regulation of the organs of the body, including the brain . . . Reflexology, particularly human reflexology, is a scientific discipline which sets for itself the problem of studying the responsive reaction to external and internal stimuli."[15]

He was at a loss, however, regarding what method could be used to implement this plan. In 1905 V. N. Boldyrev, a co-worker of Pavlov, published a description of the method for studying conditioned salivary reflexes. Attracted by the method, V. M. Bekhterev set Protopopov to work to develop a method adaptable to reflex work with human subjects. The method developed was called the "associated motor reflex." It was worked out originally on dogs and was based on the defensive paw movement which is evoked by an electrical stimulus. Adapted to human beings, it employed the reflex of the retraction of the subject's foot on the administration of an electrical shock.

Using this method, Bekhterev made a series of studies in the development of associated motor reflexes * which he published between 1907 and 1910 in two volumes entitled *Ob'ektivnaia Psikhologiia* (Objective Psychology). By 1912 he had adopted the term reflexology in place of objective psychology, and the concept of the reflex, which had been introduced as a technique of investigation, became the central explanatory concept in his system. Even when the reflex method was not used the investigation and analysis were carried out in "reflex" terms. At the time of the Revolution he had already extended his study of reflexology to pedology (child study), industrial psychology, and criminal psychology, as well as to animals and human groups.

Bekhterev was more militant than Pavlov in his opposition to psychology. Refusing to distinguish between the newer, more objective, and materialist trends in psychology and the old subjectivist psychology, he opposed psychology per se in speeches at the various congresses, in papers, and in brochures.[16] His objections were based largely on the deficiencies of the method of introspection, which he regarded as unsuitable for many of the tasks involved in studying behavior, mainly the behavior of children and animals, and on the use of subjective or metaphysical concepts by psychologists. He hoped to reduce all human and animal behavior to reflexes. For him, the study of human behavior was primarily a biological and secondarily a sociological task, but never a psychological one. The militancy of the reflexologists did not diminish after Bekhterev's death in 1928, and in 1929 his pupils pre-

* He preferred the term "associated" to "conditioned" as reflecting better the circumstances under which the reflex was published.

pared a series of papers later published under the title "Reflexology or Psychology," [17] in which they claimed the entire field of psychology for reflexology.

Since Bekhterev's work was coupled in the popular mind with Pavlov's work, the reënforced prestige of these two savants created a strong surge of enthusiasm for reflexology, which began to displace psychology in the courses of instruction in the institutes of higher learning.[18] The Ukrainian Commissariat of Education decreed that reflexology was to serve as the basis for the establishment of a scientific pedagogy and did away with all psychology for a limited period of time. But the Commissariat was shortly forced to revise its approach and commented: "At the present time it is extremely difficult to put into practice the program of founding pedagogical disciplines on a reflexological basis." [19] Even at the height of the enthusiasm for the scientific study of reflexes its proponents were forced grudgingly to add, "Not yet." A. P. Pinkevitch, in one of the important general works on education of the twenties, extols the promise which the study of conditioned and associated reflexes held for a scientific approach to education, but comments that until this promise is fulfilled, one must still employ the terminology of the old subjectivist psychology.[20]

Thus, although psychology did overcome, by the end of the twenties, the initial setback it suffered at the hands of reflexology, psychology's comeback did not mean a serious undermining of the strong position which the reflexologists had built for themselves in the early twenties. In application, however, reflexology's popularity seems to have been based on future promise rather than on present performance.

REACTOLOGY

K. N. Kornilov was the chief spokesman for psychology during the twenties. He had three distinctions: his series of pragramatic statements on the reorganization of psychology on a Marxist basis, his leadership of the Psychological Institute after 1923, and his own brand of psychology, which he called reactology. Kornilov proposed to erect an entire system of psychology around the study of reactions.[21] He had subjects respond to various patterns of stimuli and various sets of instructions by pressing a key. He measured the *speed* of response on a Hipp chronoscope, the *strength* of response on a dynascope which he himself devised, the *form* of their reactions by tracings on a drum, and the *content* (meaning) by verbal report. Subjects were run through the "gamut of reactions" extending from the "natural reaction" through the "muscular," "sensory," "discriminatory," and "selective" reaction to the reactions of "recognition" and "logic." On the basis of these experiments he "discovered" four basic reaction types: "One type of reaction, which is quick and strong, has been called by us the *muscular type;* another, which was slow but strong, the *sensorial active* type; a third type was quick but of low intensity—*the muscular passive;* and a fourth was slow and of low intensity—the *sensorial passive* type." [22] Another discovery was the "principle of the monopolar expenditure of energy": a person simultaneously engaged in mental (central) and physical (peripheral) work does so to the detriment of one or the other activity. Kornilov advocated the application of his methods and types in industry and education, and his suggestion was taken up somewhat in industrial psychology.[23]

Reactology as a system of psychology did not produce any particularly spectacular results in Kornilov's own work. Some of the young psychologists who worked under his direction, however, did interesting and original work. This is especially true of A. R. Luria and L. S. Vygotskii. In Luria's hands the method of studying reactions developed by Kornilov became a sensitive instrument for analyzing the internal dynamics of the human personality.[24]

Vygotskii and Luria, together with other younger workers at the Psychological Institute, worked out an approach to the development of the child based on the theory that development is dependent on the mastering of cultural elements such as mnemonic devices which improve the memory span.[25] Their extended program for the study of child development was conceptualized in the "theory of cultural development" and was part of a larger program of study embracing both the phylogenetic and ontogenetic development of human behavior.[26]

Whereas the work of Pavlov and Bekhterev was a native Russian product, Kornilov and his associates were part of the European and American tradition of psychology. Kornilov acknowledged his indebtedness to Wilhelm Wundt, J. McK. Cattel, Karl Lange, and N. Ach. Vygotskii and Luria were influenced by the work of Heinz Werner, and the German Gestaltists, and to a lesser extent by American behaviorism. Furthermore, Kornilov and his associates argued—some more, some less—for the inclusion of subjective report in psychological investigations and maintained the "reality of the psyche." It was on these two points that the controversy between Kornilov and his chief supporter Iu. Frankfurt and the extreme objectivists, led mainly by Bekhterev, was waged. This problem, which is to be treated in the next chapter, marks the chief point of difference between the "Marxist psychologists" and the reflexologists.

To a certain extent all Soviet psychology of the twenties was behavioral psychology, inasmuch as it was interested in the study of man's overt actions rather than in his subjective life. However, a number of Soviet psychologists traced their behavioral psychology directly to American behaviorism. The most important probably were P. P. Blonskii, who specialized in educational and child psychology, and V. M. Borovskii, an animal psychologist. M. Ia. Basov, who carried on in a measure the pre-Revolutionary functionalism of A. F. Lazurskii, was also influenced by American behaviorism.

These behaviorists are of interest to us not so much because they upheld a particular theoretical line, but rather for the role they played in applied psychology; notably in "pedology," the science which brought the concepts and techniques of medicine, psychology, physiology, pedagogy, sociology, and anthropometry to bear on the study of the child. Pedology and industrial psychology were the two main areas of application of psychology and were to be extremely important in determining the fate of psychology in the USSR. The premises about motivation, plasticity, and the determination of behavior in connection with these areas of practice will be examined in detail in later chapters.

The chief industrial psychologists were I. N. Shpil'rein and S. G. Gellershtein. Like the pedologists, the industrial psychologists derived most of their theory and technique from Western psychology. Perhaps the industrial psychologists were a little closer to German psychology than the pedologists were. Shpil'rein in particular was much influenced by Stern in the twenties,[27] although he was later to renounce his allegiance to William Stern's system of psychology and label it idealist.

Another group were those applied psychologists—chiefly pedologists—who were attached to the various institutes, such as the Institute of Communist Education and the Communist Academy, during this period, and who seem to have been the spearhead of the Party's attempts to make psychology an effective applied discipline. Chief among them was A. B. Zalkind, who was in succession a Freudian, a reflexologist, and a denouncer of Freudianism and reflexology. Another pedologist who held a more stable position was S. S. Molozhavyi.

THE TREND OF THE TWENTIES

Beginning with the years 1923–1924 psychological controversies began to be argued increasingly in terms of Marxist methodology. Much of this controversy hinged on what the Marxist authorities had to say about the nature of conscious and subjective phenomena. In 1927, in reviewing the status of psychology, Kornilov outlined three broad objectives for the establishment of psychology on a Marxist basis: (1) It must be materialist. (2) It must be determinist. (3) It must be dialectical.[28] The first two points, he said, were already accepted. Actually, since the early part of the decade, no one had disposition to argue them except the deposed subjectivists.[29] The argument concerned rather what was a proper materialist approach to psychology, and by what means one could establish determinate relations.

Kornilov said at this time that the principles of dialectics had not been accepted. These principles, as he had outlined them three years earlier, were: (1) the principles of the uninterrupted change of all that exists; (2) the principles of the universal interrelationship of phenomena, of universal lawfulness; (3) the principles of the saltatory development of processes, with quantitative changes being transformed into qualitative ones; (4) (an addition to Hegel's triad) the principle of progressive development through the resolution of conflicting tendencies.[30] No general comment can be made on the application of these principles in practice. The most accurate remark that can possibly be made is that various psychologists tried to demonstrate that the principles and practices to which they already subscribed conformed to the principles of dialectics. Kornilov, for example, argued that his theory of the monopolar expenditure of energy (essentially meaning that if mental or physical activity are carried on at the same time, one or the other suffers) was an example of dialectics because each type of energy acts negatively on the other.[31] Bekhterev went so far as to refer to the whole of reflexology as a "dialectical synthesis of the historical development of the science of human personality, the thesis of which was metaphysical psychology and its forebearer empirical psychology, and the antithesis of which was the earlier stages of reflexology." [32] Even though the reflexological institute set up a special methodological section in 1928 to consider the question of bringing reflexology in line with the methodology of dialectical materialism,[33] there is little evidence that the thinking or work of any group of psychologists was affected in any noticeable way by the principles of dialectics.

During the twenties the Marxist ideology appears to have functioned primarily as a screening device whereby certain schools of psychology were rejected as clearly unacceptable. Beyond that it was a relatively loose framework within which any school of behavioral psychology could operate. It is quite clear that psychologists were more interested in demonstrating that their own brands of psychology were consonant with the principles of Marxism than in constructing a psychology which would best exemplify those principles. From the point of view of the present day, a Soviet critic says that these early "Marxist" psychologists were guilty of the "basic error" of trying "to create their own brand of psychology." [34] A man of Pavlov's stature did not even pay attention to the prescriptions of the ideology.[35] The only appreciable trend in the work of psychology that could be ascribed with confidence to the influence of Marxism was a growing acceptance of the necessity of a social orientation on the part of psychologists. The reflexologists began to show greater interest in the social genesis of behavior toward the end of the decade,[36] and this direction does not seem to have stemmed from Bekhterev's abortive *Kollektivnaia Refleksologiia* (Collective Reflexology).

About 1928 changes began to take place which fore-shadowed closer control over psychology. In November 1928 the Moscow Society of Neuropathologists and Psychiatrists underwent an upheaval. The old leadership was replaced by a "Marxist cadre" which "brought a broad scientific and practical democratization to the society and guaranteed a further, Marxist, formulation of the basic activities of Soviet psychoneurologists." [37] The reverberations of this "October Revolution" were felt, naturally throughout the entire Union. The change was even noticed by the Psychotechnical Society—which until then had remained neutral.[38] In psychotechnics, the first major step in establishing a "Marxist basis" was taken by Shpil'rein in a speech at the Communist Academy, December 2, 1929.[39] In April 1929 the Materialist Psychoneurologists of the Communist Academy, who had begun to take the initiative in the program for developing a Marxist psychology, followed up the victory of the dialecticians in the philosophical controversy with an announcement that they would convene the First All-Union Congress for the Study of Human Behavior in January 1930 as a measure for introducing the principles of dialectics into all of the behavioral sciences.[40] In the light of what was happening throughout Soviet society in these years and the fact that the Communist Academy was an organ of the Central Committee, it is clear that the regime was moving to establish tighter control over psychology.

The nature of the change which was taking place was nowhere clearer than in the field of industrial psychology. At the first and second congresses on the "scientific organization of work" held in the early twenties psychologists were influential in protecting the individual worker from the demands of "the system." Shpil'rein, O. A. Ermanskii, and Bekhterev had fought rather successfully against the inauguration of Taylorism as a "stretch-out" system in industry.[41] In later years the early attempts of industrial psychologists to focus attention on the rationalization of the work process and to deëmphasize attempts to get more work out of the laborer by the use of strong incentives were referred to as "Menshevism" and "opportunism." It was said that "Mensheviks flocked to the institutes for the protection of labor. . . . They used these institutes as a point from which to work their counter-revolutionary agitation." Caustic references were made to "Professor Bekhterev's philanthropic position." [42] However, when a meeting of the Scientific Organization of Labor was called in April 1929, "There was no voice raised against the intensifying of labor, although a number of people complained about the inadequate procedures for the rationalization of and protection of labor." [43] This change in attitude toward labor on the part of industrial psychologists coincided in time with the introduction of the First Five Year Plan, and with the removal of Tomsky as head of the trade unions; Tomsky was noted as advocating that the primary function of the trade unions was to protect the interests of the workers.

What this shift of attitude meant in the broadest terms is that the emphasis in achieving work efficiency was to be shifted from a concern with the rationalization of the work process to an effort to improve the caliber of the worker's performance. Actually this did not mean that rationalization was to be ignored, but that the training of the worker was to be *in addition* to the process of rationalization. This shift in emphasis, coupled with the fact that a vast number of new, unskilled workers were to be introduced into industry, meant that problems of training were to come to the fore in industrial psychology.[44]

The increased interest in training which resulted from the impact of the Five Year Plan on industrial psychology meant also a heightening of certain theoretical problems connected with training, particularly the problems that involved the plasticity of abilities. Up to this point, psychotechnics had been primarily concerned with the problem of selection, and when one selects he does not ordinarily ask how a person came to have a given ability, but merely who among a group of persons has the greatest ability. "But, then, when we come to the problem of *training* we must concern ourselves with the *dynamics* of abilities. The human personality is a dynamic thing, and a test gives a photograph, but not a moving picture. Consequently, it gives us inadequate information about the personality." [45]

In education, too, efforts to apply psychology were increased. The First All-Union Congress on Pedology was called in 1928, and leaders of the prominence of Bukharin; Lunacharsky, Commissar of Education; and Krupskaia, Lenin's widow, addressed the Congress and outlined the need for the application of psychology and related disciplines to the area of child study and education. With the introduction of the Five Year Plan, psychologists began to develop subplans for pedology (and psychotechnics).

Also during the later twenties, the Agit-Prop division of the Central Committee displayed interest in the possibility of using psychological material in propaganda works,[46] and A. B. Zalkind reported to the Agit-Prop division on progress made at the First Pedological Congress.[47]

A sign of the increasing attention and importance which was given psychology in this period was the founding in 1928 of three journals, whose English titles would be *Psychology*, *Pedology*, and *Psychotechnics*. Another trend was the growing influence of German psychology, particularly Gestalt psychology. This trend was in general disapproved as being "idealist" in methodology, but was defended by some proponents because the dynamic and wholistic orientation of Gestaltism was considered consonant with dialectics.[48]

Thus, toward the end of the twenties Soviet psychology was tending to be brought more directly under Party Control and more closely coördinated with the needs of society; at the same time, the extreme objectivism of the early twenties was somewhat softened. Psychology had won its right to exist. Though it was losing some of its independence, this interference was itself an indication that psychology was taken seriously by the Party, and it seemed to be in a position to gain in importance.

5 THE MECHANISTIC MODEL OF PERSONALITY

THE ROLE OF CONSCIOUSNESS IN MAN'S BEHAVIOR

If there were a single problem around which the history of Soviet psychology could be written, it would be the role of subjective factors in behavior. The old introspectionist psychology which was driven out in the early years of the Revolution was concerned almost exclusively with the study of man's subjective reaction to his experiences. It was rejected because it reflected a contemplative approach to life, setting off thought from action, and because it was tainted with concepts like freedom of will and therefore was antideterministic. In short, it was "unscientific." This reaction was to a large measure a result of the general upsurge of objective, behavioral psychologies throughout the world, but it was abetted also by the materialist basis of Marxist philosophy. As Kornilov conceded in his first statement on the Marxist approach to psychology, many persons thought that consciousness was a concept incompatible with a materialist philosophy; and a large portion of the controversies which took place in the twenties was concerned with whether or not there was adequate doctrinal support in Marxism for the inclusion of the concept of consciousness or the psyche in psychology. The psychological controversies of the early thirties, which ushered in the modern era of Soviet psychology, revolved also around the question of consciousness—resulting in a psychology in which this concept played a leading role.

Presentation of the status of the role of consciousness in the psychologies of the twenties involves a major problem because of the role which Marxist dogma played in scientific controversies of this era. For practical purposes there was no perceptible difference in the actual work and the theoretical models of the Pavlovians, the reflexologists, the reactologists, and the independent behavioral psychologists as far as subjective concepts were concerned. There were some differences on a verbal basis in the attitudes of the various groups toward these concepts. These differences became points of departure for heated doctrinal controversies in which each side sought official sanction for its particular taste in scientific method or terminology.

Pavlov and Bekhterev, following the tradition of Comtean positivism in science, rejected the independent status of psychology as a science and insisted that man's behavior is a biosocial phenomenon, to be studied by the sciences of biology and sociology. Subjective elements had no place in their scheme of explanation. Consciousness is but a reflection of underlying physiological processes. It is true, they said, that persons have the subjective feeling of freedom, but this is illusory. It is the task of science to reduce this area of illusion and demonstrate the determinate nature of all phenomena. According to Pavlov: "There is an immediate impression, hard to surmount of some voluntary freedom of action, of some spontaneity . . . [but] the theory of reflexes constantly increases without cessation the number of phenomena in the organism which are connected with the conditions that determine them." [1]

Characteristically, Pavlov did not enter into doctrinal arguments, basing his materialism and determinism on a scientific rather than on a political basis. But Bekhterev and his pupils cited the works of Marx to demonstrate the subordinate role of consciousness in determining man's behavior, and even suggested that Marx's use of such words as "consciousness" must be reinterpreted in terms of contemporary concepts. Thus, Bekhterev, in using a well known citation from Marx, took the trouble to indicate that "consciousness" really means "behavior": " 'It is not consciousness which determines existence,' as the subjectivists have supposed and still suppose, but 'existence which determines consciousness' or (in reflexological terminology), human behavior." [2] Bekhterev's pupil, G. N. Sorokhtin, also took pains to explain Marx's use of the term "consciousness." He wrote: "Marx's law, 'social existence determines consciousness,' naturally referred not to 'consciousness' but to the external form of man's behavior. For sociology, consciousness has no significance. Its task is to talk only of behavior, of man's adaptive activity . . . " [3]

The point at issue was the one of the admissability of subjective concepts in scientific discourse. As indicated in the previous chapter, the Pavlovians, the reflexologists, and certain extreme objective psychologists such as Struminskii accused psychologists such as Kornilov of being idealists and introspectionists. They argued that employment of subjective concepts meant forsaking the principles of determinism and materialism. However, there was no mistaking the interest of the Marxist psychologists of this period in determinism. As for the incompatibility of consciousness with materialism, Kornilov argued that only persons holding to an outmoded conception of materialism could hold this point of view. The question of the compatibility of consciousness with materialism revolved throughout the twenties around fine turns of phrase reminiscent of a medieval theological argument. As early as 1923 Kornilov said: ". . . the psyche is not something opposed to matter, but is only *an aspect of the most highly organized form of matter*." [4] This, later critics agreed, permits the attribution of an effective role to consciousness in human behavior. Later, however, Kornilov fell into the "error" of adopting Bukharin's formulation that "consciousness is the subjective side of the physiological process." [5] This was gleefully pounced on by opponents who maintained that Kornilov had thereby unwittingly capitulated to them in their intention to limit psychology to the understanding of nervous processes.[6] A. L. Schniermann, a pupil of Bekhterev, claimed that this meant that Kornilov "thinks it possible to establish a casual coherence between physical phenomena, but never between physical and psychical, nor between two psychical phenomena" [7]—a point of view which the reflexologists themselves held. This form of argument went on throughout the twenties, reflecting more an attempt of these scholars to demonstrate their orthodoxy than it did their actual theoretical and practical positions.

It is true that Kornilov argued for the admissibility of subjective concepts in psychology, and further, for the admissibility of using the individual's own report of his subjective experience as part of the data in an experiment—a concession that Pavlov and Bekhterev opposed as being an entirely unscientific procedure. Nevertheless, subjective report played little role in Kornilov's experiments, which were based mainly on the objective record of the time, strength, and form of the subject's reactions, rather than on the "meaning" of these reactions. His mode of explanation, also, was nonsubjective and seemed to justify Schniermann's contention that he saw causality as taking place on a physical level. In 1928 he wrote: "The first premise . . . of relationships between psychic phenomena is that the relationship is between reactions, and not between psychic elements." [8] Not only this statement but the entire body of Kornilov's work in the twenties indicates that he actually gave very little stress to the role of consciousness in human behavior in either his work or his theory. In practice, his approach, as that of virtually all Soviet psychologists of this period, was that of epiphenominalism.

A few psychologists, among them Struminskii, Zalmonson, and Yenchman, held a position closer to that of Bekhterev and Pavlov, than to Kornilov's. Still others, like Blonskii and Basov, were close to Kornilov, but nevertheless considered conscious processes to be determined essentially by underlying physiological processes. The range of variation, in any event, was small.

If one assumes that man is responsible for his own behavior, and that he is capable of directing his own actions, then it is necessary to accord an important role to consciousness, since it is the medium by which man is presumed to integrate, direct, and coördinate his actions. As we have seen, the psychologists of the twenties accorded no such role to consciousness. In fact they considered it their scientific task to correct the illusion that man can control his behavior. To explain the integrated nature of behavior, they employed the concept of the physiological dominant, popularized by A. Ukhtomskii.

The idea of the dominant was not new. Ukhtomskii credited Avenarius, Charles Sherrington, and N. E. Vvedenskii with having anticipated it, and Pavlov and Bekhterev each entered what seemed to be well founded claims for having used it, or an approximation of it, during the first decade of the century. The general principle of the dominant [9] is that when more than one neural region is excited, the energy from all the less highly excited regions is deflected to the one region which is most highly excited. This is the "dominant" region, and all the energy from the other regions is mobilized behind the behavior associated with the dominant region. As an example of the operation of the dominant, Ukhtomskii cited the fact that a cat surprised in the act of micturition becomes, as it were, "rooted to the spot," and "does not respond with the usual defense reflexes, nor does it flee on the approach of a man." [10] Presumably it would micturate more strongly as a result of the "subdominant" stimulation of fear produced by the man's approach. The weakness of the concept, as Ukhtomskii admitted in 1933, is that the relative strength of stimulation has to be determined post factum on the basis of the behavior which is evoked. Presumably if the fear evoked by the man's approach were sufficiently strong, the need to micturate would accelerate the cat's speed of flight.

Subjective concepts being so suspect during this period of Soviet psychology, psychologists readily reinterpreted as "dominant processes" most of those concepts which are ordinarily employed to explain the integration of behavior. Both reflexologists and reactologists defined concentration, attention, and will as dominant processes.[11] Kornilov referred to the dominant as one of the basic principles of the functioning of the cerebral hemispheres, and although he did differentiate between the subjective and objective sides of attention, he defined attention on the physiological side as a condition in which, "in the event of a single dominant nexus of excitation, all other parts of the nervous system are in a state of inhibition."[12] In view of Kornilov's tacit epiphenominalism, this means that for practical purposes he too reduced attention and similar subjective processes to the status of neural dominants.

For the very reasons that consciousness was out of vogue in the twenties, the concept of the unconscious found favor. In the first place, it supplied the final link in the chain of determination of human behavior, destroying the illusion of consciously directed free behavior, and in the second place, it was considered compatible with an objective approach to the study of behavior.[13] Bekhterev said that "the unconscious is the real psychic,"[14] since the importance of unconscious processes in the subjective life of man militates against the role of conscious factors in determining behavior, and thereby affirms the determinate nature of behavior.

The search for a closed system of determination of behavior was the major goal of psychology during the twenties, and in this context the name of Freud appears time after time, beginning with 1923. "We find an ever increasing attempt at the determination of psychic processes in all phenomena which appear accidental," wrote one psychologist; "for example, Freud's work on forgetting, and on mistakes of writing and speech." [15] And, said Zalkind, "Freud's psychic pan-determinism is the best antidote to the entire doctrine of free will." [16] Similar statements were made by Luria, the educational theorist Pinkevitch, Leon Trotsky, and many other prominent figures.

This enthusiasm for the unconscious did not spread to all of Freud's doctrine. In fact, after 1925 the attitude toward Freudianism was generally hostile because the concepts ego, id, and superego were considered idealist. After 1930 even the unconscious fell into disfavor, for the very same reason for which it had previously been approved—the fact that it detracted from the role of consciousness in the direction of human behavior.

The only clear reversal of trend during this period was the work of L. S. Vygotskii and his associates, mainly Luria and Leontiev. In 1925 Vygotskii made a plea for the concept of consciousness in behavioral psychology on the ground that the psychological concepts then in vogue were not adequate for the explanation of human behavior.[17] The following year he published the results of a series of experiments designed to show the importance of conscious attitudes in the control of dominant processes. He showed that subjects given appropriate verbal instructions could counteract the effect of an electrical shock and carry out a task which conflicted with the reflex evoked by the shock. "In our experiment," he reported, "the subdominant [the shock] was by far the more intensive stimulus . . . The weaker reaction, if consciously fixed, is the dominant one." [18]

The work done by Vygotskii, Luria, and Leontiev in their

investigations of the cultural development of the child was related to their interest in the role of conscious factors in behavior. Much of this work concerned the way in which man learns to control his own behavior.[19] A present day chronicle of Soviet psychology cites these experiments as the foremost example of the reaction of "the progressive tendencies" in Soviet psychology against the prevailing antipsychological trends of the mid-twenties.[20] But, despite the fact that this work is singled out as the single favorable example of "progressive tendencies" in the psychology of the twenties, the approach of these scholars did not escape strong criticism in later years. The reason lay in the curiously oblique approach they took to consciousness and man's control over his behavior. Consciousness, said Vygotskii, is "the capacity of the organism to be its own stimulus."[21] Their general approach to the problem of the control of man's behavior is that man does this by learning certain instrumental techniques—such as mnemonic devices to improve memory—and that he uses these devices as external stimuli to direct his own behavior. "Voluntary regulation appears to us," Leont'ev stated, "instrumental regulation, 'instrumented,' realized by . . . a second series of stimuli. The controlling of behavior becomes possible only by the mastering of stimuli."[22] Such control could be only indirect; attempts to control behavior by "will power" would be unavailing. Luria wrote, "Many observations support our view that the consideration of the voluntary act as accomplished by 'will power' is a myth and that the human cannot by direct force control his behavior any more than 'a shadow can carry stones.' "[23] Thus, even the most deviant trend of the period accorded to consciousness only a mediated role in the control of man's behavior.

Soviet psychologists of the twenties, then, almost without exception, either rejected or did not deal with subjective and conscious factors in human behavior in a systematic way. To the extent that subjective processes were accepted as legitimate concepts of psychology, they were considered to be epiphenomena of physiological processes.

Causality was on a physical level, and psychical phenomena were a passive reflection of those processes. As a recent Soviet writer has said: "During the entire period under consideration, Soviet psychologists were not able to break away from the position of 'behaviorism,' a position which is mechanistic in essence. The subject matter of psychology was the behavior of man, not his psyche, and not his consciousness." [24]

THE MOTIVATION OF MAN

In the psychologies of the twenties, man was an adaptive mechanism that responded to external forces in such a way as to maintain an equilibrium between himself and his environment. This concept of equilibrium was the basic motivational concept used by psychologists, and reflected their strong biological orientation. In all probability it came into Russian biology from Claude Bernard, under whom I. M. Sechenov, the father of Russian physiology, had studied in France. The idea of man as an equilibrating mechanism, of course, paralleled and found support from the use of this general notion by the dominant Soviet social and economic theorists of the early twenties.

Adherence to the concepts of equilibrium and adaptation was almost universal. Pavlov said that it was the primary task of natural science "to ascertain completely how a living being maintains itself in constant equilibrium with its environment." [25] This view was shared by Bekhterev, Luria, and virtually every psychologist and reflexologist.[26] Kornilov, too, used this concept, but showed, as usual, a disparity between his doctrinal citations and his psychological system. He quoted Marx as saying, "Acting upon nature, man changes his own nature," and spoke of "the adaptation of the environment [to] the demands of man," as opposed to the adaptation of man to the environment.[27] Either one of these doctrinal statements implies the idea of purposive action by man, rather than adaptation to restore a situation of equilibrium. But the basis of Kornilov's system of psychology was the study of reactions to external stimuli—obviously based on the concept of adaptation—and he used the concepts of adaptation and equilibrium as integral parts of his theoretical system.[28]

Such concepts are so thoroughly rooted in biological science that it never occurred to the psychologists of the twenties to raise the question whether there was an alternative to the assumption of adaptation. As was pointed out in the philosophical controversy and later in the psychological controversies of the early thirties, it is possible to assume that the organism acts so as to disturb the equilibrium with the environment in the pursuance of some goal or purpose. The latter assumption opens the way for the possibility of there being some motive beyond the preservation of the integrity of the organism. The assumption that man acts purposively to destroy the equilibrium between himself and his environment was the necessary premise for postulating that man had higher goals than the preservation of his own life, namely the building of socialism. Hence, when this new formulation was introduced in the thirties, the older notion of man as an equilibrating, adaptive mechanism was attacked as giving too passive a picture of human nature.

As befitted psychological systems which rejected subjective concepts, little attention was given secondary, derived motivational constructs such as socially conditioned "needs" and "interests." Emphasis was on biological concepts such as instinct or reflex mechanisms. Bekhterev and Pavlov considered the reflex to be the fundamental concept on which the movement of the organism was based, and agreed that "so-called instincts" could be reduced to reflexes.[29] Neither writer paid systematic attention to derived and more complicated social motives. In his more casual utterances, however, Pavlov referred to such super-reflexes as the "slavery reflex," the "reflex of freedom," and the "reflex of purpose." The Anglo-Saxon, for example, is better at overcoming obstacles than the Russian because the reflex of purpose is more intense among Anglo-Saxons.[30] These forays into the field of social motivation, incidental as they were to Pavlov's systematic work, irked Bekhterev, who considered them loose formulations which served only as a weapon for the enemies of objective investigations of personality.[31]

Kornilov, in contrast to Bekhterev and Pavlov, favored instinct and emotion as basic motivational constructs.[32] Like them, however, he was systematically concerned with only the primary, presumably biologically founded motives.

In none of these systems, Pavlovian physiology, reflexology, or Kornilov's reactology, was there any primary concern with derived or social motives. For the physiologists and reflexologists, an unconditioned or innate reflex was taken as a biological "given" which could be elaborated into conditional or associated reflexes. The question of what moved the initial reflex was not nearly so important as the study of the mechanisms whereby the connections between this and other reflexes and various stimuli are formed and dissolved. For Kornilov it was more important to understand *how*, rather than *why* organisms reacted.

Motivation occupied essentially the same role in the systems of the animal psychologists of the period as it did in the systems of Pavlov, Bekhterev, and Kornilov.[33] The animal psychologists favored either "instinct" or a stricter physiological formulation in terms of neural mechanisms, but were little concerned with how these original biological motives became elaborated into more complicated, secondary ones.

Among Soviet psychologists of the twenties, only the educational psychologists dealt with derived, socially conditioned motives. Their approach was not that of a systematic psychologist but rather of a practical worker proceeding on a strictly empirical basis. Accepting the fact that it was necessary to know a child's interests in order to plan his education or to give him proper vocational guidance, they made a long series of studies of the interests and opinions of children of various ages and social categories.[34] This, however, was an interest in existing motives, and there was little practical or theoretical concern with how the child's interests and needs developed or could be trained. They acted on the broad social assumption, current in the twenties, that the interests of the individual and the needs of socialist society either were compatible or were not so incompatible as to call any amount of attention to the task of remaking the individual's interests by a direct approach. It was still thought that the reshaping of human nature would take place automatically as the institutions of society were changed.

In industry, work motivation was a problem from the first days of the regime, and considerable attempts were made to increase work production. But this was the work of the Party, of politicians, propagandists, and engineers; and these efforts were divorced entirely from the job of the industrial psychologists, whose task was considered to be more specifically personnel selection and instruction. The leading spokesman for the psychotechnicians, for example, attributed the small amount of activity in psychotechnics in the early twenties to the lack of need for either personnel selection or training, since the problem was *merely one of stimulating workers already on the job to greater production*.[35] The attitude of industrial psychologists to the problem of work motivation is further revealed by the fact that they resisted stimulating workers to greater efforts and advocated a primary emphasis on rationalizing the work process in order to ease the burden

of the worker. As two American students of Soviet psychotechnics said, in 1935, of the lack of emphasis given in the
twenties to problems of motivation, "The propaganda problems of psychologists in the Soviet Union have until recently
been connected only with advertising of their own wares." [36]

In many respects the approach of Soviet psychologists to
the problem of motivation paralleled the treatment of the
problem of social motivation throughout the Soviet system
during the twenties. Traditionally the two pivotal questions
posed from the standpoint of political and social theory have
been: Is man basically selfish or unselfish in his behavior; that
is, will he act primarily to preserve himself and his own interests, or will he act primarily in the service of some value
"higher" than self-preservation? And, are motives mutable—
can human nature be changed? The answers to these questions given in the period of the twenties would be: The first
question poses a false dichotomy, since in a socialist society
there is a natural concurrence of the interests of society and
the individual. By serving his own needs, man serves society.
As for the second question, human nature manifests itself dif-
ferently in different situations, and the way to change it is
not by direct attempts to modify individuals, but by altering
the social order so that the desired traits of human nature may
manifest themselves. Compared to the later periods, there was
relatively little concern with the direct reshaping of man's
social motives.

INHERITANCE AND ENVIRONMENT: THE SHAPING OF MAN

Of all questions of psychology, none has been more clearly
saturated with political and social implications than that of
the plasticity of the human organism, the question of whether
human nature is set by man's biological endowment, or can
be changed by environmental factors. Marxists have always

been sensitive to these implications. From the beginning of the Soviet regime, it was recognized that the remaking of human personality was an integral part of the social, political, and economic revolution that Bolshevism represented. Soviet psychologists, particularly those closely associated with the Party, realized that the assumption of the plasticity of the human organism was a necessary "optimistic" premise for the goal of developing a "new type of man."

While official support for the doctrine of man's plasticity was never in doubt, there was, within the field of psychology, a disagreement on the relative emphasis to be given to the environmental and the biological determinants of personality, based on the contention of some psychologists that Marxist "materialism" demanded a primary grounding of psychology in biology. Further, there developed in the early thirties another conflict over the role of the environment in determining personality, arising out of the need for holding individuals rather than the system responsible for the condition of man. The first of these two conflicts was resolved in the twenties, but in resolving the first, Soviet psychologists set the stage for the second.

The leading spokesman for the concept of plasticity was psychologist A. B. Zalkind, who seemed to be an even more direct voice of the Party * than Kornilov. He began his at-

---

* Zalkind was attached to the Institute of Communist Education during the early twenties when this institute took the initiative in bringing psychology to a Marxist basis. This institute was formed by the Agit-Prop Bureau of the Central Committee. Zalkind was the main organizer of the First Pedological Congress in 1928, and gave the key-note speech. He then worked with the Materialist Psychoneurologists of the Communist Academy —an organ of the Central Committee of the Party—in the organization of the critical All-Union Congress on Human Behavior in January 1930. Again he gave the key-note speech. He was also editor of the journal *Pedologiia* (Pedology) during the first several years of its existence. In the early thirties, he came under attack, lost his editorship, and has not been visible on the psychological horizon since that time.

tempts to introduce a "Marxist approach" to the determination of personality—that is, to emphasize plasticity and social determination—as early as 1919,[37] and returned to the same theme at the First and Second Psychoneurological Congresses in 1923 and 1924, and the First Pedological Congress in 1928.[38] In his speeches, he praised the Pavlovian conditioned reflexes as offering a theoretical basis for the plasticity of the organism. Similarly, he commended Freudian theory because it played down the primacy of inheritance in comparison with acquired social experience and afforded an opening wedge for the "dialectical study of man's mutability." [39] At the 1928 congress, he made a strong plea for the realization of the political importance of plasticity, speaking of the proletariat's crying for consideration and help in growing into the new order. He mentioned the "calumny of P. Sorokin" that "the proletariat is the 'brainless' stratum of society." [40]

Official spokesmen of the Party and government, Bukharin, Krupskaia, Lunacharskii, and Semashko echoed Zalkind's statements at the First Pedological Congress. Bukharin referred to "the silent theoretical premise of our course of action, that which we pedologists know as the plasticity of the organism, that is, the possibility of restoring within a short length of time that which has been lost . . . If we were to take the point of view that racial and national characteristics were so great that it would take thousands of years to change them, then, naturally, all our work would be absurd . . . " [41]

There could be virtually no question about the official attitude toward the plasticity of human nature. This emphasis on plasticity was related to two central points of Marxist doctrine, the dialectical principle of the continual change of everything that exists [42] and the historical materialist principle of the social nature of man. However, the official view ran afoul of the strong biological emphasis of Soviet psychology and of the broad interpretation that could be put on the doctrine of "materialism" in Marxism. While the main weight of official sanction and of doctrinal citations favored interpreting "materialism" as meaning the conditioning of the human personality by the material conditions of his existence (a sociological orientation), there was a considerable tendency on the part of many psychologists to interpret materialism as justifying or indicating a predominantly biological emphasis. One can trace an initial rise to favor of biological determinism in the very early twenties. The favor reached its peak about 1922 in the enthusiasm for Yenchman's "new biology" [43] as a reaction against the "idealist," "introspectionist," and "anti-materialist" psychology of the pre-Revolutionary period, then gradually diminished as the position that the study of man's behavior is predominantly a social problem gained acceptance. The leaders in the attack on "biologism" were, in addition to Zalkind and the Party leaders already mentioned, such persons as Kornilov, Frankfurt, and Reisner. [44]

The chief targets of the official critics were Bekhterev and the reflexologists, certain pedologists, especially the child psychologist Blonskii, and defectologists—workers with retarded and handicapped children. The defenses of those attacked always were that their approach was both objective and materialist. Blonskii, for example, said: "But when I refuse to understand consciousness without a neurological foundation for consciousness, when I say that without a knowledge of the brain one cannot understand psychology, I am not being a biologist but a materialist, demonstrating the *ABC*'s of pure materialism." [45] But the chief objections to the work of such scholars were not to their interest in studying the biological foundations of behavior, as Blonskii implied, but to their projection of biological laws to social behavior.

The particular biological concept to which the environmentalist took most exception was the biogenetic law, popularized by the American child psychologist, G. Stanley Hall.

A Soviet author once referred to this law as the "citadel around which the fight for a new Soviet pedology was waged." [46] The biogenetic law, stating that "ontogeny recapitulates phylogeny," holds that the child repeats in the course of maturation the history of the human race. Blonskii himself, for example, made detailed studies of the use of dentition as a criterion of the organism's maturity, so that one might know what behavior to expect at various stages. He described the child of the "late milktooth age" in these terms: "The child of this age . . . is a nomad . . . the activity of this nomadic period is, in the main, hunting for plants and small animals . . . At the age of five to seven years, the child begins to climb trees, and gradually, toward the beginning of the period of permanent teeth he starts to hunt for fruit and birds' eggs . . . " [47] This example is unquestionably an extreme one, but instances like this eased by their grotesquerie the task of the environmentalists, who labeled the biogentic law as a reactionary doctrine which meant that the course of the child's development was predetermined by the past history of the race. [48]

By the end of the twenties, the official position that man's behavior is primarily socially determined was accepted at least on a *pro forma* basis by the overwhelming majority of Soviet psychologists, including the biologically oriented reflexologists, [49] and environmental explanations were in full vogue. The attitude toward the environment during this period was "optimistic." It was assumed that environmental conditions would improve with the changes which were being pushed in industry and in society in general. It was good Marxism to think in terms of the social causation of undesirable as well as desirable personal characteristics of behavior. Further, since the Bolshevik regime was in the process of changing the environment, which was in its existing form a remnant of the old regime, it was in no sense critical of the

Bolsheviks to make such explanations. Rather, it was a statement of optimism for what the new regime would produce.

The influence of the environment became an *idée fixe* with most pedologists. During 1929, of forty-two empirical studies or discussions of methods printed in the journal *Pedologiia*, eighteen, or 43 per cent, were primarily concerned with the differential effect of environment on the child's development. One study was on "Child Newspaper Vendors and Their Environment." [50]

Environmental influence was invoked especially to explain differences in intelligence. Consistent differences in intelligence were found between children of the various social classes, with the children of workers always faring poorly. [51] Such differences were accepted as natural results of environmental influence. "For us, there is no quarrel over the existence of social differences in manifestations of intelligence . . . since in every circumstance an associated reflex is formed under the influence of the stimuli of the environment." [52] Similar differences between nationalities were found, and explained on the same basis. F. P. Petrov explained the fact that Chuvash children were considerably behind Russian children in intelligence on the basis of socio-economic conditions. [53] Ionov found in turn that Russian children were two years behind Western European children in their mental development, and that the average IQ for Russian children was seventy-five. [54] Again, the environment was blamed.

Critics occasionally pointed out that intelligence tests used in these experiments had been standardized on children of America and Western Europe, with occasional modifications for the Great Russian population. They raised the methodological question of whether these tests could be applied with equal validity on a group against which they were not standardized. Nevertheless, the critics of this practice still agreed that the authors were right in principle in explaining differences in IQ between nationalities and classes on an environmental basis.[55]

It would be incorrect to give the impression that all findings by psychologists were unflattering to the Soviet environment of this period. Zalkind, for example, said that the new environment enabled children to mature without the *Sturm und Drang* of adolescence,[56] and Gur-Gurevich discovered a "precipitous drop" in the number of suicides among growing children after the Revolution.[57]

It would be equally incorrect to conclude that the fight to establish the importance of the environment as a determinant of personality meant an abandonment of biological considerations. Even the most extreme environmentalists held to the "two-factor theory" that the individual's personality is determined by his inheritance *and* his environment. In practice, however, there were vast differences in the emphasis which individuals placed on each of these factors, and for many, the acceptance of biological factors was purely nominal.

What is essential, however, in understanding the attitude of Soviet psychologists toward the environment in this as contrasted to later periods, is that not only was environmental explanation encouraged, but that there was no resistance to explanations which cast an unfavorable light on the environment.

The controversy over the relative importance of inheritance and environment served to reënforce the determinist tendency of Soviet psychology of the twenties, and to give strength to the picture of man as a passive accommodator to his environment. In the broadest sense, the passivity of the organism in relationship to its environment was a direct function of the attempt to explain behavior in social and biological terms, of the insistence on using for explanation such "final" causes as inheritance and environment, and rejecting such proximal causes as man's thoughts and intentions. This epitomized the scientific hopes of the Marxist pedologists of the time.

Until Pavlov, human life was considered to be governed by psychophysical lawfulness . . . (where the lack of clarity of the term "psycho" confused the whole affair) . . . After Pavlov's works, a new phenomenon arose which had real laws, a phenomenon which we call behavior, and which is, in reality, the activity of two basic factors: the environment (social and physical) and the organism (biological).[58]

Bekhterev, in discussing the biological and social conditioning of crime said that "one must acknowledge the fact that crime is fatalistically determined," [59] and similar views were current in the bulk of psychological writings.

This passive conception of man's nature was strongly illustrated in the field of educational psychology. Psychological studies of deficient and retarded children focused on the biological and the environmental causes of these faults, and maintained that the school could do nothing to rectify these conditions.[60] In the journal *Pedologiia* for 1929—the year in which the journal printed eighteen articles on the influence of the environment—there was not a single article devoted primarily to the process of instruction and/or learning of school material.

This attitude toward the role of environment in education was, in turn, reflected in the prevailing conception of training and instruction. It is here, too, that one finds the bridge between the equilibrium theory of motivation and the problem of plasticity. The assumption behind the project method, which reigned until the early thirties, was that the child learns best by doing rather than by conscious indoctrination. Much of what he learns, it was said, comes indirectly, implicitly. The content of knowledge is often the by-product of some specific activity in which the child is engaged. The "rules" of correct procedure are learned—if at all—after one has learned to do something concretely. As Shul'gin, the proponent of the "withering away of the school," said, "Formerly . . . the school taught reading, writing, and arithmetic. The child was *taught*. And now? The school takes him on excursions; it conducts campaigns; it fights against flies . . . and all this in the company of adults, all outside the walls of the school." [61] Another leader in educational thought, the pedologist Molozhavyi, elaborated this position, saying, "Education is not the ordering or systematization of the thoughts, concepts, and ideas of the child. It is the organization and order of his behavior and actions—of his behavior as a whole—thus giving him directiveness and maximum adaptability. It is not our ideas or our examples which train the child, but the fact of his existence." [62]

The psychological assumptions behind this theory of education were that the child learns in the process of equilibrating with his environment, and that each act of equilibrating leaves a definite trace in the organism which determines the course of future behavior.[63] The point of departure for the educator is the surrounding environment to which the child responds.[64] The task of the educator is the organization of an appropriate environment in which the child will acquire the required skills and knowledge.[65] But in order that the process of learning should take place, "the skilled hand of the educator must always maintain a state of disequilibrium between the child and his environment so as to direct the child along the road to his perfection." [66] The absence of any conscious participation in this process by the child is underscored by such statements as ". . . it is erroneous to assume that the child's attempt to increase his powers by exertion will yield positive results. In actuality this effect will disrupt the relationship of the child to his environment, and the results of his labor will be decreased." [67]

With this as the prevailing conception of the process of education, it is easy to understand the statement of a later critic of the project method, who said, "Shul'gin reduces the educational process exclusively to exerting influence on the environment which surrounds the child and the adult." [68]

Despite the enthusiasm of Soviet educators for Pavlovian conditioning and reflexology, these psychological systems never received appreciable application in pedagogy. Nevertheless, it is worthwhile to consider briefly the possible relationship of some of the assumptions of associative conditioning to the assumptions of the psychologists and educators who espoused the project method in education. Ordinarily, associationism has been considered an optimistic doctrine since it assumes the plasticity of the individual. There are indeed these optimistic elements in associationism, but at the same time it can be argued that the role assigned the individual tends to be a rather negative and passive one. The external relationship of stimuli—their spatial and temporal contiguity—rather than the individual's active comprehension determines the course of learning. To the extent that the element of meaning is brought into associative conditioning, it seems to me that the whole intent of Pavlov's and Bekhterev's insistence on objective concepts has been violated. The model of training by associative conditioning is that of an external agency (in this case, the teacher) which arranges events so that certain associative connections will be made. According to the principles of associative conditioning, therefore, the teacher would remain in the role of an organizer of environment. If the broad gap between the theoretical work of associative conditioning and the applied work of "progressive" education had been bridged, there would have been considerable compatibility in the two approaches to the individual. Under the theory of associationism, the teacher's role could have been more active, but the child's role would have remained essentially passive.

THE CONCEPTION OF MAN IN THE PSYCHOLOGY OF THE TWENTIES

We have seen that the conception of man implied in the psychological theory of the twenties was that of a relatively passive individual whose over-all motive was the maintenance of a state of equilibrium between himself and his environment. There was some conflict over the extent to which his personality was plastic and his behavior determined by environmental —as opposed to biological—forces, but official sanction was clearly on the side of environmental determinism, and attention to the social determinants of personality and behavior increased throughout the decade. But there was little or no interest in the plasticity of motives. This circumstance seems to have stemmed, in Soviet society, from the premise that man's motives are innately good, and that changes in environment would bring about the spontaneous expression of his better motives. In psychology, the lack of concern with the subjective constructs abetted the absence of interest in derived motives. All in all, the responsibility for man's character and actions, and the initiative for action, lay in his environment.

Particularly striking, in the light of later developments in psychology, is the minimal role accorded to subjective, and particularly to conscious subjective, factors in the determination of human behavior. To the extent that subjective factors were considered in psychological work, unconscious factors received a warmer welcome than did conscious ones. Consciousness was shortly to be regarded by Soviet psychologists as man's most important tool in remaking his environment, but the psychologist of the twenties regarded consciousness as the least reliable element in his scheme of psychological analysis. He was more concerned with the errors it brought to science than with the positive knowledge it afforded. The predominant model of man was a physiological one which saw causality as operating on a physical level. Man's subjective experiences were but reflections of the underlying physiological processes. At the risk of overstating the position held by psychologists of this period, one may say that in their scheme of thought man might at best know what he was doing and why he was doing it, but could do nothing to control it.

The tendency was strong to present man as a hollow shell of his psychological self, as no more than a convenient meeting place in which biological and sociological factors worked out their interrelationship. The premises of objectivism in science have great merit, but they also present difficulties when one attempts to construct an adequate model of human behavior. By the end of the decade the pressure for a revision of the model of personality was beginning to develop both within and outside the discipline of psychology. To some extent, the plea that the mechanistic model did not offer an adequate explanation of the totality of behavior was over-ridden in the early twenties by the enthusiasm for what it was hoped it *could* do. As the decade proceeded, however, as psychology established its position, younger Soviet psychologists began to be attracted somewhat by the more wholistic and dynamic psychology developing in Germany—on the basis that it offered a more adequate model of human behavior.[69] Many factors militated against the adoption of Gestalt psychology—its idealism, its deëmphasis of the influence of experience on functions such as perception, and so on—but pressure for a more adequate psychological model was developing in the Soviet Union, just as it was developing in the world of psychology in the West.

At the same time, the demands of the social order on its human material were beginning to become clearer and more insistent. We saw in Chapter IV that it was not until the end of the decade that the demand for training in industry became important for industrial psychology. In a measure, the same statement may be applied to educational psychology. It was not until the turn of the decade that the training needs of the educational system became firmly crystallized. Until the end of the twenties it was still possible to proceed on the semi-anarchistic assumption that if a child were given something useful and interesting to do, he would, in some way, "become educated." But as the decade ended, the problem of training was in the process of clarification, and as Shpil'rein remarked about the changing role of psychotechnics, education too was placing new demands on psychology.[70]

If one adds to these two sets of pressures—demands within psychology as a science and those on psychology as an applied discipline—the changes that were taking place in the social system at large at this time—the victory of the dialecticians in philosophy and a shift away from "spontaneous" to "consciously controlled" social processes—one will have an appreciation of the positive forces which were acting for the introduction of a different set of constructs to represent man's personality.

The question why consciousness and purpose were excluded from the psychology of the twenties may be answered in summary again. It seems quite clear that once Engels' *Dialectics of Nature* was published in 1925, there was a sufficient doctrinal support for the introduction of such concepts. Yet, such concepts were not introduced to any appreciable extent, and were, in fact, to meet considerable resistance even when there was marked official pressure for their adoption. The reasons were twofold. The temper of the entire psychological world at the beginning of the twenties was such that subjective concepts were suspect. In the process of rooting out the "idealist" psychologists in the early twenties, the Soviet system had lost the effective voices of a large group of those psychologists who might otherwise have supported such subjective concepts. Second, despite the fact that the "dialectical" position was "proven" on paper by the middle of the decade, the dialecticians had not established their point of view as official until 1929; hence, there was no *effective* doctrinal support for subjective concepts in psychology until the beginning of 1930.

With these considerations in mind we may turn to a study of the first half of the next decade, the period in which consciousness and purpose were restored to the model of man in psychology.

6 | CONSCIOUSNESS COMES TO MAN

The period from January 1930 to July 1936 marked the razing of the psychological systems of the twenties and the laying of the foundations of present-day Soviet psychology. The years 1930–1932 were years of criticism and reformulation. The implications of the general theoretical conceptions established in the philosophical controversies were spelled out for psychology, and the various schools of psychology evaluated on this basis. In these same years the applications of psychology were scrutinized closely for conformity to the newly established criteria of "political vigilance." Following on and slightly overlapping these years of criticism and reformulation, was a longer period (1931–1936) in which psychologists changed their applied and theoretical work in response to the newly defined policies. In the light of later development these changes seem not to have been drastic enough to keep pace with the demands of a rapidly developing Soviet society. On July 4, 1936, the Central Committee of the Party took formal notice of these deficiencies in a decree "Concerning Pedological Perversions in the System of the People's Commissariat of Education," in which the accumulated ideological and practical problems of psychology were given summary treatment, and the major period of adjustment of psychology came to an end.

While to some extent these developments were an implementation of policies developed in the philosophical controversies, they were also influenced to a large degree by social changes taking place after 1930.

MAN ACQUIRES CONSCIOUSNESS AND PURPOSE

The first major step in the revision of psychology was the clarification of the meaning of the results of the philosophical controversies. The four methodological principles of importance for psychology which emerged from the victory of the dialectical philosophers of the twenties were: (1) The laws of dialectics apply to all areas of science. (2) Each level of organized matter has its own laws which cannot be reduced to the laws of any "less complicated form of matter," that is, subjective phenomena cannot be explained *entirely* in terms of physiology, physics, biology, or chemistry. (3) The ordinary state of matter is motion and each system of matter or events has autogenetic movement; it moves itself. (4) A dialectical system of explanation provides for chance and accident, although, of course, not denying determinism.

The first of these principles is important only because it demands that the other three must be applied in psychology. The last three, however, were the basis for introducing consciousness and purpose into the psychological model of man. If conscious processes cannot be wholly explained in terms of physiological laws, then conscious processes must be treated as events having their own order of causal relationship. Psychology, therefore, has the status of an independent science whose subject matter is the study of these subjective processes. Furthermore, if each system has autogenetic movement, then man is more than an equilibrating mechanism. The initiative for action lies within him, and not with his environment. Consciousness, and man's own intentions, therefore, have a role in behavior.

The final principle, that chance and accident are compatible with determinism, is merely a doctrinal rationale for the implementation of the second and third principles, for making consciousness and purpose consistent with a determinist philosophy. It maintains that under certain conditions it is possible to treat man as though he were free to act contrary to the course of history. First, there is no system of explanation in which the trend of historical events is so rigidly predictable that man has *no* latitude for affecting the course of events. Second, it is true that if we regard man at any one point in time, everything that he is has been determined by previous events. Nevertheless, his thoughts, motives, values—all these things which are a product of the past—can be studied as they are and as they may effect the future. They may be regarded as independent factors in the historical process. With the establishment of these two chinks in the walls of determinism it is always possible to treat any individual action of man as free or voluntary, and thereby to hold him responsible for it.

The clarification of these ideas in psychology was begun at the First All-Union Congress on Human Behavior, called in January 1930 by the Society of Materialist Psychoneurologists of the Communist Academy to implement the decisions of the philosophical controversy. At the congress the irreducibility of the psyche to physiology and the general importance of the role of consciousness were established. But the notion of autogenetic movement was either poorly understood or unenthusiastically received at first. Its importance was not fully elaborated until 1931 in a series of discussions held by psychologists as an aftermath of the second philosophical controversy. The main issue of the latter controversy was the necessity for a closer tie between science and the needs of the social and political order. The doctrinal support of the militant philosophers who argued for the closer tie was the "Leninist theory of reflection," based on Lenin's theory of epistomology which holds that man perceives the universe by acting purposefully on it. For psychology the Leninist theory of reflection meant two things: a more positive statement of the purposive nature of human activity, and a more pragmatic approach to the truth of scientific theories. (The second consideration is more directly the topic of the following chapter, and the supporting theoretical argument will be developed there.) The first point facilitated the introduction of the concept of autogenetic movement into the theories of Soviet psychologists, and established firmly in psychology the generally purposive picture of man which was being developed throughout the social order.

The affirmation of the "reality of the psyche"—of subjective factors as accessible to study and as having their own order of lawfulness—resulted in the establishment of psychology as a science independent of physiology. Although this trend was resisted in the early thirties by a few reflexologists and co-workers of Pavlov, the independence of psychology became increasingly firmly established from this time on. This did not mean in any sense that it was assumed that psychology could proceed independently of physiological knowledge. The importance of understanding "the material substratum of the psyche" continued to be accepted, and the study of conditioned reflexes has continued as an important branch of physiology. In 1950–51, there has been even a reënforced interest in the relationship of psychology to physiology. But the basic principle that psychology is a science independent of physiology has remained in continuous effect since 1930.

The criticisms which were brought to bear in the clarification of the new doctrinal line in psychology struck at the essence of all the existing schools of Soviet psychology—reflexology, reactology, behaviorism, eclectic child psychology, and attempts to use Pavlovian concepts as an exhaustive explanation of human behavior. "For Marxist psychology," Party representatives in psychology said, "it is equally unacceptable to reduce psychic processes to either the conception of 'reaction' or 'reflex' . . . "[1] Such concepts, ran the argument, presuppose the reduction of all of man's complex behavior and thoughts to simple reactions to external stimuli. They deal with the process of behavior "in general," too abstractly; they do not provide a means to study the historical conditioning of man. Finally, such concepts "are based on the theory of equilibrium and ignore completely the problem of autogenetic movement." [2]

Party spokesmen hurled the charge of ignoring autogenetic movement and of relying on the twin concepts of equilibrium and adaptation at every Soviet psychologist except Blonskii, who earned this distinction only because he drew the more serious charge of projecting the laws of biology onto society. [3] The concepts of equilibrium and adaptation were said to give a passive, mechanical conception of man. It is true, they argued, that there are elements of adaptation in man's behavior. But the behavioral, objectivist psychologists stress too much the continuities between human and animal behavior, and ignore the distinctive, conscious, purposive aspects of man's behavior. Primary reliance on the concepts of equilibrium and adaptation, or of any concept that implied them was condemned. The Adlerian principle of compensation, for example, came in for criticism. Vygotskii had used it as the basis for explaining the development of the child's organism. He contended that the child develops as a result of responding to the needs and demands with which the organism is faced; that the child grows and develops in the process of accommodating to disequilibrating forces. His critic argued, however, that the initiative for action lies with the individual, and not with his environment. "The basic driving 'motive' of the child's development is involved in the process of his continuous active cognition—of practical activity in interaction with the surrounding milieu." [4] It is not the child's perception of the demands of the environment which determines the course of his development, he continued, but the child's perception of the disparity between *his* demands and the means of satisfying them that serves as the stimulus for his development. Thus, the argument of the mechanists and the dialecticians concerning whether force is a construct external to the system or the system has "self-movement" was repeated in psychology, and with the same result. The new position was that the system has autogenetic movement, and man is purposive.

The use of the concept of equilibrium, and the entire passive conception of human nature that is implied in the earlier theories was linked with "right opportunism" in politics and with political conservatism in general. The mechanistic model of man was said to be a fit model for the capitalists to use. *They* would like to think of the working class as robots entirely under their control!

The entire reactionary nature of this approach to man is completely clear. Man is an automaton who can be caused to act as one wills! This is the ideal of capitalism! Behold the dream of capitalism the world over—a working class without consciousness, which cannot think for itself, whose actions can be trained according to the whims of the exploiter! This is the reason why it is in America, the bulwark of present-day capitalism, that this theory of man as a robot has been so vigorously developed and so stubbornly held to.[5]

Not only did the older theories present an inadequate image of the "conscious builder of socialism," but they furnished an inadequate foundation for educational policies for training such citizens. One school of psychology after another was rejected as an inadequate theoretical basis for training Soviet citizens. The Western theorists Karl Bühler and Alfred Adler were criticized because Bühler's theories saw man as too narrowly individualistic and Adler—with his "drive for power"—presented him as too antisocial. Pavlov did not offer a basis for understanding how man acquired the concrete content of his particular culture. Reflexologists, reactologists, and all behavioral psychologists were criticized because they assumed that human personality could be explained exhaustively in terms of reflexes, reactions, neural processes, and other "objective" constructs. "How," one of the critics asked, "can this machinelike personality be reworked independently and creatively so that it, itself, in turn, may—in a corresponding manner—refashion the social environment? It is impossible to understand how this might be." [6] Freudian psychology, said Zalkind, the keynote speaker at the First Congress on Human Behavior, could not serve the needs of Soviet society because it is oriented toward the past. The Freudian, he continued, can tell why a person is the way he is, but can give you little help in making him what he should be. Furthermore, Freudianism puts too much emphasis on internal, unconscious processes, and too little on conscious processes and man's relationship to society.

Suppose we receive the assignment of studying the child or the adult in an institution composed of Freudians. How would this collective of Freudians carry out their assigned task? Now, *for Freud* man exists entirely in the past. This past is at war with the present, and it is more powerful than the present. *For Freud*, the personality poses an elemental gravitation toward the past, and attempts to fight the past from the standpoint of the present lead to profound tragedy. *For Freud*, the conscious is subordinate to the unconscious. *For Freud*, man is preserved from the demands of society in a private little world in which he constructs a special strategy of behavior. *For Freud*, man is a pawn of internal, elemental forces.

What sort of results will we get . . . ? How can we use the Freudian conception of man for socialist construction? We need a socially "open" man who is easily collectivized, and quickly and profoundly transformed in his behavior—a man capable of being a steady, conscious, and independent person, politically and ideologically well trained.

Does the "Freudian Man" meet the demands of the task of socialist construction? . . . From such an institution composed of Freudians, we would get from their study of human behavior such very "significant" statements as that man selects "unconsciously," and that the past directs all of his behavior. The consciousness of this man is subordinated to the unconscious . . .[7]

The new conception of man in Soviet society and psychology was crystallizing, and the task of training future Soviet citizens was beginning to have an influence on psychological theory.

CHANGING APPROACHES TO MAN IN INDUSTRY AND EDUCATION

Changes in psychology and in industry and education continued to develop in close interrelationship. As the new economy expanded and grew more complex there was an increasing demand on the mental capacities of workers, and an increasing acceptance by industrial psychologists of the importance of subjective, conscious factors in training, fatigue, and other problems of industry.[8] Whereas in 1929 a system of rote training in very restricted mechanical skills prevailed in Soviet industry, by 1931 the Central Committee of the Party clamored for "completely educated men possessing a good foundation in the sciences" to serve in industry.[9] This change was due not only to the altered demands of industry, but also to the newly formulated ideological line—itself, of course, a function of the developing society of the twenties. The "economic base" and the "ideological superstructure" continued their course of interaction, and fashionable ideological precepts reënforced the shift of industrial psychologists to a consideration of intellectual factors in work performance. Psychotechnicians learned that Lenin had said, ". . . the consciousness of man not only reflects the objective world, but it creates the world," and that Marx had said, ". . . a well-formed will expressing itself in attention is necessary during the entire work period . . . "[10] Increasing emphasis on "will" and "conscious discipline" began to appear, paralleling the public statements of Soviet leaders that there was a greater need for discipline and responsibility. As the lure of self-interest paled, the attempt to move man by the spur of social motivation began.

This shift toward a greater interest in subjective factors in industrial psychology was in agreement with developments in German industrial psychology, developments with which Soviet psychologists were familiar.[11] Nevertheless, the weight of evidence suggests that except for developments in industry and the ideological revolution in the late twenties the scrapping of methods of rote training would have taken place more slowly, if at all. The ethos of the twenties would have impeded this change. That of the thirties facilitated it.

The demands of industry for persons well equipped with basic knowledge had their effect on the educational system. The project method and the generally "progressive" techniques of education which had been in effect since the early days of the Revolution had produced children who were very bright and alert, but who lacked specific knowledge and skills. One story which was widely circulated at this time alleged that at a meeting of the Central Executive Committee one member after another rose to complain that his own child was bright, eager, and well acquainted with the conditions of labor in capitalist countries—*but* he could not spell! [12] Whether the story is true or apocryphal, it gives an accurate picture of the status of Soviet education at the close of the twenties. On September 5, 1931, a decree was issued restoring discipline in the schools, introducing the three *R*'s in place of the project method, and reënstating a system of examinations and grading.

The earlier educational policies of Shulgin and his associates were labeled "leftist." Official critics, with a magnificent command of both the complexities of the situation and the flexibility of language, pointed out that while these theories were "leftist" in form because of their ultra-radicalism, they were "rightist" in substance because their policies led to in-action in education. This inaction came from hyper-environ-mentalism, from reliance on the "spontaneous" relationships between the child and his environment rather than on con-sciously directed pedagogical processes. The affinity of such hyper-environmentalists in pedology as Zalkind, Molozhavyi, and Zaluzhnyi for the leftist pedagogues who espoused the project method and the doctrine of the withering away of the school was explained by the fact that "the leftists [in ped-agogy] were in the process of dissolving the school in the surrounding environment, and were making the spontaneous process dominant over the pedagogical process. *For them the child becomes the passive product of the environment.*" [13]

As a corollary to the opposition to spontaneous process in education the Party began a campaign to "restore the teacher to his rightful position" in the school, and to bring psychology (more especially pedology) more directly into the service of education. "Up to now pedology has been di-vorced from the immediate pedagogical process. An end must be put to this state of affairs." [14]

The introduction of consciousness and purpose in psychol-ogy meant an end to a mechanistic conception of man, and meant also a marked decrease in the emphasis on objectivism and determinism. We even find in the statements of the early thirties a questioning of the strong environmentalism of the twenties. Of the reigning premises of the twenties only that of the plasticity of man's organism remained.

What had been "correct" was now "incorrect." "That which I considered to be my virtue—regarding objective reality as the direct source of the laws of psychological de-velopment—became its opposite," wrote one Soviet pedologist, "or nearly so. It became the vice of 'tailism,' of the passivity of the personality. In a word, the personality was seen as fixed by 'objective lawfulness'." [15]

7 THE TURNING POINT IN APPLIED PSYCHOLOGY

THE PRINCIPLE OF PARTY VIGILANCE

Beyond affirming the purposive nature of man, the establishment of the "Leninist line" in philosophy amounted to a very strong statement of the necessity for "a unity of theory and practice" in all science. The latter point is of primary concern here.

The slogan of the "unity of theory and practice—with practice leading theory" is integrally related in Bolshevik thinking with the idea of *partinost*, literally "Partyness," which can best be translated as "Party vigilance" or "political acuity in the interest of the Party." The principle of political vigilance means that every citizen must always be alert to sense the implications of any theory or action from the point of view of the political program of the Party, and that the "truth" of any theory or the value of any action is determined on the basis of whether or not it contributes to the Party's program.

It is typical of the Bolshevik system that such a highly political, virtually anti-intellectual approach to science is based in a very sophisticated manner on a highly intellectual foundation, Lenin's theory of epistomology.[1]

As developed by Soviet theoreticians after 1930, the essential point in Lenin's theory of knowledge (known in Soviet literature as the Leninist theory of reflection) is that there is an *absolute* truth, but that at any point in time man knows only relative truth, and that he knows this relative truth by virtue of his action on the real world. Absolute truth is approached by successive approximations as each partial truth is discarded and revised in the light of man's attempt to apply it in practice. However, the nature of man's activity, the nature of his understanding of the real world is conditioned by the social order in which he lives, and by his class membership in that order. Every theory is conditioned by *and* serves the interest of some social class. (Note the conjunctive *and;* the fallacy in the argument which follows hinges on the addition of the second verb in the sentence.) Membership in any social class places limitations on one's ability to perceive reality as it is. But the further advanced in the historical sequence any class is, the better equipped its members are to know reality. Each successive order of society permits its members to approach more closely absolute truth, and the most advanced type of society, socialist society, in which the proletarian class (the only class which is not blinded by prejudices and rationalizations) rules, creates the most favorable conditions for discovering truth. Since all truth is relative and serves some class interest, and since the proletarian class has the closest approximation of truth, thus the theory which serves the interest of the proletariat is the closest approximation to absolute truth. Therefore, the primary criterion for validating a scientific theory is the exercise of "party vigilance." A theory is true if it serves the interests of the proletariat, or, more accurately, the vanguard of the proletariat, the Bolshevik Party.

The particular elaboration which Leninist epistomology has been given in this context is fitted especially to the task of keeping science under political control and is not strictly consistent with the application of the Leninist theory of knowledge to other topics. The very argument by which the Party is made the vanguard of the proletariat in Leninist theory is itself in contradiction to the contention that every theory is conditioned by *and* serves some social class. Leninists contended that the working class can never by itself rise above "trade-union consciousness"; that is, the ideas of the working class are so conditioned by the class environment that the proletariat cannot see those truths which serve its own interests. Therefore, it is the task of the Party, liberated from this limitation, to lead the workers. Hence, in at least one critical instance, Leninists argue that ideas are conditioned by class membership, but that they are antagonistic to the interests of that class.

However, to argue the logic of this argument is to obscure its intention, and it is only the intention that is of importance in this context. The most far-reaching consequence of the Leninist theory of reflection and of Party vigilance is that under the guise of being anti-pragmatic it is an extremely pragmatic approach to scientific theory. According to the Leninist theory it would be as great an "error" to contend that there is no objective basis for testing the truth of a scientific theory, as it would be not to exercise Party viligance. If a theory serves socialism, it *is* true. "Every theory in a class society is a partisan theory and serves as a weapon in the class struggle. But it does not follow from this that every theory is false, and subjective. Today only Marxism defends absolute truth, i.e., fundamental science." [2]

Thus the establishment of the Leninist line in 1931 was the signal in psychology for the reëvaluation of both theory and practice from the viewpoint of their contribution to the task of building socialism in one country. During the twenties Soviet psychologists had assumed that a proper Marxist approach to science consisted of adherence to certain principles of methodology but that, by and large, the empirical findings of science, no matter what assumptions of method or methodology were involved in their discovery, were to be accepted as "facts." Now, in the early thirties, "facts" themselves came to be scrutinized on a political basis, and "objectivism" came to be a term of abuse.[3] As one psychologist said:

One of the inescapable conclusions to be drawn from the Marxist-Leninist doctrine of the unity of theory and practice and of Party vigilance in science is that every theoretical mistake, every error in the field of methodology is inescapably transferred into a political error. Similarly, in the present state of things, every such error not only weakens the front of socialist construction, but it arms our enemies.[4]

THE CHALLENGE TO EMPIRICAL FINDINGS

The dangers which the regime saw in politically harmful psychological "fact-finding" were dramatized in 1931 in a hit play, *Fear*,[5] depicting counterrevolutionary activity in the "Institute of Physiological Stimuli." Spurred on by "class enemies" in the institute, the director, a distinguished scholar, Ivan Illitch Borodin, conducts a series of investigations on the social motivation of the population. By deliberately selecting dissident elements he manages to bias his findings so as to support the conclusion that 80 per cent of the citizenry is motivated primarily by "the unconditioned response of fear." From this he concludes that a new social order must be developed in which people are not subject to fear. The plot is exposed, and Borodin is replaced by a young woman activist. Later he repents and is welcomed back to the institute, but the counterrevolutionaries who mislead him are suitably punished.

It is doubtful that anyone thought seriously that psychologists, as suggested in this play, were deliberately biasing their findings in order to discredit the regime, even though some psychologists were later to be sentenced for "Trotskyism." However, the warning was clear: the theories and applications of psychology must be scrutinized closely for their political implications.

What this new policy meant in practice can be demonstrated vividly by contrasting the attitude of Soviet psychotechnicians toward bourgeois science in 1928 and then in 1931. When the journal *Psikhofiziologiia Truda i Psikhotekhnika* (Psychophysiology of Work and Psychotechnics) was started in 1928 the editors granted that it was necessary to combat bourgeois theories in the humanities, in philosophy, and even in theoretical psychology. However, they said, "It is another matter in psychotechnics . . . It is scarcely possible to oppose bourgeois techniques to Marxist or socialist techniques." [6] But by 1931 Soviet psychotechnicians shocked their foreign guests at the Seventh International Conference for Psychotechnics in Moscow by the sharpness of the line they drew between psychotechnics in a socialist order and psychotechnics in a capitalist order. [7]

To some extent the line they drew had a basis in fact. In 1931 there was mass unemployment in capitalist countries, and Western industrial psychologists were mainly occupied with techniques for selecting the best among the multitude of job seekers; whereas Soviet psychotechnicians were instructed to place primary emphasis on developing techniques of training in order to fill the enormous demand for workers in the newly expanded economy. That there was a difference in the main problems which faced Soviet and Western industrial psychologists is undeniable. Soviet critics pursued this difference further, however, and claimed that bourgeois psychotechnics was based on the premise of the immutability of abilities and skills and was designed to perpetuate the class order in capitalist society. As evidence they cited the preferential selection of Negroes and members of various nationality and class groups for certain types of unskilled labor. [8] These facts were drawn from the work of Western psychotechnicians and could not be disputed. What was distinctive of the new attitude, however, was the interpretation: that industrial psychology in capitalist countries was designed to perpetuate the existing class order.

Within Soviet psychology, a wide variety of theoretical positions and practices had to be reconsidered from the point of view of Party vigilance. In pedology, for instance, the "bourgeois" concept of the "antisocial period of development of the child" was labeled counterrevolutionary, and a critical review of everything written by Soviet pedologists was called for.[9] Kornilov's theory of the monopolar expenditure of energy was condemned as being opposed to the principles of "the unity of theory and practice," and "the unity of physical and mental work." He had found, with the aid of his theory, that there is a conflict between physical and mental work, and had come to the conclusion that it would be easier to make a manual laborer out of an educated person than to educate a manual laborer.[10] Thus he undermined the class policy of the regime, and its program for raising up the working class. Kornilov protested that his theory and the conclusions he drew from it were based on experimental findings, and that no contrary empirical evidence could be introduced. Thereupon Zalkind, one of his critics, replied, "This theory (even though it may be 'experimentally' established! All the worse: there must have been something rotten in the experiment) is methodologically perverted and leads to harmful practices."[11]

Other psychologists were criticized for the way in which they used statistics. It was claimed that the pedologists in particular fell into the practice of becoming slaves of "empty correlations"; that they discovered some empirical uniformity, such as the correlation between school failure and the age of the mother when the child was born, and then assumed that this was a necessary, invariant relationship which psychologists and educators must accept as a fixed condition.[12] Griboiedev, the leading figure in the study of retarded children, was accused of "arithmetical tailism, with a terrible panic in the face of 'objective facts,' without a precise Leninist Party acuity and vigilance in his approach, without any attempt to work out the system of study on a dialectical basis." [13]

To some extent all of these criticisms could be translated into terms that are familiar to Western scholars. Experimental results can be interpreted in various ways, and experiments can be loosely conceived. Social systems do affect the work of scientists. Also, many Western psychologists have objected to reliance on statistical regularities without an understanding of what lay behind them. But this similarity must not obscure the basic point of difference that according to the Leninist doctrine of the unity of theory and practice "practice *leads* theory." This definition of "practice" includes ideological correctness, and the right of investigators to come to whatever empirical conclusions their data and reason lead them is challenged on political grounds.

THE DILEMMA OF APPLIED PSYCHOLOGY

The more psychologists attempted to apply their techniques to concrete social problems, the clearer the political and social implications of their work became. In many instances these implications conflicted with the interests of the regime. The demand for political vigilance and the demand to make psychology an applied science—both integral parts of the Leninist line—exerted conflicting pressures on psychology and led ultimately to a sharp reformulation of the areas in which psychology was to be applied.

The dilemma in which applied psychologists found themselves was exhibited most clearly in the first few years of the decade of the thirties, the period which saw the most enthusiastic attempts to apply psychology to the tasks of building socialism and simultaneously the first application of the new principles of political vigilance. The main conflicts arose in the study of political and social attitudes, of class and nation-

ality differences in intelligence, and in the treatment of retarded school children.

The study of political and social attitudes had a feeble
beginning in the early twenties, but became an area of concentrated interest with the inauguration of the First Five Year
Plan. Many psychologists felt that in a period of accentuated
ideological conflict they should study the attitudes of the
people involved as a guide to the political reëducation of dissident groups. Shpil'rein, for example, called for a speedy investigation of "deviations of an ideological order such as characterize our period of transition." [14]

In the first years of the Five Year Plan psychologists probed
the attitudes of children and adults on such questions as "Is
there a God?" and "Which people are best?" and on the relative merits of the issues of class war which was taking place.
The repercussions were rapid. When only one child in an
Uzbek school gave the "correct" answer, "All peoples are the
same," to the question "Which people are best?" the *Uzbekhistan Pravda* carried an angry editorial that claimed, "The children in School FES No. 35 are taught to be chauvinists." [15] On
the strength of this editorial the department of pedology of the
Uzbekhistan University set up a special commission to study
the problem of the use of attitude tests, and found that such
instances of the "misuse" of attitude tests were not unusual.
They concluded that the Party must exercise vigilant super-
vision over the study of attitudes. The Culture and Propaganda
division of the Central Committee said that posing political and
social issues as open questions to which there might be more
than one acceptable answer was "politically harmful, and contrary, to the basic principles of our propaganda, educative, and
agitational work." [16] Such an approach, it was said, was part
of the reliance on "spontaneous" processes that characterized
the "leftist" trend in pedagogy. [17]

The criticism was so strong that by 1935, a half dozen years after the first flurry of interest, Soviet psychologists had virtually stopped the study of attitudes. As Razran, an American observer of the time, stated: "Such aspects of behavior are seen as things to be changed rather than to be experimented with." [18] Finally, in 1936, a blanket condemnation of this kind of research was invoked. "Such questionnaires as concern the subject's political views or probe into the deeper and intimate side of life," it was said, "must be *categorically banned* from use." [19]

Studies of the psychological characteristics of children of different nationalities and different social classes passed through much the same phases as did the studies of attitudes. During the early period of industrialization and collectivization there was an increased interest in studies of this type. It was felt, for example, that the impact of collectivization was bringing profound changes into the lives of the children of national minorities in the USSR and that special efforts should be made to understand the children of these groups.[20] However, the results of the studies proved to be politically unpalatable. They indicated consistently that the children of the national minorities scored lower on intelligence tests than the children of the Great Russian nationality did. It was found that from 15 to 75 per cent of the children of these nationalities were not fit, on the basis of various criteria, either for physical or for mental work. Psychologists tended to regard nationality differences as the natural result of poor environmental conditions and to accept this as inevitable. Some pedologists even suggested a new program, new textbooks, and special schools for Uzbek children to take account of the low mental capacity of these children as indicated by the investigation of Uzbek scholars.[21] Such conclusions were considered evidence of a chauvinistic attitude on the part of the researchers, and less frequently, the product of professional incompetence. In either case, the conclusions themselves were rejected. Virtue, though seldom found, was richly rewarded. Two psychologists who concluded that Buriat children were the equal of Russian children were singled out for praise. "These authors give us a more comforting picture than did those 'brilliant' Uzbek pedologists who discovered with the aid of Binet and Simon that the local children were complete idiots." [22]

During the twenties any defect of any social group could be explained on the basis of environmental influence. But in the early thirties one begins to find, for the first time, hints of the rejection of an environmental explanation of group differences in ability. The criticisms of the findings of differences between the nationalities implied that there was a limit to how much could be blamed on the environment, particularly when the implications of such findings were "pessimistic." In at least one instance this point of view was made explicit, and an author who explained the retarded state of Chuvash children on the basis of inferior environment was accused of taking a counterrevolutionary position. It was pointed out for his benefit that the environmental conditions on which he blamed the deficiencies of these children had been created by the Communist Party.

> The school failure of the great number of Chuvash children is explained by Petrov on the basis of contemporary socioeconomic conditions; i.e., those conditions which have been created by the Soviet state, by the workers under the leadership of the Communist Party. It is these conditions, according to F. P. Petrov, that account for the low average performance of the children who were investigated. F. P. Petrov, neither understanding nor wishing to understand the real conditions for the development of the children in the Soviet Union, speaks from the point of view of COUNTERREVOLUTION.[23]

Similar ideological complications began to arise from the application of psychological tests in industry and education.

It was not sufficient to explain away class differences in test performances on the basis of environmental effects. What counted in the eyes of the critics of these tests was the fact that when they were applied as a means for selection of persons for advancement in school, industry, or the Army, they operated in such a manner as to favor the representatives of political groups which were not in the favor of the present regime.

Beginning in 1929 there were complaints that the sons of kulaks, the wealthy peasants opposed to the collectivization of agriculture, were being selected by psychotechnical tests for command positions in the Red Army.[24] These complaints were not taken very seriously at the time and the use of tests was developed widely in the next few years. In 1931 and 1932, after the introduction of the Leninist line, criticism of the results of the use of tests became sharper. It was said, as in the criticism of bourgeois psychotechnics, that they "perverted" the class policy of the regime; that they were "bourgeois" instruments constructed to favor systematically the ruling groups of bourgeois societies. Psychotechnicians were directed to take into consideration the class origin of testees in order to give adequate opportunities for advancement to the children of workers and peasants who fared poorly on these tests. Two general suggestions were made: either different norms of performance should be established for each class, or a quota should be set up for each social class and tests used only to rank candidates within their class quotas. The latter system was actually put into effect by the All-Ukrainian Institute of Labor.[25]

Soviet refugees who worked in education and industry in the Soviet Union report with considerable uniformity that an additional problem arose, one which is not mentioned in the published literature. Party personnel scheduled for responsible positions in industry and education did proportionately more poorly on these tests than did non-Party individuals. This proved something of an embarrassment to the Party in its program to advance political activists to key positions in society. The result was that the testors made enemies on the lower and intermediate Party levels.

Wherever psychological tests were used in the early thirties, they seem to have produced complications. In addition to the problems already mentioned, there were difficulties in "defectology," the study and treatment of retarded children. Tests were the main criteria for deciding whether children should be kept in the regular schools or sent to special schools designed for children who were judged not capable of benefiting from instruction in the regular schools. The testors encountered an ironical impasse in their relationship to the theoreticians of defectology. The defectologists assumed that any child who fell below a certain level of performance on the intelligence tests was "oligophrenic," that he was congenitally defective and incapable of profiting from instruction. Therefore, if one of these children, after being sent to a special school, improved to the extent that he could be returned to a regular school, the tendency was to assume that the original test result had been wrong, rather than that the child had improved.[26] On the other hand, the defectologists themselves were under fire for the extent to which they assumed that children were innately so defective as not to be amenable to training. Critics maintained that the Binet test was misapplied, and that a diagnosis of oligophrenia should be made primarily on the basis of psychiatric examination.[27] If the defectologists were right, then psychologists were inept in their use of tests. If the critics of the defectologists were right, then there was no place for psychologists in the study of retarded children. In either event, defectology was another area in which psychological testors were in difficulty.

*   *   *

The difficulties which psychology faced in the earliest years of the thirties, 1930–1932, were but a preface to the revolution which was to take place in the succeeding few years. In these early years, however, one finds an increased emphasis on political control, a questioning of empirical findings, a more querulous attitude toward the practice of blaming things on the environment, and a general tendency to restrict the application of psychology while simultaneously urging psychology to turn to more practical problems. A crisis was brewing.

8 THE
DECREE
AGAINST
PEDOLOGY

History is usually written in a chronological sequence, from the remotest events to the most recent. All events have the appearance of following more or less inevitably upon the preceding ones. In writing thus, the historian plays something of a fraud on the reader, because he really writes history in inverse chronology, selecting the most recent events as his point of departure and organizing and analyzing preceding events in order to give a reasonable explanation of why what happened did in fact happen.

Nowhere is this more true than in writing a history of events in the Soviet Union. Soviet history is full of surprising twists and turns which few persons anticipated, and those mainly for the wrong reasons. Looking back on them in perspective these events make sense, providing of course that one understands the distinctive characteristics of the Soviet system that comes into play in decision making. The search for the explanation of such events is in fact one of the most fruitful sources of insights into these distinctive characteristics. The decree of the Central Committee abolishing the discipline of pedology and drastically revamping the science of psychology is such an event, and the history of Soviet psychology in the early thirties, and most particularly in the years between 1932 and 1936, must be considered in the light of this decree.

To understand why the decree was issued it is necessary to

consider the extent to which the policies promulgated in the
first years of the thirties were carried out, the problems which
applied psychology encountered after the first flurry of "Party
vigilance," and the course of social change in Soviet society
at large.

THE WORK OF PSYCHOLOGISTS AFTER THE PSYCHOLOGICAL DISCUSSIONS

The years immediately following the psychological discussions of 1930–1932 showed the beginnings of a shift of research interest of Soviet psychologists, and something of a
tendency to conform to the prescription for a theoretical
model of a conscious, purposeful builder of socialism. This
tendency, although in the right direction, proved, in the light
of later criticism to be inadequate.

Blonskii, for example, departed from his behavioristic position and published two major works more in the spirit of
Western Europe psychology—one on Memory and Thinking
and another on The Development of the Thinking of School
Children.[1] Vygotskii continued his work on the theory of cultural development, did work on the psychology of speech, on
the mental development of the child, and on principles of
didactics. Even in the light of stringent later criticism, this
shift of interest to the study of conscious processes was applauded. But some of the old assumptions remained. The
child's development was regarded mainly as a process of immanent maturation, and too little weight was given to the influence of training in the development of the child.[2] Furthermore, the theory that the child "learned by doing" remained
in Vygotskii's principle of didactics. He maintained that learning proceeded from the unconscious to the conscious; that is,
general principles could be understood only after one had
learned how to do something. Thus, in the learning of gram-
mar and syntax the role of instruction, said Vygotskii, is not

to teach new grammatical habits, but to bring to consciousness the principles of what the child already has learned by
rote.[3] According to the standards set up in later years, he
underestimated the role of conscious understanding in the
process of instruction.

Behaviorism and mechanistic, objectivist psychologies seem
to have been on the wane, but they had not disappeared by
any means. Borovskii, the leading behaviorist animal psychologist, and Kornilov were accused of having retained their old
positions essentially unmodified up to 1936, and Thorndike,
one of the fathers of behaviorist learning theory in American
psychology, continued to be translated and used as a basic
text in 1935.[4] Bekhterev's reflexology disappeared. Pavlov's
study of conditioned reflexes continued, but this work became
progressively more clearly defined as physiology, and attempts
to replace psychology by physiology decreased sharply.

Other developments were more in harmony with later
trends. The Leninist theory of reflection with its strong
emphasis on the process of cognition stimulated the development of an interest in "sensation and perception as the primary points of departure in the cognition of the world."[5]
L. M. Shvartz and V. A. Artemov, for example, approached
the problems of typography and military camouflage from the
point of view of the psychology of perception,[6] and Kravkov
began a series of publications on the psychophysiology of
vision.

Two publications of S. L. Rubinshtein probably came
closest to the position of present-day Soviet psychology.[7] In
an article called "Problems of Psychology in the Works of
Karl Marx," published in 1934, he made what is regarded as
the first adequate formulation of a Marxist theory of motivation and ability, stressing the plasticity and social conditioning
of these psychological traits. His text, *Osnovy Psikhologii*
(Foundations of Psychology; 1935) despite the fact that it was

later criticized, was actually the foundation for his monu-
mental text, *Osnovy Obshchei Psikhologii* (Foundations of
General Psychology; 1940), which, again despite later criticism, remains the classic of present-day Soviet psychology.

The problem of heredity versus environment which divided
Soviet psychologists of the twenties began to come to a
sharper focus. Attacks on an extreme biological approach continued. But for the first time extreme environmentalism was
criticized. The relationship of these criticisms to developing
political conditions was outlined in the preceding chapter.
Additional criticism was made on more general theoretical
grounds. It was said that one cannot ignore biological factors
in development, and that extreme environmentalism could be
just as dangerous as ignoring environmental influence. The
unfortunate experience of the "leftist" pedagogues had shown
that one had to take more cognizance of the actual capacities
and maturational curve of the child. The earlier emphasis on
the plasticity of the organism remained, but the question of
inheritance versus environment was posed more concretely.

Interest in working out a more precise understanding of the
relative contributions of inheritance and environment was reflected in a very extensive series of twin studies which began in
the early thirties. By 1934 the Medico-Biological Institute in
Moscow had under permanent observation 750 pairs of twins
who were being studied from the standpoints of biology,
pathology, and psychology.[8] S. G. Levit experimented with
different techniques of instruction, comparing the results when
different methods were used on each of several pairs of twins,
and found that the method of "wholes" was more effective
than the method of "elements" in teaching children block-
building.[9] Similar studies were made by Luria, Minerova, and
others. The full value of these studies was never realized,
however, since they were terminated after the decree of 1936.

If one takes the criticism voiced after the publishing of the decree as a criterion, it would seem that despite certain "steps in the right direction" psychologists of this period did not devote enough attention to problems of conscious learning, and that in studying the effect of environment and inheritance they did not treat the child as an active participant in his relationship to the environment.

APPLICATIONS OF PSYCHOLOGY

Psychology, particularly applied psychology, reached its peak in 1932 and 1933. We have seen in the preceding chapter that just as applications of psychology began to boom in the first years of the thirties, these applications began to run into difficulties as a result of the policy of increased political vigilance. The difficulties of applied psychology did not end there. Psychologists began to run into conflict with workers in other fields. Ex-Soviet citizens who worked in education, industry, and the arts during this period are unanimous in stating that applied psychology, especially the use of tests, reached its peak about 1932, at which time the resistances it generated began to mount and the tide of psychology began to ebb.[10] Both teachers and parents resented the claim of the testors that certain children were inherently incapable of instruction beyond defined levels. One former Soviet psychotechnician explained the conflict between teachers and pedologists in these terms: "It was a conflict between determinism and freedom of will." The artists of the children's theaters felt that the educators and psychologists who were attached to these theaters were needlessly pedantic and dried up the artistry of the theater.[11] Throughout the years 1932–1936 pedologists continued to have important functions in the school system, but the attacks on them, particularly those launched by educators, became increasingly severe. About 1934 the opposition to pedology and psychological tests began to sharpen in Party circles. An American working with tests at the Psychological Institute in Moscow was warned privately that he would do well to finish this work before the Party made a final statement.[12] Psychotechnicians in industry, hearing that tests were being criticized as anti-Marxist, began to be more cautious in their use. About the same time, as we have seen, the use of attitude tests was also cut back severely.

These attacks on applied psychology, partially a matter of changing ideology and the demands of changing political and social conditions, and partially a matter of interprofessional rivalry, were facilitated by mistakes and incompetency on the part of a large portion of applied psychologists. From all indications, the rank and file of these workers were poorly trained—as was the great mass of workers of all types of this period. The evidence for the low professional qualifications of the average pedologist can be found in the constant criticisms in Soviet educational journals between 1932 and 1936. This evidence is supported strongly by the testimony of ex-Soviet educators and psychotechnicians. This increased the antagonism of teachers, industrial engineers, parents, and others who had contact with psychotechnics, and weakened the arguments of defenders of applied psychology.[13] Furthermore, neither in industrial nor educational psychology did the promised work on training of new citizens and new workers develop.

Psychological journals reached a peak circulation in 1932; but at the end of the year *Psikhologiia* (Psychology), *Pedologiia*, (Pedology), and the journal of Bekhterev's institute, *Voprosi Izucheniie i Vospitaniie Lichnosti* (Questions of the Study and Training of Personality), all stopped publication. *Sovetskaia Psikhotekhnika* (Soviet Psychotechnics) continued with diminished circulation until the end of 1934, when it too stopped.

Thus, by 1935–1936, the signs that psychology was in difficulty were unmistakable, but the magnitude of the reaction which was to take place cannot be understood apart from the changes which were taking place at this time throughout Soviet society.

1934–1937, YEARS OF CONSOLIDATION

In Chapter III we noted that basically new lines were laid down in many areas of Soviet life—in law, education, philosophy, history, literature, et cetera—immediately preceding 1932. These revisions were reaffirmed with unusual violence in 1936 and 1937. To some extent there was an actual lag in the implementation of the policy decisions of the later twenties and early thirties. This occurred largely because many prominent figures of the twenties were still in positions of power, and complied reluctantly or in a *pro forma* manner to the new line. But the violence of the attacks of the years 1936 and 1937 was also a result of the fact that the basic problems with which Soviet society had been faced in the early thirties were sharply aggravated by the repercussions of industrialization and collectivization.

The years 1934 to 1937 were, as we have said, the years in which the Bolshevik regime turned serious attention to the solving of the "human problems" resulting from the tremendous social upheaval of the First Five Year Plan. While the industrial and social base of the old society had been largely destroyed, the "remnants of capitalism" still lingered in the minds of men. "You," Stalin told Party members in 1933, "as Marxists should know that in its development the mentality of man lags behind his actual condition. In status the members of collective farms are no longer individual farmers, but collectivists; but their mentality is still the old one—that of the owner of private property." [14] Problems of social control were mounting in all areas. At the same time, the demands for skilled personnel continued to mount. By 1935, Stalin announced that the critical demand of Soviet society was no longer material, machinery, or organizational changes in industry and agriculture, but trained people. "Under our present conditions, 'cadres decide everything.' " [15]

A whole series of changes were introduced, the intent of which was to increase the effectiveness of the individual members of society, to make social control more adequate, and to stabilize social relationships. The Stakhanovite movement began in August 1935. The new constitution, bringing the "stability of law" to the Soviet Union was discussed and adopted in 1936. Marriage and family laws were changed to bring greater stability to the family. The legal system was revised to increase the strictness of control over behavior. Dissident or potentially dissident elements in society were rooted out by drastic purges.

The main idea behind the social changes of the mid-thirties seems to have been the decision to bring all possible facilities of society to bear on the problem of training and controlling its individual citizens. It is only in the light of such a decision that it is possible to understand the changes which took place in education, and thereby in psychology.

THE DECREE

On July 4, 1936, the Central Committee of the Party issued the decree "on Pedological Perversions in the System of the People's Commissariat of Education." [16] This decree blamed the Commissariat of Education for undermining the role of the teacher in the school by handing over to the pedologists the most vital functions of the school. The decree charged that the pedologists carried out their work "in complete isolation from the pedagogues and from scholastic studies." The work of the pedologists "amounted to pseudo-scientific experiments and numberless investigations on pupils and their parents in the form of senseless and harmful questionnaires, tests, et cetera, long since condemned by the Party." Pedologists were accused of attempting "to prove from the would-be 'scientific,' 'biosocial' point of view of modern pedology that the pupil's deficiency or the individual defects of his behavior are due to hereditary and social conditioning." Chief among the "pseudo-scientific" and "anti-Marxist theses" singled out for condemnation was the "principal 'law' of modern pedology —the 'law' of the fatalistic conditioning of children's fate by biological and social factors, by the influence of heredity and invariant milieu. This profoundly reactionary 'law'," the decree continued, "stands in flagrant contradiction to Marxism and to the whole practice of Socialist reconstruction which successfully reëducates men in the spirit of socialism and liquidates the survivals of capitalism in economics and in human consciousness." This "law," ordinarily referred to as the two-factor theory, was considered to be the heritage of bourgeois pedology, "which for the purpose of preserving the supremacy of the exploiting classes aims, on the one hand, at proving the special giftedness and the special right to existence of the exploiting classes and 'superior races,' and on the other hand, at proving that the working classes and 'inferior races' are physically and spiritually doomed." Psychological tests were formally characterized as instruments for perpetuating the class structure of bourgeois societies.

To a great extent the criticism made of pedology and psychology in the decree of 1936, and in the discussions which followed it were repetitions of changes which had been made in the years 1930–1932. On such points as the importance of conscious factors, the plasticity of the organism, autogenetic movement, and so on, little new was added. Certain charges, however, were either new or much more heavily stressed than they had been. These were: (1) that test methods tended to perpetuate the existing class order; (2) that pedologists took a negativistic and passive attitude toward school failure, considering it a function of factors external to the school and a matter about which little could be done; (3) that pedologists gave too little weight to positive efforts to mold the child; (4) that stressing the environment as a determinant of the child's personality could be pessimism and fatalism. The first of these points reflects the embarrassment of the regime from the persistent fact that the children of workers and peasants and Party cadres in industry did relatively poorly on psychological tests. The last three points, however, may be summarized under one general rubric, that every possible resource should be directed toward concrete steps of training, and any activity which tended to turn attention away from the actual process of training or tended to deprecate its effectiveness should be stopped. The rejecting of testing, too, was closely related to the emphasis on training. The Party seems to have decided that it was willing to forgo whatever benefits to easing the manpower shortage that might come from systematic means of selection, and pose the issue dramatically as one of training versus selection.

Writers who elaborated the implications of the decree in the Soviet press charged that pedologists were not sufficiently trained, that they were extremely arbitrary in their relations with children, and that their tests were inadequate. But especially it was said that they were professionally more oriented toward finding an excuse than toward the development of a cure. Numerous anecdotes were recounted of the pedologist's tendency to divert attention away from positive educational attempts. For example, a story was told of a new teacher who arrived at a kindergarten fresh from a course in pedology in a normal school. Immediately he detected that several of the children were "difficult to educate." The writer proceeds in an ironical style to tell what followed.

In order to bolster up his contention, he investigated the families of the children with the purpose of demonstrating their negative influence on the children. As a result of the investigation, the teacher collected material which depicted the negative influence of the environment and of inheritance on the development of these children.

Then he selected fourteen children and sent them to the Central Pedological laboratory in Moscow. The pedologists, naturally, confirmed the contention that these children were difficult to educate, and also agreed that the blame lay on environment and inheritance.[17]

Instead of facilitating work to prevent "repeating" in school, the pedologists were accused of regarding repeating as a natural phenomenon, and, in fact, encouraging it with the "two factor theory" that the individual's personality is determined by his inheritance and his environment. The preoccupation of the psychologist and the educator with these two categories of determinants, as exemplified in the above anecdote, was said to have turned attention away from training. In response, a "three factor theory," the determination of the child's personality by inheritance, environment, and *training*, was introduced. In setting up the category *training*, Soviet educators and psychologists carved out from the category *environment* an area of positive action directed toward the molding of the child. This was, on one hand, a final step in "restoring the teacher to his rightful place in the school," and on the other hand, an attempt to implement the policy of directing all possible energies to educating the child by drawing a formal distinction between the directed and nondirected influences on the child and to fasten the responsibility for his development on the directed influences, notably the school. In place of the "fatalistic theories" of the pedologists, the following explanations were offered as the "fundamental causes of repeating": "(a) Poor quality of presentation of lessons. (b) Insufficient training and poor qualifications of teachers, particularly in the lower schools. (c) Lack of attention on the part of the teacher to the task of giving opportune aid to students who begin to fall behind in their work, and the fact that the teachers do not take special measures against school failure. (d) Lack of responsibility for the problem of repeating on the part of the school and the organs of education." [18]

The decree against pedology meant in practice that: (1) The role of the psychologist in the schools was to be sharply curtailed, his policy making functions virtually eliminated, and the educator made the dominant partner in his relationship to psychologists. (2) The testing movement was to cease in school and industry. (3) Industrial psychology was virtually to be abolished. (4) The model of man in psychology was to be, if anything, more purposive and conscious than that prescribed by the Leninist line of 1931. (5) The influence of the environment was to be played down, and the influence of "training" emphasized. (6) Psychologists were more definitely to shift their attention from the investigation of the determinate relationships between external phenomena and behavior toward the task of developing Soviet citizens.

9 | THE "NEW MAN" IN SOVIET PSYCHOLOGY

On one point, all sources (official Soviet statements, the testimony of émigrés from the USSR and that of foreign visitors) agree: the decree against pedology threw Soviet psychologists into confusion and panic. Students of the Institute of Psychology in Moscow complained that they looked in vain to their instructors for leadership and spoke of "the confusions, spinelessness, and panic which reign among our leading workers." [1] The editors of *Pod Znamenem Marksizma* called a meeting of leading psychologists and took to task Kornilov, Blonskii, Kolbanovskii, Leontiev, Luria, Teplov, and a number of lesser persons.[2] Shpil'rein and Zalkind disappeared from the psychological scene and Shpil'rein is reported to have been convicted of Trotskyism and sent into exile, where he continued some form of psychological research.[3] Departments of psychology were closed, and teachers of psychology wondered what to teach.

It was more than a year before the new line began to emerge. In 1938 a group of psychologists, led by Kornilov, who has shown an astonishing ability to remain on top in the rough and tumble of Soviet controversy, published a series of articles setting the "correct" position for various topics of psychology (the subject matter of psychology, the physiology of the nervous system, attention and memory). A bibliography with specific page references to the treatment of such topics in the classics of Marxism-Leninism was included in these articles.[4] Soon thereafter it was announced that this same group was attempting to work out a program which would cover *all* topics of psychology from the standpoint of the criteria set by the decree on pedology,[5] and shortly there followed a detailed outline of the course of psychology to be taught in teacher-training institutes—virtually the only places in which psychology was then being taught—giving the material to be covered in each section, the point of view to be adopted, and the amount of time to be devoted to each topic.[6] Later in the year the first general text written after the decree appeared,[7] but the authors—among them Kornilov, of course—cautiously refused to commit themselves on some of the most controversial topics such as mental development, needs, and talent and abilities. The authors excused the absence of chapters on these topics, saying, "We prefer consciously to leave a whole series of gaps—small or large—rather than include unverified positions." [8] Within the next few years, appropriate formulations were reached on each of these topics. In 1940 the first complete text appeared—Rubinshtein's *Osnovy Obshchei Psikhologii* (Foundations of General Psychology).[9] The publication of Rubinshtein's book marked the final definition of the line which evolved out of the decree of 1936, and the book remains the most adequate statement of that line.

In general, the period since 1936 marks so great a shift from the previous period that despite minor fluctuations from time to time it can be considered as a unit. There have been variations and developments, but for the most part they have been an intensification of the line of 1936. Certain gross trends within the period should be noted, however. With the approach of the Second World War, emphasis on the individual and his responsibility to the state was strengthened throughout the Soviet system. In 1941 and 1942 character training began to be stressed in education and educational psychology more than it had been previously. Interest turned to emotional, as opposed to intellectual, traits; and articles by both psychologists and educators on "strength of character" and loyalty to the state began to appear. Research in medical psychology was stimulated by the war. After the war, beginning in August 1946, Soviet psychology began to reflect the increasingly critical attitude toward the West which appeared in all Soviet intellectual circles. Late in the forties, the Lysenko controversy in genetics made a slight stir in psychology.[10]

Certain slight reversals of trend are noticeable since the Second World War. After 1946, both pre-Revolutionary and early Soviet psychologists began to be extolled as the founders of "scientific psychology." The old scapegoats of reflexology, reactology, and pedology are retained, but a somewhat milder attitude has been taken toward such semi-heroes as Vygotskii. Rubinshtein, for example, was criticized for appropriating Vygotskii's concept of "the leading role of instruction," [11] a concept which had once been under official attack as taking too passive an approach to the role of instruction. Such a shift is illustrative of the programmatic nature of many Soviet pronouncements. In a period in which the order of the day was to put greater stress on the active role of instruction, a principle which seemed insufficiently militant was condemned. Later, when the first program had been sufficiently implemented, it was possible to revive the earlier theory, because it happened to fit in with the current theme that Russian and Soviet scholars have been the "most progressive" agents in developing the world of science.

Of potentially greater importance, however, have been the discussions, which began in the summer of 1950, about Pavlovianism in Soviet science. It is too early to assess the eventual significance of these discussions. In all probability they do not herald any significant reversal of direction in psychology per se, but they unquestionably indicate that the precautionary isolation of psychology from physiology which took place after 1930 is at an end, and that there will be a closer working relationship between the disciplines (see discussion below, pages 170–175). With these exceptions, the period since 1936 may be considered as a unit.

The problem of dealing with variations from trend is very difficult for the period after 1936. Without a doubt closer control is exercised over the content of psychological research and writings than in earlier periods. Furthermore, the range of "acceptable" positions is much narrower than it was. It is safe to say that no psychologist would be permitted to teach or write anything that ran counter to the trend, *if* he and/or the appropriate reviewing agency knew at the time that his writing or teaching was counter to the trend. Yet there are constant critical articles in the Soviet press pointing out the failure of psychologists to hew closely enough to the established line. Whether or not the work criticized should be regarded as variations from trend is hard to say. In most instances the extent of deviation is from the viewpoint of Western psychology so minute that we would be inclined to view the criticisms as prophylactic measures designed to prevent any real deviation. If it had been possible to make a more systematic survey of the full range of empirical research done by Soviet psychologists, it would be possible to treat more satisfactorily the problem of deviation from trend. As it is, our present discussion is limited mainly to the "official" position. For this reason, the pedagogical journal, *Sovetskaia Pedagogika*, is the main journal source employed for this period. In the absence of any specifically psychological journal after 1934, this educational journal has been the main medium for the expression of the official view in psychology. Theoretical journals such as *Voprosi Filosofii* and *Pod Znamenem Marksisma* have also been of help in understanding the official point of view.

THE DOCTRINE OF CONSCIOUSNESS IN MODERN SOVIET PSYCHOLOGY

"Conscious, purposive action" has become not only the norm of conduct of the Soviet citizen, but the central focus of psychology, and the principle of "conscious understanding" is the fundamental tenet of Soviet pedagogy. Any tendencies which might undermine the idea that man is in conscious control of his behavior are opposed.

Soviet psychology is in contradistinction to bourgeois psychology in this regard—bourgeois psychology takes the "unconscious" as a point of departure, as though it were the central core of man's personality, but Soviet psychology has explicitly fostered the theory that consciousness is the highest most specifically human level of development of the psyche, and has indicated the dominant role which conscious influences play as compared with unconscious influences. In this regard, Soviet psychology is hand in hand with Soviet pedagogy. Soviet pedagogy maintains as the basic principle of didactics the doctrine of conscious understanding. And, in questions of training, Soviet pedagogy holds the principle that it is the conscious personality of man, his conscious behavior, and his conscious discipline that are to be molded.[12]

The Soviet conception of consciousness is above all tied to action. The most important function of consciousness, says the Soviet psychologist, is to free man from the constraint of the immediate situation, and to permit him to direct his actions toward goals and tasks beyond that situation. It is through the development of consciousness and through the acquisition of needs and interests that lie beyond the immediate situation that behavior becomes voluntary.[13] "*The first* [characteristic of voluntary movement] *is the preliminary consciousness of a goal and the presence of striving for its achievement.*" [14] As a matter of fact, the distinction between voluntary action and involuntary action is almost entirely one of whether or not the individual is conscious of the relationship among elements in a situation of action. The epitome of an involuntary movement is a reflex. One is unconscious to the extent that he does not understand the relationship between his feelings and his actions. The process of becoming conscious is the process of understanding relationships.

Soviet psychologists are alert to distinguish between their conceptions of will and voluntarism and the "idealist" conception which can comprehend will only as "free will." The freedom which voluntary action gives man, they argue, is not freedom from determinacy, but the freedom to carry out the necessary. "Freedom," they echo, "is the recognition of necessity."

The freedom of a voluntary act consists in its independence of the impulse of the immediate situation, and means that the behavior of man is not determined directly by his immediate surroundings, and naturally, *not* that it is in general undetermined; it is just that the lawfulness and determination involved are of a different order. Immediate determination becomes mediated determination. Voluntary action is mediated through the consciousness of the person.[15]

It is true, they continue, that conscious goals play an essential role in voluntary action, but these goals are themselves determined by previous experience. The stimuli of the immediate situation are mediated through the conscious goal determined by previous events.

This formulation, in addition to reconciling the traditional Marxist doctrine of determinism with voluntarism, serves a number of other purposes. By postulating that conscious man is free from the determination of the immediate situation, it makes him responsible for his immediate behavior. By stating that consciousness is the understanding of relationships and that "freedom is the recognition of necessity," it offers a rationale for the subjugation of the individual to the demands of society. By arguing that the possession of needs and interests lying beyond the demands of the immediate situation frees man from the situation, it suggests and implements a program whereby social needs and interests which will articulate the "voluntary" action of man with the demands of the social system are developed by the state as a matter of deliberate policy. Consciousness is the concept whereby the Soviet citizen is, in fact, liberated from determinism and tied to the service of the state. It is also the pivotal concept of modern Soviet psychology.

One of the most difficult doctrinal tasks with which Soviet psychology has been faced has been to formulate a conception of the relation of mind to body which offers consciousness a leading role in directing man's behavior and yet avoids the trap of idealism. Introspective psychology studies conscious phenomena apart from behavior. Behaviorist psychology studies behavior apart from consciousness. Each treats behavior and consciousness as though they could be studied apart from each other. Idealist psychologies offered an adequate role to consciousness but had to be rejected on ideological grounds.

The resolution of the psychophysical question—the relation of mind to matter—which Soviet psychologists accept is that of *psychophysical* unity.[16] According to the principle of psychophysical unity, subjective and objective factors are functionally interrelated aspects of the same phenomena. "The psyche," it is said repeatedly, "is an aspect of highly organized matter." It is both a function of the underlying nervous system—"the material substratum of consciousness"—and a reflection of things in the "real" world.

In holding this position, Soviet psychologists walk a very thin chalk-line. "Consciousness is determined by existence," but if one stresses too strongly the relationship of man's consciousness to the real world, he runs the danger of ignoring the fact that it is mediated through physiological processes, and

thus may fall into idealism. Even so adroit a person as Rubinshtein has occasionally fallen into this error. A critic of this
error comments: "Marxism maintains that consciousness reflects existence, but no Marxist has ever thought that existence
may determine consciousness except through the prism of the
human brain." [17]

On the other hand, if one stresses too strongly the fact that
man's consciousness—his perception of the world—is mediated
by physical processes, then there is a danger of falling into the
position of extreme subjectivism, by implying that what man
knows is more a product of the structure and functioning of
his nervous system than of the reality of the external world.
According to this view, man knows only his own sensations.
To the extent that they avoid these two traps of idealism,
Soviet psychologists have, with the aid of their philosopher
colleagues, developed a formula reconciling materialism with
a conception of consciousness that sees consciousness as an
effective agent in the direction of man's behavior.

The Soviet doctrine of consciousness is tied to action not
only in that consciousness is accorded an important role in
directing man's actions, but also in that it is shaped by the
results of his actions. Consciousness is "approximate" truth.
According to the Leninist theory of reflection consciousness
is developed in man's purposive action on the world which
exists externally of him. Thus, consciousness does not evolve
from the "immanent laws" of its internal dynamics (Hegel's
position), but it develops in interaction with the "real" world.
Man learns by acting, by testing his knowledge in practice.
Therefore, it is argued, one must study man in action to understand his consciousness.

The range of implications of this doctrine of consciousness
for the work and theories of psychologists may be summarized as follows:

1. There is no longer any question but that psychic phenomena may be treated as having their own order of lawfulness, provided always that relevant physiological knowledge for understanding these processes is adequately exploited.

2. Conscious processes are studied almost to the complete exclusion of unconscious ones. Only in the field of physiology, much more closely allied with psychiatry than psychology in the Soviet scheme, has there been systematic work on unconscious processes.

3. The psychologist's approach to a series of theoretical problems is affected by the a priori position that man's knowledge of the world is not "betrayed" by unconscious processes. The Soviet psychologist does not deny the existence of unconscious processes, but he rejects the idea that they are as important as conscious processes in determining man's behavior.

4. The position that consciousness liberates man from the immediate situation by focusing on goals beyond that situation stimulates the study of motivation and the training of motives in educational practice.

5. The idea of man as a purposive actor means that the study of psychic functions is always related to man's motives and goals.

6. The doctrine that "consciousness must be understood in action" combines with the dialectical principle of the "unity of form and content" (actually they are only aspects of each other) to support a more concrete, and hence a more applied approach to the study of psychological processes. "Soviet psychology studies all the psychic processes—sensation, memory, thought, etc.—in action. It studies them in concrete activities, whether these be practical or theoretical, and in the context of real motives and tasks. In this way, we overcome the abstract analytical treatment of traditional functional psychology." [18]

THE MODERN CONCEPTION OF MOTIVATION

The modern doctrine of motivation in Soviet psychology is based on two concepts: autogenetic movement and the "historical nature of man." As we have seen, the concept of autogenetic movement was introduced to displace the concept of equilibrium, in order to transfer the initiative for action from the environment to the individual. "The historical nature of man" serves, among other things, to implement the concept of autogenetic movement. By focusing on socially conditioned, specifically human motives, the Soviet psychologist is able to treat man "as is." The focus is on man as the *end product* of the historical process. The specifically psychological constructs employed are *need* and *interest*, and—with less precision—*ideals* and *duty*.

The first hints of an attempt to develop a doctrine of motivation based on social rather than biological concepts are found as early as 1931.[19] A fairly successful approach was formulated in 1934 by Rubinshtein in his article on problems of psychology in the works of Marx,[20] but it was not followed up. Further attempts were made in the years immediately following the decree on pedology. However, it was not until 1939, fully three years after the decree, that an acceptable formulation was arrived at and the modern doctrine of motivation was adequately stated.

The statement of motivation made by L. A. Gordon in his article "Needs and Interests" (*Sovetskaia Pedagogika*, 1939) is the one which is presently accepted by Soviet psychologists dealing with problems of human motivation.[21] In treating the concept of needs, Gordon describes the historical development of human needs—with due reference to the works of Marx and Engels—and underscores the fact that general biological needs (instincts) become transformed in the course of development of society into social needs. Thus, the sex drive becomes the specifically human need of love. He makes two essential points: Human needs "can in no way be reduced to drives and instincts"; and, "Human needs know no limits on their appearance and growth." [22] The significance of these points become clear in his criticism of bourgeois psychologists —Edouard Claparède, Freud, and Kurt Lewin. Lewin is applauded for having demonstrated the enormous plasticity of needs, but criticized for not having considered the conditioning of needs by social-productive relations. Freud and Claparède, says Gordon, are too biological in their orientation; socially conditioned needs cannot be reduced to biological drives.

A special fault of Claparède, in Gordon's eyes, is his statement that "need is a disturbance of the equilibrium of the organism." Gordon comments: "From this it follows, obviously, that the fewer needs a man has, the better off he is, that needs are an interference with his efforts to maintain himself undisturbed." [23] Such a conception of motivation is incompatible with the idea of the New Soviet Man as a creature of expanding needs and interests, a person who pursues ideals rather than reduces tension. Man, says Gordon, is not a system that strives for passive equilibrium, but is a conscious being who through his interests and activities constantly broadens his horizon and enriches his life. "In actuality, as we have seen, the greater the scope of human needs, the more varied they are, the richer and broader is one's life, the greater are the materials for his development, for the growth of his powers, the more he becomes a real man and is distinguished from animals, and their strictly organic needs." [24]

Accordingly, while needs cannot be reduced to drives and instincts, it is nevertheless true that they vary greatly in the extent to which they are conscious or unconscious, biological or social, the property of all animals or specifically human. This is not true of *interests*. Interests are built upon needs, but are distinguished from them in three respects: (1) They are focused on relevant objects; (2) they are uniformly conscious; (3) they are uniformly the product of concrete social, political, economic and educational conditions. Being entirely derived motives, interests are the social motive par excellence. In combination with consciousness they free man from the immediate situation. "Thanks to the basic nature of interests—their mediation by meaningful elements—man proceeds beyond the limitations of the immediate data of the situation." [25]

With interests, as with other human motives, the object is not the reduction of tension—the reëstablishment of equilibrium—but the pursuit of some goal. Gordon quotes Ushinskii as saying that "the more successfully our affairs go, the more the subject arouses interest in us." [26] Furthermore, interests are conscious motives, and within their framework all such psychic functions as thought, emotion, will, and attention may be observed. "The basic cardinal trait of the psychological nature of interests that distinguishes them from needs, drives, and instincts and makes them a really human characteristic is the fact that they are mediated by consciousness, by thought." [27] Finally, in addition to being completely conscious and completely socially conditioned, they are directed at definite goals and objects. "Interest is a purposeful orientation which is associated with striving toward this or that object, and it influences our activities in a relevant manner." [28]

Gordon's formulations of the theory of needs and interests are the basis, with some elaboration, of modern motivational theory in Soviet psychology. The essential aspect of these motivation constructs is that they are "functionally autonomous," to use the term coined by the American personality theorist Gordon W. Allport.[29] Needs and interests, once formed, say Soviet psychologists, have a dynamism of their own. Being formed under social conditions, and further, being the form in which all "more basic" motives are eventually expressed, needs and interests are an exemplification of the social nature of man. And, since interests are both conscious and functionally autonomous, the pursuit of interests is the ultimate in voluntary behavior.

In addition to needs and interests, the concepts *ideal* and *duty* occupy an important but poorly defined place in Soviet conceptions of motivation. These concepts are treated as a mixture of motive, goal, and ethical norm, and are very important for understanding how man is assumed to become responsible for his own behavior and his own personality, and how his behavior becomes integrated into society. An ideal, according to Soviet theorists, is an image of conduct or personality which a person acquires from the people around him, and to which he tries to mold his own behavior and personality. It is an orientation point, a norm whereby he guides his conduct and his efforts to better himself. While consciousness, needs, and interests make man independent of the demands of the immediate situation, the presence of appropriate ideals makes it possible for man to direct his efforts to himself. It makes possible "self-training." "When man lives only for the day without the constant necessity for self-development, when all his behavior is determined by private goals and by immediate motivation, when his life is not guided by an overall unifying idea, then the valuable aspects of his personality do not develop." [30]

Duty, according to Soviet theorists, is one's conception of what should be done in the interests of society and/or other people. As we saw in the discussion of the nature of voluntary behavior, internal conflicts are usually those between one's "feeling of duty" and other conflicting motivations. Obviously the "feeling of duty" is regarded as the highest of motives, the one to which all others are to be subordinated. The theorists argue that a person has achieved the ultimate of conscious freedom when his personal needs and

those of society are one. "Feeling of duty" is, however, not
a unitary motive but a resultant of such social motives as "love
of fatherland, devotion to the Party, a feeling of military
valor, et cetera." [31]

Since the content of so much of Soviet motivational theory
is preëstablished in political and ideological thinking, it is not
surprising that despite the emphasis on the "purposive nature
of man" there is little actual empirical work done on this topic.
In no year in the last decade and a half are there more than a
scant half dozen titles on motivation. The absence of empirical
work on the specific topic, however, does not mean that motivation concepts are not important in Soviet psychology. First,
as shall be seen in the next chapter, motivation is an integral
part of the theoretical treatment of psychic functions. Second,
it is a focus of interest in education. Whereas educators of the
twenties studied the existing interests of the child in order
to find out which subjects he would study most eagerly,
present-day educators turn their attention to shaping the interests of the child so that he will study what the state, as represented by the educational system, happens to want him to
study. [32]

Of particular importance is the way in which the present
doctrine of motivation, taken together with the doctrine of
consciousness, becomes a rationale for subordinating the interest of the individual to that of the state and for making him
personally responsible for serving the interests of Soviet power.
Soviet theoreticians contend strongly that it is only under
socialism that the individual can realize his full capacities and
the full satisfaction of his needs and interests. [33] Conflict between the individual's needs and those of society, they argue,
is a reflection of the conflicts in society itself. In socialist society, there are none of the internal contradictions of capitalist society, and therefore there is no conflict between individual and society. Gordon wrote:

At certain stages of the development of productive forces and of the social relationships conditioned by those forces, there occur conflicts between personal and social interests. But this conflict is a characteristic of class society and it cannot be concluded that this is inherent in the relationship of personal and social interests. With the destruction of capitalist society and its replacement [by socialism] this conflict disappears.[34]

The present-day Soviet theorists contend that only in socialist society is there a resolution of the conflict of the interests of the individual and the interests of society. To understand the significance of this contention, we must ask the question of how the conflict of interests is to be resolved. Is it to be resolved, as originally implied by Marxist classics, by the creation of a society that is innately harmonious with man's natural wants and desires, or is it to be resolved by shaping man's wants and desires to the interests of society? A Marxist would answer that the posing of this question is "undialectical," that the interests of the individual and society cannot be set in opposition to each other in this way, that there must always be some mutual adjustment. Yet the leading role must be assigned to one or to the other: either the individual takes precedence, or society does. It is obvious that since 1930, the emphasis has shifted more and more to the primacy of society over the individual. The Bolsheviks have clear objectives toward which the individual and his motives are being molded,[35] and these objectives have as their goal the proper functioning of the Soviet system as a whole.

Interests in the plasticity of motives arises out of the desire to shape the citizen's motives to the needs of the state. When the individual has acquired the desired needs, interests, and ideals, and is in conscious control of his behavior, then he is capable of "disciplined behavior." Disciplined behavior, says the psychologist Kornilov, is behavior which serves society. "By the word 'disciplined,' we understand the capacity to

unite with, and where necessary to subordinate one's behavior
to, the collective; or, as Lenin said, 'to devote his work, his
powers to the general concern', 'to serve the world' as Marx
liked to say." [36]

THE SHAPING OF HUMAN NATURE

Soviet theoreticians are extremely adept at the use of words.
For example, we have seen that the old slogan of the absence
of conflict between the needs of the individual and the needs
of society has been retained throughout Soviet history, but
that the meaning of the slogan had been completely inverted.
This device of retaining the form of an old slogan while reversing its meaning is one of the established techniques of
Soviet theorists. Another device is the manipulation of categories; things are arbitrarily redefined and then treated according to the new definition. A third tactic is the formulation of
programmatic statements which are essentially nonempirical in
that there is no meaningful way in which they can be proven
either "right" or "wrong." They are statements designed to
get somebody to do something, and are implicitly prefaced
with the phrase, "You should act as if . . . " The latter two
techniques, manipulation of categories and use of programmatic statements, are especially evident in the contemporary
Soviet doctrine of the shaping of the human personality.

The intent of the present-day doctrine is to accomplish the
following purposes: (1) To direct as much attention as possible to the potentialities for shaping human nature without
denying the reality of biological endowment. (2) To place the
responsibility for developing the New Soviet Man on a limited number of agencies within the society, including the
individual himself. (3) To direct away from society responsibility for difficulties without in any way depriving society of
credit for any advantages which may be claimed for the
present state of affairs in the USSR.

The plasticity of the organism is as much a "necessary optimistic premise" today as it was in the twenties. As long as there are "remnants of capitalism in the consciousness of man," it will be necessary for the Soviet regime to attempt to change human nature. In the twenties, as has been seen, the main determinant of human nature was considered to be the environment; human nature would change when the social order changed. Then environmental explanations began to be viewed with something of a jaundiced eye in the early thirties. These explanations were embarrassing to the regime, which was becoming responsible for the environment. They distracted attention from the concrete steps which could be taken in education, and in a few cases, hyperenvironmentalists seem to have paid too little attention to the biological realities underlying human development. The classic categories of inheritance and environment posed a dilemma for Soviet theorists. As the Western psychologist and the pre-1936 Soviet psychologist ordinarily use them, they are intended to represent a logical exhaustion of reality. The Western psychologist generally regards the distinction between heredity and environment to be a very tenuous one, with each factor being in extremely close interrelationship with the other; but, without in any way minimizing the difficulty of telling in specific cases just what *is* inheritance and what *is* environment, he feels that what is not inheritance is environment and vice versa. For the Soviet psychologist there was no retreating to a biological explanation; this would be "fatalism." But he had to escape from the "all-powerful influence of the environment." This was done by replacing the "two factor" theory (inheritance and environment determine personality) with a "three factor" and then a "four factor" theory, that personality is determined by inheritance, environment, *training*, and *self-training*. The categories *training* and *self-training* are essentially jurisdictional inroads on the category environment, designed to direct the teacher to teach, the psychologist to aid the teacher, and the individual to assume the responsibility for his own actions and his own personality.

Neither as materialists nor as psychologists concerned with the training of growing children can Soviet psychologists avoid taking the individual's biological endowments seriously. The idea that the organism is a *tabula rasa* is rejected. In order to avoid the taint of "fatalism," however, inherited characteristic are referred to as "potentialities," which can be realized only by appropriate training. Man's biological endowment is not something which impedes training; it is rather the necessary premise for training.

We have here a certain inevitability. It consists of the fact that a human being is born, with human capacities for development, and that these capacities are based on inherited human prerequisites. Obviously the acceptance of this inevitability has nothing in common with fatalism. It is not an obstacle to the realization of our educative tasks, but it is a necessary natural premise.[37]

The position that has consistently been held to be correct is that "only the anatomophysiological traits of the organism may be innate. These traits do not in themselves determine directly the abilities of man, since abilities are formed only in the process of development of relevant activities and consequently are dependent on the concrete conditions which make a given activity possible." [38] Any suggestion of "improving the race" by eugenic selection is attacked as the epitome of "bourgeois racism." Even the stability of inherited characteristics is challenged, though the challenge is a circumspect one, designed to reënforce rather than undermine the importance of training. A distinction is drawn between that which is "innate" and that which is "inherited." That which is *innate* already has its history of development and presumably has been affected by nongenetic factors. Thus, the possibility of the influence of prenatal environment is introduced, though it has not, apparently, been systematically studied.

The victory of "progressive Michurin biology" in the recently highly publicized Lysenko controversy in Soviet genetics posed the further possibility of postulating the inheritance of acquired characteristics.[39] Lysenko has for almost two decades preached the doctrine of Michurin, the Russian Burbank, that gene structure is subject to controlled change, that man can direct the process of inheritance. Only in 1948, however, did this position gain full official support. As early as 1940, G. S. Kostiuk suggested in a very tentative fashion that "the newest data in modern biology," namely the work of Lysenko and Michurin, offered "the possibility under certain conditions of hereditary reënforcement of acquired characteristics."[40] But despite the attacks which Soviet psychologists have joined in making on orthodox genetics, and despite their praise of Lysenko's point of view and its implications for psychology, there is no evidence that they have tended to adopt a neo-Lamarckian point of view. Kostiuk, the very man who raised the question initially, carefully side steps the question of the inheritance of acquired psychological characteristics in a later article on the implications of Michurin biology for psychology. He says it is true that training may operate on inheritance, but one can inherit only certain endowments and there is no one-to-one correspondence between man's physical endowment and his psychological characteristics. The determining role in human development, he continues, is that of training.[41]

Thus the individual's biological endowment is considered to be a real factor in his development, one which must be taken into account; but every effort is made to concentrate attention on the mutability of innate characteristics and to direct efforts toward what can be done by training, with the implication that there are no limits to what can be done.

THE PARTITIONING OF THE ENVIRONMENT

It is no coincidence that the 1936 decree against pedology occurred in the same year as the inauguration of the new Soviet constitution and the declaration that socialism had been achieved. With the achievement of socialism—by declaration— it was possible to announce that all the necessary conditions for the full development of the personality of the individual were attained, since, by definition, a socialist order has none of the fundamental conditions which, in capitalism, produce personality deviance. If a person is imperfect, then the responsibility lies in his earlier environment—or in him personally. "Divergencies from the moral norm in a socialist society are the manifestations of the remnants of capitalism in the consciousness of man." [42]

The "attainment of socialism" meant that one could no longer consider fundamental environmental changes as a means of improving human nature; it meant that the task of eradicating these "remnants of capitalism in the consciousness of man" had to be assigned to some functions within the framework of the existing order. This function has been called "training," and it is set in opposition to "environment" for pragmatic purposes only. It is, in fact, part of the environment as we ordinarily understand it. "Training" is that aspect of the social order that can be directed systematically to the shaping of man.

Training is the basic form of influence which the social environment exercises on the psychic development of the child. This constitutes all social activity that is directed at the nurture of the juvenile generation, the creation of conditions for their development, the communication to them of necessary knowledge, the development in this generation of a definite ideology and of norms of social behavior.[43]

One of the reasons for partitioning "environment" in this fashion was apparently to make the teachers aware of the fact that they were themselves an effective part of the environment. Thus, one writer commenting on the decree of 1936 spoke of "the tendency to overestimate the influence of the social environment in kindergarten work," and commented that "the teacher failed to understand the fact that he himself was a central figure in the child's environment." [44]

The term "training" is not by any means restricted to the activities of the school. It extends, roughly, to all of the individual's social relations, the influences which other people have on him by their example and precepts. The family, of course, is such an agency of influence, and interest in the family as a factor influencing the child's development has grown ever since 1936. The distinction between training and environment is drawn mainly to deprecate the importance of such aspects of the environment as the actual material conditions under which the child lives.

All attempts of certain pedologists to find such a dependent relationship as that, for example, between the individual characteristics of the unsuccessful school children and the sizes of their living quarters, the average number of times a day they had a certain type of food . . . were pseudo scientific. These attempts only disorganized the educators, deflecting their attention from the explanation of the fundamental causes of the individual characteristics of these school children and of their failure in school. [45]

In other words, it is precisely those "social-productive relations" and economic factors which Marxists stress so much as determinants of personality in a capitalist order which are excluded from consideration in the modern Soviet system.

The curtailed role of the environment in the explanation of the development of the individual is not only a reflection of the arbitrary designation of certain elements in the environment as "training," but also of a reinterpretation of the individual's own relationship to the environment. This began, of course, with the postulation of "autogenetic movement" in 1931, and became particularly pertinent in the struggle against the "all-powerful influence of the environment" after 1936. It is said that factors of the environment are not immutable, unchangeable, that "they are not only changed by people, but by the child himself who enters into active relationships with them and thereby alters their influence on himself." [46] In the course of time, the Soviet psychologist has come to hold that man is not only responsible for his isolated actions, but that he is responsible for his own character. "A man takes part in the shaping of his own character and he himself bears a responsibility for that character." [47]

The process whereby the individual shapes his own character is known in Soviet literature as "self-training." [48] Soviet psychologists have not been entirely clear about just when self-training begins, just as they have not been completely explicit about when the individual becomes "responsible" for his environment. Development of self-training is apparently a continuous process with small beginnings. "In the process of development there are gradually *created new internal conditions for self-development* . . . " [49] Self-training becomes an effective force as the individual develops ideals, a definite image of the course of life along which he will guide himself. It is for this reason that ideology and "communist morality" play so large a part in Soviet education. The individual is instructed to aid in molding himself to such a life ideal by giving himself self-encouragement, and particularly by constant practice of those traits of character which he is striving to develop in himself.[50] There is no empirical psychological research on this topic, even though psychologists often write about it. For illustrative material they use the example of fictional and actual persons—invariably Russian or Soviet heroes —who have been particularly successful in lifting themselves by their own bootstraps.

Positing self-training as a factor in personality development is the last step in a doctrine which sees the individual's personality as almost infinitely plastic. Soviet psychologists not only believe that the child can be shaped from birth, but that the human individual remains plastic into adulthood, and can continue to shape his fundamental character at a relatively mature age—if he is equipped with an adequate ideological picture of himself and the world. Rubinshtein, in his text on general psychology, has written:

The early years of childhood play an essential role in the development of character. However, the Freudian notion that character is fixed in early childhood is erroneous. This error arises from the failure to understand the role of consciousness in character development. Man takes an active part in reshaping his own character to the extent that it is related to a *Weltanschauung* . . .[51]

10 | MODERN SOVIET PSYCHOLOGY

Modern Soviet psychology differs from the psychology of the twenties in a manner more fundamental than the contrast in the content of the two positions. It differs in the extent to which its most general propositions have been imposed from outside the discipline by social and political considerations. Even though trends in Soviet psychology have paralleled *some* trends in Western psychology, it would be difficult to argue that the extent of the repudiation of behaviorism, or the adoption of the present-day positions on consciousness, inheritance, environment, and motivation had been forced on Soviet psychologists by the discovery of new empirical data. Behavioristic psychology involved the same methodological assumptions that had been dominant throughout most of the political and social structure of the USSR. The collapse of these assumptions—or perhaps more accurately, the resolution of the conflict between these assumptions and more activist assumptions throughout the Soviet order between 1930 and 1937—produced the changes in psychology that are the subject of this book.

It would be erroneous, nevertheless, to imply that Soviet psychology is no more than a series of deductions from general Bolshevik tenets. Modern Soviet psychology is rather a result of the critical review of the accumulated body of world psychological knowledge as refracted through the general premises of the new Soviet civilization. However, because of the peculiarities of the relationship of Soviet psychologists to world psychology since the mid-thirties it is not always easy to trace the precise source of many recent developments. It is nevertheless clear on the basis of citations in Soviet literature and by the flow of American and other psychological literature to the Soviet Union that Soviet psychologists are adequately aware of the work of their Western colleagues.

Bolshevik spokesmen from the time of Lenin to the present have continually stressed the need for making maximal use of the knowledge of bourgeois scientists, without, however, falling into bourgeois errors. This would seem to be a difficult line to hold, if one may judge by the volume of criticism which has been directed at Soviet psychologists for being too friendly toward bourgeois psychology, for failing to expose the "reactionary nature" of Western psychological theories, and for underestimating the work of Russian and earlier Soviet psychologists. Despite the fact that Soviet psychology has become increasingly distinctive, the pressure on Soviet psychologists, as on all other intellectuals, has grown progressively stronger throughout the history of the regime and has reached a peak in the postwar period.[1] Psychologists meet the demand for increased "Party vigilance" with studies of the contributions of Russian psychologist to world psychology,[2] with "exposés" of the political and social role of Western psychology, and with drawing falsely sharp lines of distinction between Western and Soviet psychology. For example, from reading Soviet descriptions of the work of Western psychologists on questions of aptitude and ability, one would never suspect that American psychologists have done a very large amount of work on raising children's IQ's. The Soviet version draws a clean-cut line between the "progressive" attitude of Soviet psychology, and the imputed "reactionary," bourgeois doctrine that the IQ is immutable. It would seem that the attacks on and criticisms of Western positions are necessary prophylactic measures which the Soviet psychologist must take if he is to maintain any positive contacts with world psychology.

The difficulty of establishing the exact source of many modern positions in Soviet psychology can be demonstrated by one example. It is a matter of principle in present-day Soviet psychology that experimental conditions should approximate as closely as possible the natural conditions of everyday life. This practice is referred to as the "natural experiment," and often consists of more or less controlled observation of a natural situation, or of some degree of active intervention in the natural situation. One of the typical expressions of this principle is the dictum that the child shall be studied while being taught. If one turns to Rubinshtein's 1935 text, he will find Lazurskii, a pre-Revolutionary psychologist, and modern Gestalt psychologists, especially Kurt Lewin, cited as the developers of more natural techniques of experimentations.[3] The reference to the Gestaltists and Lewin is entirely missing from the 1946 edition of Rubinshtein's book, and all modern Soviet treatises give the impression that Lazurskii is the sole source of this technique. This is only a single instance in which the difficulty of source ascription can be documented, but it is obvious to the person acquainted with Western psychology that such covert borrowings are frequent. Many elements of Gestalt psychology have been adopted. Also, the influence of William Stern on much of Soviet personality theory may be suspected, on the basis of the generally concrete approach to the individual personality employed by Soviet psychology and on the basis of some of the specific criticisms made of psychological tests of ability. We know, further, that Soviet psychologists of earlier periods were well acquainted with Stern's work.

Thus, though we have emphasized in this book the effect of factors internal to the Soviet system in shaping Soviet psychology, we must not overlook the fact that these factors have always been in a state of interaction with developments in world psychology. To some extent these factors have exerted influence in the same direction as world trends. Behaviorism has slipped somewhat from its dominant position of the twenties in America; but not nearly as drastically as in the USSR. Subjective concepts have tended to come back into favor; but, again, not as markedly as in the Soviet Union. On the other hand, these factors have just as often impelled Soviet psychology counter to world trends. The use of depth concepts such as the unconscious has increased steadily in Western psychology and has as steadily decreased in Soviet psychology. Psychotechnology has continued to flourish and the study of public opinion has grown into one of the most important branches of social science in the West. In the Soviet Union both are proscribed. The vigorous growth of refined statistical techniques of psychological investigations in the United States has been matched by a countertrend in the USSR, where a simple arithmetic mean is about the most complicated statistic employed. It has been the task of the Soviet psychologist, given a prescribed ideological line and policy directive, to shape a system of psychology out of the body of knowledge available to him.

SOVIET NEO-FUNCTIONALISM

The psychology which has evolved in the Soviet Union in recent years is a functional psychology. The current trend in functionalism began with the publication of Rubinshtein's *Osnovi Psikhologii* in 1935. Though the author himself later criticized this work as being an "abstract" approach to functionalism, it was in fact an important point of departure in the development of the present position. In 1935 it was still possible to be frank in acknowledging one's debt to foreign psychologists, and Rubinshtein indicated that his work was strongly influenced by the work of American functionalists and by the German Carl Stumf.[4] Later Soviet works do not acknowledge such sources. However, it seems clear from the detailed criticisms and discussions of the works of the Swiss functionalist, Claparède, in recent years that he, too, must have had a strong influence on Soviet psychologists. Surprisingly, the indigenous functionalism of the pre-Revolutionary psychologist A. F. Lazurskii and of M. I. Basov is seldom referred to, despite the strong disposition of Soviet psychologists to find native roots for their work. Lazurskii's functionalism was extremely introspective,[5] and would be unacceptable on that ground, but there are some elements in the early work of Basov—written before he turned so strongly to behaviorism and before the drive for the elimination of subjective psychology became entirely effective—that sound very much like present-day Soviet psychology.[6] As it stands, however, the origins of present-day functionalism are not entirely clear.

Functional psychology has always been an applied psychology. As such it suits well the needs of both ideologists and educators. As we know, the broadest view of man promulgated by both Soviet psychologists and educators is that he is a purposive actor. If one is to come to grips with the problem of how to train such purposive actors, the most concrete contribution that psychology can make is to study in action and development those processes or functions * whereby man relates himself to the environment in which he lives. Hence, the typical chapter sequence of the central section of Soviet

---

* The tendency in recent years has been to use the term "processes" rather than "functions." Apparently this is largely an attempt to avoid the taint of "abstract functionalism." "Function" was used in the first edition of Kornilov et al., Psikhologiia (1938), but was replaced by the term "process" in the second and third editions. Nevertheless, the approach was identified as a functional one—and an "abstract" functional approach at that. Cf. S. L. Shnirman (The Second Edition of the Teaching Manual "Psychology"), Sovetskaia Pedagogika, 1941, no. 9, p. 90.

textbooks of psychology is: Sensation, Perception, Images, Memory, Thought, Speech, Imagination, Emotion, Will, Attention. These processes are thought of as the tools with which man learns the nature of the real world; retains, conceptualizes, communicates, and reworks this data; and brings it to the service of his needs. In line with the ideologist's conception of human nature, in which consciousness liberates man from the constraint of the immediate situation, these processes are conceived as being in a genetic sequence representing successive stages of liberation from the influence of the immediate situation. Sensations, by themselves, evoke reflexes, the most involuntary of all actions; whereas imagination permits man to transcend circumstances which he has experienced and conceive of new combinations of elements, or of qualitatively new conditions.

However, Soviet psychologists make two basic criticisms of traditional functionalism; functions cannot be understood when abstracted from the personality in which they operate, and they cannot be understood apart from the material on which they operate.[7] Both of these criticisms stem from the conception of man as an actor. The basic fact of the situation of action is that the person stands in relation to some object.[8] The process of perception, for example, cannot be understood merely in terms of the object perceived or merely in terms of the personality of the perceiving individual. It must be understood in terms of the relationship of *that* individual to *that* object. The structure of the perceived object is important, but the purposive orientation of the individual toward the object is equally important in determining how it shall be perceived.

The effect and/or intent of these strictures against traditional functionalism has been to restrict the level of abstraction on which Soviet psychologists work, and to tie their investigations to more concrete practical problems. It is held, for example, that there are no "general" laws of learning, but that the laws of learning vary with the type of material being learned and with the stage of development of the person doing the learning. Therefore, Soviet psychologists and educators study the laws of the mastery of arithmetic, or of correcting writing and spelling. This point is also related to certain principles of Soviet didactics. Mental functions are to be trained in concrete activity. "We, obviously, are not opposed to the development of abstract thought, attention, memory, and the development of mental abilities in general. [But] . . . we must remember the most important tenet of Marxist dialectic philosophy, *the unity of form and content*. Content and form are inseparably connected, but *the leading role belongs to content*." [9] This principle is used, also, to reënforce the Soviet faith in the role of training. It is reasoned that since faculties are developed in concrete activity, the direction and guidance of that activity and the presentation of proper material will bring the faculties to full fruition.

PSYCHOLOGICAL WORK SINCE 1936

Psychology and education have drawn progressively closer throughout the history of the Soviet Union. The development of the pedological movement was an abortive expression of this trend. The decree on pedology not only brought psychology and education still closer to each other, but it forced a complete restatement of the relationship between the two disciplines. Present-day psychologists point out that the point of view which prevailed before 1936 was that of such scholars as Munsterberg and Maiman who held that educational psychology is a form of "applied psychology"; that is, educational psychology applies in practice principles derived from general psychology. There are, say present-day psychologists, two fallacies in this position. The first is the assumption that "methods of instruction and training must be directly and entirely derived from the nature of the child . . . therefore, that instruction and training cannot actively direct and affect development, but must, on the other hand, conform to the 'natural course' of this development. . ." [10] The second fallacy is the premise that the psyche is "a complex of separate abilities and traits that develop by their own independent laws" without respect to the *content* of the child's experience; that is, the earlier psychologists were guilty of "abstract" functionalism. If it were possible for abilities and traits to develop apart from the content of experience then "it would be completely logical to study general laws of memory, etc., under laboratory conditions, and from these studies deduce pedagogical principles." But the premise is fallacious and "the value of such 'applied' psychology in pedagogical practice is nil." Since 1936 "pedagogical psychology has become much less the 'application' of general psychological laws, and has become the psychological study of the pedagogical processes." [11]

Such declarations are better understood in terms of what they are intended to accomplish rather than in terms of their overt meaning. There is no disposition for Soviet educators to deny in practice the characteristics of the growing child, as the criticism of the first "fallacy" would seem to imply. The intent of both this point and of the criticism of "abstract" functionalism is to direct the attention of psychologists away from laboratory studies toward work of more immediate use to educators.

Psychologists everywhere have always stated the goals of their discipline as the traditional goals of all science, to understand, predict, and control. The sequence in which these goals are stated implies that the first goal, understanding, is a prerequisite for the second, and that both the first and second are prerequisites for the third. Soviet psychologists, however, stress the goal of control to such an extent that the other two objectives tend to trail in its wake, and attempts to understand

and predict are focused on those areas where control is desired. Ideally all psychological investigation should take some practical task as its point of departure. "Our basic defect in this regard," said the psychologist A. A. Smirnov in a public speech, "is that we do not start out with practice, but we try 'post factum' to apply our results in practice." [12]

The main objective of Soviet psychology, to do work of practical importance for education and training by studying first the psychological aspects of the process of education, and second the development and operation of those functions whereby man relates himself to the external world, virtually determines the range of work done by Soviet psychologists. By 1938, educational and child psychology were the dominant fields of interest, with general psychology, the psychology of art, and "pathopsychology" trailing behind. The psychology of labor and animal psychology were poorly represented. [13]

The same relative emphases have obtained since that time. In 1949, if one excludes historical articles, book reviews, bibliographies, and articles on administrative problems and controversy, there were 248 articles in the Directory of Psychological Literature complied by *Sovetskaia Pedagogika*. [14] Slightly over half (52 per cent) of all articles fell in the categories of child and educational psychology. General psychology came next with 29 per cent, pathopsychology with 12 per cent, and other categories—such as personality, psychology of art, zoological psychology, and defectology—trailed behind with no one category representing as much as 5 per cent of the total literature. It is my impression that these figures are representative of any non-war year since 1937. Figures for all postwar years vary only a few percentage points for any category.

The large quantity of work done in the field of child and educational psychology is not matched, however, by an equally high quality. In educational psychology particularly a pretentious title may frequently cover a report of a teacher's classrooom observations.

What is striking is the almost complete disappearance of all work connected with psychotechnics and the testing movement. Only from three to six articles a year on the psychology of labor remain. There is no literature on psychotechnics after the mid-thirties. Intensive questioning of scores of persons from different walks of Soviet life—psychologists, journalists, engineers, former psychotechnicians, military personnel—gives a slightly confusing picture of whether or not the use of psychological tests has disappeared *completely*. There are indications that psychomotor tests are used for selection of such personnel as chauffeurs. Also there is apparently a very limited use of some tests in the military. There is no question, however, that there is *no mass use* of tests. I have not heard of the use of intelligence tests in any form. Most "testing" is medical or physiological.

Animal psychology is very limited.[15] Since 1936, each year a very small number of items (never over six) concerned with problems of phylogenesis or the study of animal behavior per se appear. The content of research in these areas is considerably different from that done by American psychologists working with animals. "Zoöpsychology" is concerned with problems of phylogenesis or with the study of animal behavior per se. Attempts to work out on animals general laws of psychology which might be carried over to human beings have been proscribed since 1936. Work on conditioned reflexes, too, has been primarily on animals and has been focused on discovering the physiological laws that lie behind psychological phenomena.[16]

Investigations of conditioned reflexes included under the category general psychology in recent yearly indexes have amounted to approximately 5 per cent of the total number of articles listed. If one were to include all the work on conditioned reflexes published in physiological journals, but not listed in the psychological index, this proportion would increase. It might, perhaps, double. This surmise, however, poses the vexing question of deciding where to draw the border between psychology and physiology. By some criteria, these investigations would be included as psychology. Just as significant as the fact that this work has been done, however, is the additional fact that up to 1950, Soviet psychologists considered it to be primarily physiology rather than psychology.

Soviet pathopsychology is, by our standards, more properly a branch of medicine or physiology. There is none of the continuity among Soviet general psychology, pathopsychology, and psychiatry, that there is among general psychology and clinical or abnormal psychology and psychiatry in the United States.[17] "Defectology" is concerned almost exclusively with the problems of handicapped children. In 1949, for example, six of the seven articles listed were on the psychology of blind and deaf children.

An especially interesting feature of the distribution of research interests of Soviet psychologists is the amount of work done on sensation and perception. For more than a decade this has been overwhelmingly the largest field of interest in general psychology. In 1949 it accounted for forty-four items in the directory (60 per cent of those under general psychology, 18 per cent of the total). The concentration of work in this area is apparently a result of three circumstances: (1) It is a topic of research that has strong doctrinal support in the form of the emphasis on perception in Leninist philosophy and in the conception of man's purposeful relationship to the environment. (2) Although there is a defined political line in this area, it is one which is broad enough to encompass almost any research. By refusing on methodological grounds to fall into either extreme of approach to perception—an exclusive concentration on the structure of the stimulus as the determinant of perception, or an exclusive preoccupation with the "learned" elements in perception—Soviet psychologists are left free to study the full range of perceptual phenomena. Similarly, on the basis of the philosophical premise that form cannot be divorced from content, Soviet psychologists have doctrinal support (in fact, an injunction) to work on problems of sensation. To study perception apart from sensation would be "abstract formalism." To study sensation apart from perception, particularly apart from man's purposeful orientation toward the object sensed, would constitute going over to the side of idealists and regarding man's knowledge of the world as a passive record of sensory stimuli.

(3) Problems of sensation and perception are of traditional interest to psychologists, and there was work in progress on many of these problems by Russian and Soviet psychophysiologists before there was any active doctrinal support for such research. Kravkov's work on the psychophysiology of the eye was begun several years before the introduction of the Leninist line in the early thirties. Research on sensory interaction (the study of the effect of one sense organ on the functioning of other sense organs) is hailed as an example of the application of dialectical principles to psychology and physiology, but this work began before the Revolution. There is evidence that the more purely psychological forms of perception research were stimulated by official encouragement after 1931, but the study of sensation and perception is as a whole an example of an area of research in which the prescription of Marxist doctrine are so broad that much of the work has gone on from the time of the Revolution as though Marxist doctrine did not exist. Soviet psychologists have found here a compatibility of dogma and science, and have done some of their most intensive and best work in this field.[18]

Thus, since 1936, all the work of Soviet psychology has become progressively tied to a relatively few fields of application, principally aiding the educator and secondarily giving help to the sick and handicapped. These areas of application account for about two-thirds of all applied and theoretical work. The majority of the remaining works are in the field of sensation and perception, a providential oasis in an ideological desert. And, just as the fields of work of Soviet psychologists have become progressively constricted, so has the range of theoretical models used. As far as the psychology of normal persons is concerned, just one theoretical model obtains, and it is essentially the image of the New Soviet Man.

THE NEW MAN AND THEORIES OF PSYCHOLOGY AND EDUCATION

The picture of the New Soviet Man as a conscious, purposive, builder of the socialism, who is capable of change and modification to the ideals of the socialist state even as an adult, permeates theories of psychology and education. It is possible here to cite only a few examples for illustration.

The basic principle of modern Soviet didactics is the principle of conscious understanding. The basis of this principle is that the child learns better if the teacher proceeds from an explanation of general principles to practice rather than starting with practice and either letting the child infer these principles or explaining them to the child later. The motto "learn by doing" is rejected. A recent writer cites seven ways in which consciousness enters into the process of education, ranging from an explicit knowledge of the goal and tasks of education, to the conscious application of one's knowledge in practice.[19]

The theories of learning of Soviet psychologists are congruent with this approach. Behavioristic learning theories are criticized on two points: (1) Above the animal level one encounters intellectual, intelligent behavior that is qualitatively distinct from automatic habits. (2) In such behavior, the na-

ture of habits is different from habits in animals, since human
habits are generally formed in the process of conscious learning and become automatic later.[20]

The contention that human learning is qualitatively distinct from animal learning is used also in criticism of Gestalt
learning theories. The famous Gestaltist experiment of Wolf-
gang Köhler in which an ape hit on the solution of pushing
one stick into the end of another in order to reach a banana
which was otherwise out of reach was repeated with variations
by Vatsuro. However, Vatsuro put a series of holes in the side
of the main stick. He found that the ape was just as likely to
stick the second stick into the side holes as into the end of the
stick. Thereby it is argued that the original experiment was so
structured as to create the illusion of animal intelligence.[21]

Soviet studies of learning are carried out almost exclusively
with human subjects—a reflection of the doctrine of the qualitatively distinct nature of human intellect—and they are almost invariably studies of the learning of some relatively concrete activity—a reflection of the doctrine of the unity of form
and content, which says that there are no "general" laws of
learning.

The basic content of education is the "acquisition of a system of knowledge, coupled with the mastery of relevant
habits." [22] Much attention is given to the problem of mastery of
correct habits, and in this process conscious understanding is
given a prominent role. There are, it is said, two kinds of
habits, simple mechanical habits and complex habits. Complex
habits are not formed mechanically, as behaviorist theorists
have argued, says the Soviet psychologist. The automaticity of
complex habits is the last stage of their formation. The first
stage is learning *how* a thing is done. Next one must *acquire
the skills* involved in doing the thing. Finally he must *practice*
so that the action becomes automatic. Thus a student may be
able to write perfectly from dictation but begins to make

spelling mistakes when he tries to write something original. The reason, it is said, is that the habit has not yet become completely automatic and writing per se demands the child's full attention.[23]

The principle of two basic stages in learning, learning how to do a thing and fixing what is learned so that it becomes automatic, was used in a typical piece of research designed to improve techniques of teaching arithmetic. Pupils' errors were analyzed and those errors which were unpatterned were assumed to be the results of faulty remembering and to demand more intensive drill. Those errors which were systematic were assumed to be the result of incorrect understanding and to demand more adequate explanation.[24] The Soviet doctrine of learning and training is, therefore, highly dependent on conscious processes.

Lest this presentation lead to oversimplification, we should point out that Soviet psychologists have demonstrated that there are conditions under which involuntary remembering can be more effective than deliberate memorizing; that is, if the involuntary memorizing takes place in the context of some appropriate activity. P. I. Zinchenko, for example, set for his subjects the task of describing a picture placed before them. They remembered the details better than other subjects who were instructed to memorize the contents of the picture. Smirnov carried out a similar experiment.[25] Despite this work, however, Soviet theories of learning rest much more strongly on conscious processes and understanding than do Western theories.

Finally, the concept of purposiveness affects Soviet learning theories. Many Western theorists hold to the "law of effect," which states roughly that the organism learns those responses which are followed by a reduction of tension. Soviet theorists reject this statement and postulate the operation of such auxiliary motives as curiosity, the desire for knowledge for its own sake, the acquisition of knowledge as a tool, and so on. To accept a theory which said that the New Man learned only that which returned him to the level of inactivity would be unthinkable.

Soviet psychologists usually insist that all their psychology is personality psychology. This is true, however, only in that they study the separate psychic functions in terms of the personality in which they are imbedded. Both from the standpoint of any general theory of personality and from the standpoint of empirical work done, personality psychology is a very poorly developed field in Soviet psychology, and Soviet critics constantly lament this fact.

The basic concepts of Soviet personality theory may be sketched briefly. The concept closest to our concept of "personality" is their "character." The literal word for "personality," *lichnost'*, implies something more concrete than our understanding of personality. *Lichnost'* must often be translated as "person." "Character" is all those traits which are *essential* to understanding a given individual. It is explicitly stated that not *all* aspects of the individual are part of his character.

Underlying character there are varieties of temperament (choleric, sanguine, melancholic, and phlegmatic) which are presumed to correspond to Pavlov's four types of nervous system (impetuous, lively, weak, and quiet). Temperament is determined largely by its physiological base, but in no way determines the individuals' aptitudes and abilities. "Great abilities may be found just as often in connection with any type of temperament." [26] In addition to predispositions toward certain types of temperament, man inherits certain endowments. As indicated in the discussion of plasticity, these endowments are regarded as potentialities which have to be developed through appropriate experience.

According to the dominant theory of personality development current in the Soviet Union, these endowments and man's psychic functions in general develop in a series of "leading activities." [27] Such "leading activities" are the changing series of social relationships—play, study, work—through which the child passes to assume his adult role in society. His needs, interests, skills, and traits of character develop within each activity to the point that he is prepared to move into the next more advanced system of social relationships.

This theory is characteristic of Soviet psychology in its emphasis on the leading role of social over maturational factors and in the use of qualitatively distinct stages to depict the course of the child's development. The emphasis on "leading activities" in no way detracts from the importance of training. The activities of play, study, and labor are part of the system of relationships *within* which the child develops and is trained. Rubinshtein, for example, devotes a fifty-page chapter to the discussion of the psychological nature of activities, and the motives, skills, and so forth, that are employed and developed in work, play, and study.[28]

In the process of development the individual's psychic functions are trained. The higher functions—thought, speech, imagination, emotion, will, and attention—reach their full expression, and man becomes conscious and independent. Endowments become aptitudes and abilities. The concepts of aptitude and ability are tailored, as are most Soviet psychological concepts, to facilitate training.[29] They are regarded as "synthetic" concepts, which means that any one ability may be made up of various combinations of skills, and any one aptitude may be made up of various combinations of abilities. The possibility of achieving a high level of aptitude by various combinations of skills and abilities means that the teacher must be alert to capitalize on the strengths of each student, and develop those skills and abilities in which the child is especially gifted in order to compensate for his weakness. Furthermore, aptitudes and abilities are regarded as "historical" concepts and as "dynamic" concepts. This means that any ability, for example, is always the product of past development and is always subject to future development. "In psychology we cannot speak of an ability as it existed up to the moment at which it began to develop, just as we cannot speak of an ability reaching its full development." [30] In other words, the potentiality for improvement always exists.

The way in which ability and aptitude are conceived is closely related to the techniques of measurement advocated. Ability and aptitude are developed in activity and are defined as the capacity to carry out some activity. Therefore, it is argued that they can be measured only in terms of actual performance and not by "abstract tests." The slogan in pedagogy is that "the teacher studies the child while teaching him." Assessment of abilities is partially on the basis of common-sense ratings, and in schools, on the basis of regular subject-matter examinations. The argument for the necessity of assessments of abilities and aptitudes in terms of actual performance is buttressed by the contention that the "synthetic" nature of these traits makes the use of standard, generalized tests of ability impossible.

In Soviet theory the dynamism of personality is of central importance. The basic motivational concepts—need, interest, ideal, and duty—have been mentioned above. Related to these are such concepts as emotion and will. Emotionality—in the pursuit of a consciously fixed goal—is a highly valued trait of the Soviet Man, as is a strongly developed will, whereby this emotional drive can be effectively channeled. Emotionality is in disfavor only if man becomes a victim of it, if his will and consciousness cannot retain control.

However, despite the facts that "autogenetic movement" is presumably the result of the internal dynamics of personality and that such limited dynamic problems as conflict of motives are dealt with, the Western psychologist will find very little of internal dynamics in the Soviet model of personality. This is mainly a result of the fact that all depth psychology is ruled out. Preoccupation with conscious factors to the exclusion of unconscious factors makes impossible entire areas of psychological investigation which have contributed greatly to the development of Western psychology. This tendency is further facilitated by the relative lack of continuity between normal and abnormal psychology, a relationship that has been very effective in the cross-fertilization of Western psychology.

Another fertile field of personality study, social psychology, has become virtually a proscribed area. Studies of group differences are ruled out because of their political implications. Many of the instruments of social research—tests and opinion studies—have been condemned. But more basically, empirical investigation of the formation of personality under concrete social conditions, as much as it is urged on Soviet psychologists, can have little meaning because the conclusions are performed in official literature.[31] Whether or not one agrees with these conclusions, the fact of their existence makes superfluous a large area of personality research. There has been considerable pressure on Soviet psychologists in recent years to study the New Soviet Man to determine how his particular traits of character are formed under the conditions of Soviet society.[32] Both the traits of character (consciousness, strength of will, fervor in building socialism, love of motherland, high morality) and the conditions under which they develop are defined for the psychologist. If it were possible to conduct empirical research that bolstered these conclusions, the psychologist who accomplished the feat would become an official hero overnight. No one has done this, however, for obvious reasons. What could have been a very valuable psychological premise, that the concrete conditions of existence determine man's personality, has actually become a barrier to research in the very area it promised to open.

PSYCHOLOGY AND PHYSIOLOGY

A sharp line between psychology and physiology is always hard to draw. In fact there are a variety of criteria which can be employed, each of which would result in drawing the line at a different point. I have followed the practice of Soviet scholars and included in the discussion of modern Soviet psychology those writings and materials to which they apply the label "psychology," even though this meant excluding occasionally some work which we might label "physiological psychology."

The ever-increasing gulf that developed after 1930 between Soviet psychology and Soviet physiology never brought about a complete denial of the relevance of physiology for psychology. At all times, Soviet psychologists paid at least lip service to the importance of the "physiological substratum of the psyche." Every text devoted a chapter to physiological principles and was sprinkled with occasional passages indicating physiological data relevant to the psychological topic being discussed. After 1936, however, there was no trace of any tendency to reduce psychological concepts to physiological terms. It would seem, in fact, that the separation of the disciplines beginning with 1930 was a prophylactic measure designed to insure the independence of psychology as a discipline and to protect psychological constructs from reductionism.

In the summer of 1950 developments occurred which probably herald a closing of the gap between the disciplines. One year after Pavlov's one hundredth birthday, and shortly after a revolution in Soviet linguistics, Soviet physiologists and other scholars were enjoined to "return to correct Pavlovian principles." [33] The occasion seems to have been more the revolution in linguistics, than Pavlov's anniversary, since it followed a year after the anniversary, and since it carried an injunction for physiologists to work on Pavlov's "second signal system," which is concerned with man's use of words.

In recent years, work on conditioned reflexes has taken three main lines: the relation of the cerebral cortex to internal receptors and organs (a group led by K. M. Bykov), a sophisticated elaboration of the Pavlovian system which challenges many of Pavlov's formulations (P. K. Anokhin), and work on the sympathetic nervous system (L. A. Orbeli). The latter two lines of work have now been condemned. Of Orbeli's work official spokesmen in the "Pavlovian discussions" said that by concentrating on the automatic nervous system he depreciated the importance of the cerebral cortex (the material substratum of consciousness) and thereby of consciousness in man's behavior. These scholars and the distinguished Georgian physiologist Beritov (or, in Georgian, Beritashvili) were criticized and instructed to reorganize their work along "correct Pavlovian lines."

At the same time, educators, physical-training instructors, and psychologists were all instructed to establish their disciplines on a "Pavlovian basis." [34] After more than a year, however, there is no indication of substantive changes in the discipline of psychology. It seems almost inevitable that work on conditioned reflexes will be increased and that psychologists will pay more attention to physiological findings. But there is no indication that Soviet psychology will return to reductionistic theorizing and that subjective constructs will be reduced to physiological ones. In all the literature on the Pavlovian discussions all authors carefully avoid such a suggestion. In fact, the injunction to physiologists to study the cerebral cortex, designated as the material substratum of consciousness, suggests the possibility that the rewedding of psychology and physiology may result in psychology having the dominant position. Certainly these developments cannot be interpreted as a simple return to traditional Pavlovianism. The "second signal system" occupied a very minor role in Pavlov's system, and there are only occasional passing references to it in his later writings. In the stenographic transcript of Pavlov's seminars—the place where one would expect to find the most advanced and speculative of his thoughts—the index contains references to only four short passages in three thick volumes.[35] Rather than psychology's being reduced to physiology, it may be that physiology is being brought into the service of psychology.[36] In the twenties, an attempt was made to do away with psychological concepts and explain human behavior exhaustively in physiological terms. Today, the tendency seems to be to retain psychological concepts, and to see *how much* physiology can contribute to understanding them.

One should never discount the possibility of momentous changes in Soviet science or ideology. However, if the Pavlovian discussions of 1950–51 were to mean a complete reversion to the physiologically oriented psychology of the twenties, then the implications of this change would reach into the essentials of Soviet ideology and philosophy. It would mean a reversal of the formulation of the relationship of the ideological and sociopolitical superstructure to the economic base (as outlined in Chapters II and III), and a denial of the importance of consciousness in man's behavior. Since recent doctrinal pronouncements have continued to stress the importance of both consciousness and the superstructure, it seems hardly likely that such a counterrevolution is taking place. One can only wait and see.

The highly fluid state of Soviet psychology at the time the manuscript for this book was completed (September 1951) suggested the need for a last minute review of developments as of the time the book went finally to press (February 1952). The truth of the matter is that the picture has become very little clarified in the intervening period. Certain suggestive items may be recorded, but their interpretation remains very much in doubt.

It is the "second signal system" of Pavlov which continues to be stressed in articles pertaining to the psychological implications of Pavlov's doctrine. This emphasis, in turn, is related to Stalin's letter on linguistics of 1950 and seems largely to be directed at increasing the attention psychologists pay to the study of language. Engels' theory that man developed from the ape in the process of labor has been related to the development of the second signal system, and it is thereby argued that this "characteristically human" bit of adaptive equipment, language, has evolved in true Marxist fashion as a result of man's active relations with his environment.[36] Animals possessing only the "first signal system" respond only to immediate excitation, whereas man can signal himself, and thereby free himself from domination by immediate stimuli.

Discussions of the relationship of Pavlovian doctrine to perception stress the materialist basis of Pavlov's doctrine, and the fact that man's percepts reflect the real world.[37] Writers are careful to deny some of the passive implications of older associationism. The suggestion that man forms associative connections mainly on the basis of the accidental concomitance of events in the external environment is denounced as anti-Pavlovian.

Pavlov contrasts this "simple accident" to that circumstance in which we have the simultaneous action on the nervous system of two phenomena which have a stable relationship in reality, and a connection is formed between these phenomena. This is still another type of association, which is the foundation of knowledge, the basis of the chief principle of science—the principle of causality, of lawfulness.[38]

One gets the impression from reading these recent articles that Soviet theoreticians are trying simultaneously to achieve a variety of objectives which place conflicting demands on theory. The "scientific" nature of all Soviet theory is underscored by reaffirmation of the principles of materialism and determinism in Pavlov; at the same time, every effort is made to retain the principles of rationality, of the dominant role of consciousness, of man's ability to know reality. For example, Soviet psychiatrists are criticized for using the operation of leucotomy, one of the criticisms being that it produces a passive type of personality. "What a fortunate and convenient type of personality is created [by American psychiatrists] out of the [American citizen] in behalf of the Wall Street monopolists." [39] While the independence of psychology is reaffirmed (Pavlov is cited to this effect), attempts are made, not too successfully, to spell out the implications of Pavlovian doctrine for psychology. Although the present agitation is conducted in the name of Pavlov, it is actually little known portions of Pavlov's work which are stressed, and these seem to controvert the characteristic aspects of Pavlov's main line of thinking.

In the midst of this, the main intent of the new line in psychology and physiology (this is not equally true in other areas) seems to be to stimulate research on problems of language from the point of view of Pavlov's second signal system. Work in psychology, judged by the directory of psychological literature for 1950 [40] seems virtually unchanged for that year. This is perhaps too early to expect a change. Since 1950, however, work of physiologists on the second signal system has increased. There is a prospect, however, of a real ideological difficulty that Soviet theorists do not seem to have anticipated. The second signal system of Pavlov, as treated in both Pavlov's and recent writings, sees words, symbols, as instruments which mediate between the individual and his environment. They are signals which man directs at himself to direct his own behavior. This view of language is astonishingly similar to the theories of cultural development proposed by Vigotsky and Luria at an earlier period (see above, Chapter V). While such views might well be the basis for fruitful psychological research, they may also be interpreted as a species of idealism which sees man as reacting to symbols rather than to the "real world" which these symbols represent. Soviet theorists have, in the past, directed violent criticism at the semanticists for this type of idealism. Now they may be smuggling general semantics in through the back door. Certain suggestions of the importance of the role of language in the etiology of mental disorders strengthen this possibility.

All this, however, is in the realm of speculation. The full meaning of the Pavlovian resurrection remains unclear.

11 PSYCHOLOGY AND THE SOVIET SYSTEM

The most sincere compliments often come under the guise of abuse. As long as a substantial number of leaders of the Soviet regime thought that ideas had no important role in history, there was a relative freedom of expression and scientific inquiry. The increasingly stringent control over ideas in the last twenty years is a tribute (albeit a left-handed one) to the importance which is attached to ideas by Marxists in the Leninist tradition. True, ideology has changed drastically under the impact of social and economic change. But the urgency with which these revisions of ideology were forced through by the leadership is in itself a testimony of the seriousness with which ideas are taken. What is peculiar to the Soviet approach to ideas, however, is its highly instrumental nature. The Soviet leaders are concerned with what ideas *do* far more than with their truth or falsity. Perhaps more than any people in history they have come to concern themselves with the relationship of ideas to social behavior. The history of psychology under the Bolsheviks, and of the changing conception of man in both science and politics, is a case study of such a concern for the relationship of ideas to action.

THE SOVIET CONCEPTION OF MAN

In considering the Soviet approach to man, the three words that come to mind are *responsibility, rationalism, individual-*

ism—all seeming contradictions in a totalitarian society. Totalitarian society is a "rationalized" society. It exemplifies the principle of functional rationality which maintains that the components of the social system shall be so constituted and so organized as to contribute maximally to the effective functioning of the system. Functional rationality has ordinarily been considered to be in opposition to substantial rationality, the situation in which the individual acts rationally in the pursuit of goals. In such a situation, his behavior is rational from his own viewpoint, even though it may not be articulated into the functional requirements of the social system. The basis for the seeming contradiction lay in the assumption that in a rationalized society the individual must obey blindly, that the individual is not responsible for the substance of his behavior, but only for obeying. He performs actions the rationale of which he does not understand, actions which make sense only in a larger context. That the Bolsheviks think of their system as a rationalized one should be sufficiently clear from the discussion in Chapters II and III. They maintain, however, that the Soviet citizen understands the rationale of his behavior in the larger social context. His behavior is considered to be "rational" in both senses.

The contrast is most marked when one compares Bolshevism with Nazism, the other important totalitarian system of modern times. The Nazi held that man was moved primarily by unconscious, nonrational motives. The Nazi valued "elemental" drives. The Bolshevik, however, stresses consciousness and rationality to the point that he finds the idea of behavior being determined by unconscious forces extremely disturbing. The Nazi would have preferred to control the behavior of people largely by appealing to motives which the individual did not understand. The Bolshevik controls man by training his motives and shaping his ideology; he then expects an individual consciously, and unfailingly, to carry out the task assigned to him. "Freedom," he says, "is the recognition of necessity." The characteristics of the good Bolshevik are that he can foresee the course of events, and that he is loyal to the Party (whose decisions are defined as embodying truth). Basically the Nazi did not see man as responsible, but stressed rather his weakness, his helplessness in the face of events, the necessity for the ordinary man to submit himself blindly to a leader. The Bolshevik insists on man's responsibility for his behavior and on his ability to make his own destiny. He follows the Party line because the Party is "right" and because he presumably understands why it is right. For the Nazi, man was a marionette who moved when one pulled the strings. For the Bolshevik, he is a robot who can be trained to act independently within specified limits. The Bolshevik reconciles the rationality of the social system (functional rationality), which characterizes totalitarianism, with individual rationality (substantial rationality), ordinarily considered to be opposed to totalitarianism, with the statement that the goals of the individual and of society are identical. According to the Bolshevik formula, consciousness liberates man from the immediate situation only to tie him to the demands of the social system.

The evolution of the present-day Soviet conception of man cannot be understood apart from the role which assumptions about human nature play in society, or apart from the heavy emphasis which the Bolsheviks place on ideological consistency.* The conception of man held in society is a theory for the prediction and control of human behavior, a rationalization of the system of rewards and punishments used in that society, and a model for the training of future members of that society.

---

* The theoretical basis for this emphasis on ideological consistency is discussed below, and its importance as an organizing principle in Soviet society outlined. At this point it is sufficient to say that without an insistence on ideological consistency *per sc*, there is no logical necessity for attempting to effect a point-for-point correspondence between ideology and action.

To the extent that the deterministic conception of man of the twenties was applied in action, and to the extent that the disparity between ideology and action was a source of concern, this early conception of man failed on all counts. When put into practice as a theory for explaining or predicting behavior, it led to such circumlocutions or absurdities as the abolition of the concept of guilt in law. In most instances the determinist conception of man was not used in action even by persons committed to it "in theory." The operating principle of Bolshevik propaganda, for example, was always direct, rational appeal, and clearly assumed the consciousness and responsibility that the determinist conception denied.[1] For the man in the street, it is doubtful that the determinist conception of human nature had any meaning whatsoever.

Further, the determinist conception of man did not offer the ideologist an adequate rationalization for the system of rewards and punishments used. It is difficult to remain consistent with a theory which holds that society and not the individual is responsible for antisocial behavior and attempt to mobilize the moral indignation of the citizenry against deviant individuals. If the individual is said to be not responsible for his behavior, then it is logically difficult to hold that he is in any sense blameworthy.[2] Finally, the determinist conception of man furnished a poor ideal for molding new citizens. There would have been little point in urging parents and teachers to raise the new generation in the image of a passive product of the historical process.

The new model of man, defining man as conscious, rational, and purposive, conforms to the assumptions which the Bolsheviks used in political practice. It also directs the attention of educators, psychologists, legal theorists, et cetera, to the thoughts and motives of the individuals whom they are trying to mold, rather than to the environmental and biological factors which are the ultimate determinants of these thoughts and motives. It offers an adequate rationalization of the system of rewards and punishments by which behavior is controlled. Finally, it serves as an ideal of the type of citizen which is desired—the New Soviet Man.

Beyond the above considerations, the conception of man held in Soviet society has served certain mythical functions. It has served to rationalize the deficiencies and extoll the merits of the system. As Soviet society has evolved, the demands put on the myth have altered. During the twenties the Bolsheviks had no vested interest in the existing order; it was something they planned to change. Environmental determinism, in that situation, served the function of derogating the old and existing orders and emphasized the hope of what would come out of the new order. Once the new order was achieved and there were no further major changes to look forward to, the requirements of this myth changed. The old order was kept responsible for the undesirable traits of character of the Soviet citizens—the "remnants of capitalism in the minds of man"— and the new order was credited with producing the New Soviet Man, to whom are ascribed all the desirable traits of the same citizens. By shifting the responsibility for molding human nature from the "environment" to "training," the Soviet order is able to capitalize on the myth of the New Soviet Man as being a product of the system, while fixing the responsibility for shaping people to this ideal on a relatively small group of "trainers" and on the individual himself.

The preceding passages have emphasized the ideological aspects involved in the changing conception of man. But ideological considerations, as we noted in earlier chapters, were closely related to practical considerations, particularly to increasingly difficult problems of controlling human behavior. This is reflected in the evolving patterns of social control. Bearing in mind that all delineation of "stages" must be highly abstract, one can see in this progressive convergence on the individual three distinct analytical stages in the development of social control in the Soviet Union. At first, there was a strong tendency to underestimate the task of social control. It was more or less assumed that once a socialist government came to power, most of these problems would solve themselves. In successive areas of life it began quickly to be realized that one had to intervene actively to direct human behavior in and out of various activities. This second stage, characterized by heavy emphasis on active intervention, reached its peak during the first half of the thirties. About the end of the First Five Year Plan the cumbersomeness of attempting to direct all the day-to-day activities of people became evident, and the campaign began to make the Soviet citizen a more or less automatically functioning member of the system, by shaping his motives, sharpening his consciousness, and training him in "disciplined" behavior.

Trends in the pattern of Soviet social control are reminiscent of the familiar image of getting a horse to move by dangling a carrot in front of his nose and whipping him from behind. The Bolsheviks first overestimated the extent to which the horse wanted to go in the same direction as the driver did. Having been disillusioned on this score, they tried both the carrot of positive incentive and the stick of police power. But this took too much energy and produced inadequate results. They decided then to remake the horse without relinquishing, for the time being, either the carrot or the stick. The immediate goal is better performance on the part of the horse. The ultimate goal may be the hope of relinquishing some of the external controls.

Any relaxing of external controls would depend, of course, on the success of attempts to mold the Soviet citizenry in the image of the New Soviet Man. The consensus of observers is that character changes have taken place in the Soviet citizenry since the Revolution.[3] In contrast to persons who emigrated before or immediately after the Revolution, the recent Soviet émigrés are more overtly disciplined and less spontaneous. They are more practical and less contemplative; more concerned with results and less with the means whereby they are gained. They are more manipulative and better extemporizers. Rationality is more prominent, and emotion less so. They are more militantly self-confident. They exhibit, in short, the "reflex of purpose" which Pavlov found lacking in the Russian. It is difficult to say whether these specific traits of character are more directly the result of deliberate training by the Soviet regime or the consequence of learning how to live under conditions of political insecurity, in which one has to learn to control his every word and deed and to struggle tenaciously to survive. The émigrés themselves attribute these traits mainly to their life experience under the Soviet system. Since these traits characterize many persons who are too old to have been products of the Soviet school system of the last two decades, and many persons who seem to have been markedly anti-Soviet throughout their lives, it seems more reasonable to assume that the new traits are actually a result of day-to-day living under the Soviet regime. Regardless of their origin, these are traits that enable a man to live and operate more effectively in a modern industrialized society and particularly in a tightly controlled system such as the Soviet one.

However, these traits are not sufficient to permit the relaxation of external controls. Only the development of appropriate social motives in the citizenry could bring about this condition. Whereas Soviet life conditions seem to facilitate the development of a more disciplined and goal-oriented character structure, and thereby facilitate the shaping of this aspect of the New Soviet Man, these same life conditions seem to alienate the sentiments of the Soviet citizen. Here, accordingly, the system of indoctrination which seeks to develop appropriate social motives must succeed in the face of life conditions.

To this obstacle must be added the further circumstance that the very presence of rigid external controls in the form of the secret police is in itself a source of alienation, and thus the external controls tend to become self-perpetuating. Whether in the face of these difficulties the Soviet regime can succeed in indoctrinating its citizens with the desired social motives is impossible to answer at this distance.

The ideal for which they seem to be striving is eloquently stated by a young anti-Bolshevik refugee who had been reared under the Soviet regime. When asked her opinion of what a citizens' responsibilities to his state are, she replied:

It must consist in readiness to defend one's state when it is necessary, and in following the laws and rules of communal life. The most difficult manifestation is the ability in some instances to subordinate oneself to the purposes of the state *without any application of external pressure*. For instance, if it is necessary for a physician to work in the village, *he should see that this is necessary for his country*, and consequently do it.

The phrases which I have italicized indicate that many of the premises which the regime is striving to inculcate have penetrated into the minds of even those who reject the system. Whether this will become widespread or not, we can only wait and see.

THE SOVIET SYSTEM AND CONTROL OVER PSYCHOLOGY

Any science, it is true, is affected by the social system in which it develops. The only meaningful questions to ask are how much a given system affects a given science and in what distinctive ways it exercises its influence. The Soviet system is distinguished from liberal societies in both the extent and manner of influence it has on psychology, and the distinguishing aspects of Soviet influence on this discipline can be understood only in terms of certain fundamental aspects of the Soviet order.

The most basic consideration which distinguishes the USSR from a liberal society is the fundamental premise that Soviet society is an *organized* society, a society in which—insofar as possible—all the parts are coördinated to the service of the whole by the deliberate decisions of persons who are in a position to implement that decision. In terms of the preceding section, it is a rationalized society. True, there is inconsistency and malcoördination in Soviet society; especially malcoördination between ideology and practical affairs. But the existence of malcoördination only highlights the extent to which Soviet leaders value and strive for consistency. For example, time after time psychologists have tried to go off in their own direction, or have lagged behind official directives. The disparity between official policy and actual performance is a reflection of the fact that there are practical limitations on the extent to which any regime can implement so drastic a policy. The constant complaints and exhortations, and the occasional firm intervention of official agencies demonstrate, however, the degree to which consistency and rationalization is valued.

The premise that society should and can be consciously organized and directed is in itself an element of Marxist doctrine, with a characteristic Leninist twist—the emphasis on conscious intervention in the social process. This premise is fortified by other elements in Marxist-Leninist theory. Stressing the rational analysis of the interrelationship of social institutions, Marxist theory, as elaborated in the last thirty years, provides the Bolsheviks with a theoretical tool for the coordination of society. Like any theory, and more than some, it has its defects. But it is sufficiently thorough-going and systematic to offer operating principles for most of the problems which face the Soviet politician.

Marxist ideology is simultaneously a tool and a problem. It not only helps in "solving" problems, but it creates them. It would seem, for example, that the principles of materialism and determinism may have lost their initial importance in Leninism-Marxism. Today they retain mainly their symbolic value as signs of Marxist orthodoxy. By and large, they serve mainly as a test of the ingenuity of scholars in reconciling their work to the principles of philosophical materialism. The problem of resolving the relationship of consciousness to matter is one example of such a difficulty in psychology.

The Marxist theory of the sociology of knowledge, with the added refinement of the Leninist theory of reflection, is an especially pertinent example of the way in which Marxist doctrine is used in coördinating Soviet society. It is the basis for holding each theory up for scrutiny and asking, "Does it contribute to the goals of the Party?" We have seen how, in psychology, this doctrine has been used to constrict the range of psychological theory and practice, and to bring psychology ever more narrowly into the service of a restricted bracket of practical problems. We have seen that under the banner of the Leninist theory of reflection psychology has become subordinate to politics.

Another Bolshevik premise of importance here is that of the unitary nature of truth. The ideology of Soviet society, it is maintained, is "scientific" and self-consistent. Therefore, there can be only one correct theory in any area. In fact, there can be only one correct general theory—Marxist ideology— and all particular theories must be consistent with it. This premise, while now imbedded in Marxist ideology, is a continuation of the traditional Russian belief in the unity of truth. The result is a considerably lower tolerance of divergent theoretical positions than would seem to be optimum for the growth of a science. There can be only *one* "correct" theory in psychology, in politics, in genetics, in linguistics.

The effect of ideological premises on restricting the range of psychological theory is augmented by restrictions on the range of applications of psychology. Any science is stimulated in its theoretical development by the practical problems with which it is faced. Application poses new questions and provides an opportunity for trying out in practice ideas of theoretical importance.

Particularly with the advent of modern techniques of research, often demanding large staffs and expensive equipment, the development of theoretical interests is dependent on the enlistment of financial support from some interested party. In America, for example, research on group processes has been facilitated in recent years by the growing interest of government and industry in the contributions of psychology to solving problems of human relations. Theoretical work in public opinion has been possible largely because of funds from market research. Without financial support from the applications of science, many theoretical advances would have taken place much more slowly. In a liberal society the allocation of psychologist man-hours to various fields of application and theory depends on the free competition of the market. Furthermore, a psychologist who so prefers may continue along a given line of work even though it pays poorly and offers little chance of advancement. No one can force him to abandon it. In a closed system like the Soviet one, however, some decision has to be made about the allocation of resources. The result of having to face this decision explicitly seems to be that resources are concentrated only on the *most* urgent problems. Centralized coördination of scientific research is frequently cited as one of the strengths of the Soviet system. That there are certain short-run benefits for the system is not to be doubted. It would seem, however, that the long-range development of any scientific discipline depends on a system of loose controls which will permit a multiplicity of lines of work. The variety of applications of psychology and other social sciences which is possible in a liberal society may be the most important single factor in facilitating the development of research along a wide variety of theoretical lines, and this may be the only condition under which such disciplines can flourish. It is not simply an arithmetical matter of *adding* to the amount and types of research that is done that is involved here. Science advances by challenging what is accepted. It is the possibility of attempting divergent approaches to a problem, of challenging accepted scientific propositions—not only with words but with concrete research—that is important. It is the possibility of trying out a new approach or of investigating a new field of inquiry without first having to convince some one central authority that the expenditure of funds on such an innovation is worth risking his bureaucratic neck. Inevitably in a society in which it is possible to seek funds from a variety of sources, involving peoples with varieties of interests, the probability of finding a market for a new idea is proportionately increased.

Ultimately the system of controls in any society comes to bear on individuals, in this case on the individual psychologist. Even in a liberal society there are techniques of selection and coercion, some subtle and some overt, which affect the composition and behavior of the psychological community, and thereby the development of the science. Sanctions are brought to bear against the individual who deviates either in his professional or his political views. Most psychologists in the United States know instances in which a person lost or was refused an academic post because of his political views. Such sanctions operate more strongly, however, against the psychologist whose theoretical or research interests do not conform to current trends. An antibehaviorist, for example, might have had some difficulty getting a teaching position in the United States during the twenties, although possibly not as much as he would have had in the Soviet Union. That such selection takes place in a liberal society is unquestionable and unavoidable (although in some instances one might wish it could be reduced). This, however, is a situation in which a difference in degree is actually a difference in kind. Even though such selection affects the composition and behavior of the psychological community, it is never sufficiently drastic to eliminate all representatives of a point of view.

Under the Bolsheviks, control over the individual psychologist seems to move in five stages. First, the Party uses propaganda. Psychologists as well as other citizens are urged to adopt the beliefs of Marxism and accept the program of the Party as their own. Second, the Party proceeds by infiltration, by persuading psychologists to become members of the Party, and by training Party members to be psychologists. Third, by controlling appointments to academic posts, editorships of journals, and so forth, the Party rewards reliable personnel and puts them in positions of power. Fourth, those who deviate from the prescribed line are criticized by their colleagues and by the Party, and they may be relieved of their posts if their deviation has been sufficient or if they respond too slowly. Fifth, the supreme coercive power of the state has seldom been used against psychologists,[4] but it stands as an implied threat and must have an inhibiting effect on any psychologist who is tempted to deviate in his work.

In both the Soviet system and in a liberal society many of the same isolated mechanisms can be seen at work, but the ultimate effect of these mechanisms is conditioned by the nature of the over-all system. There is a certain parallel, for example, between a Central Committee member who complains about a piece of scientific research in the USSR and United States congressmen who have at times clamored for cuts in the budgets of government agencies doing research of which they did not approve, or conducted the investigation of a public opinion organization whose results favored an opposing political party. But the congressman has to run counter to an ideology that condemns interference in freedom of inquiry. Furthermore, he is not in command of a control system with which to implement his taste in research quickly and ruthlessly as can the member of the Central Committee. And, only in a very few instances can he exert influence beyond the limited range of research which is directly under government jurisdiction.

The controls of the Soviet system, whether operating to produce a uniform ideology, to concentrate research and application on a small range of problems judged by some central agency to be most important, or to assure the "correct" behavior of individual psychologists, all have the effect of constricting the discipline. It is not so much the content as the extent of political interference that is deadly to the science. A discipline such as psychology, as has been said many times in the course of this book, is many-sided. It has a wide range of problems facing it, and its theoretical development can proceed only if a wide range of models and methods are open to it. Regardless of the particular views that are suppressed or espoused, the mere fact of having eliminated from consideration so wide a variety of potential views would inevitably be destructive. Because of these factors, any centralized system must always be a poor climate for the development of social science. As a matter of fact, *any* dogmatism on social and political matters, even if not pushed to its extreme and implemented to the hilt by a centralized system of control, is a threat to the social sciences. The social scientist must forever be disabused of the notion that he does or can work in an ivory tower. To the extent that his theories have meaning for mankind—to that extent they are potential threats to special interest groups and may evoke restrictive measures. Even in a liberal society, freedom of inquiry depends on more than the absence of state controls; it demands vigorous and positive protection.

It is not sufficient for the psychologist to be aware of the dangers of dogmatism imposed on his science from outside the discipline. Particularly he should not undervalue dangers that come from dogmatism, no matter how involuntary, within the science. This is most likely to happen with the broad premises of the science. The history of Soviet psychology indicates that it is precisely at the most general level that the discipline is subject to the most efficient manipulation. It is difficult to dictate the content and conclusions of all specific empirical research. But if certain methods and broad assumptions can be imposed, then the probability of certain types of research being done and certain conclusions being reached will be heightened. A scientific theory has importance beyond its initial statement of fact. By saying "thus and such is true," each theory suggests certain directions of research rather than others, because it says that certain variables and certain relationships are more important than others. The decision about which variables to include in an investigation is frequently the most important step in the whole course of study. It can virtually dictate the conclusions which will be reached.

Yet, scientists who would be horrified at the suggestion of political or other dictation of specific empirical conclusions are relatively undiscriminating in their selection of methods and methodology. Many times they accept the implicit assumptions of their culture or the scientific fads of the moment,[5] without first considering their suitability to the demands of the problems on which psychologists are working. Psychology in America has been exposed to waves of "objectivism," "wholism," "operationism," and recently to consideration of highly complicated mathematical models. These trends came into psychology from other sciences, and unquestionably each has had a very constructive effect on psychology. But in each period there has been also a tendency for enthusiasts to say that theirs was *the* scientific method and that problems which fell outside the scope of this method were not the proper topics of scientific study. Whereas the Bolshevik says that the *conclusion* is all-important, there is something of a tendency for

American psychologists to say that the *method* is. Science investigates *problems*. There is no point in investigation if the conclusions are prejudged. On the other hand, problems are not to be selected on the basis of their amenability to treatment by certain methods; rather the methods are to be judged by their adequacy to the problems. Science has many methods, and dogmatism from within the discipline can be just as stifling as dogmatism imposed by a political regime.

THE SOCIAL ROLE OF SOVIET PSYCHOLOGY

One of the criteria for estimating the strength of any social system is the extent to which it makes use of its resources. Obviously one of the most important resources of modern society is science, or even more broadly, the free play of the human intellect brought to bear on the problems of society. Marxism has always prided itself on its scientific pretensions. Yet Soviet Marxism has demonstrated some marked inabilities to make use of the full range of applied social science or to tolerate the free play of scientific inquiry. Many problems which are considered in our society to be the province of social science specialists are handled in the Soviet Union on a common-sense basis by politicians, engineers, journalists, teachers, physicians, and similar persons. In this category of problems may be included: principles of propaganda, industrial motivation, interpersonal relationships, community studies, assessment of public opinion, evaluation of abilities, personal counseling—all areas in which the specialist has demonstrated his ability to produce valuable practical results.

Largely this is a result of the claims of Marxism-Leninism that it *is* social science.[6] It is further a function of the apparent inability of Marxist-Leninist dogma to permit expression of a variety of theoretical views. Supporting the common-sense approach to human problems is, also, the strong emphasis on rationalism, the contention that man's behavior can be understood and controlled without resource to complicated, deep psychological constructs. In addition, there are, of course, the concrete historical circumstances which affected the suppression of certain of these areas of application. These circumstances, as has been seen, were sometimes partially "accidental" in that they were not systematically related to essential aspects of the regime. For example, some of the factors leading to the decree against pedology, the rivalry between teachers and psychologists, and the apparently poor quality of pedological work cannot be considered as inherent in the system.

Lying behind these overt factors leading to the restriction of the activities of social scientists seems to be a complicated pattern of supporting factors, much more subtle in their operation, about which one can only speculate. The Bolshevik is primarily a man of action, and not a detached scholar. A "common-sense" approach to human behavior seems to be more comforting to the activist for a variety of reasons. It does not challenge the adequacy of his own premises for action. More complicated explanations of human behavior make the world more difficult for him to deal with. This is particularly true if the existence of unconscious motives is postulated. One of the premises of Soviet ideology which has evolved with greatest clarity is that man, or at least Soviet man, is infinitely capable of controlling the universe, and in successive areas of life propositions which implied limitations on man's ability to control the universe have been rejected.[7] It must be assumed that one of the motives behind the progressive restriction of applications of psychology and the rejection of unconscious factors in the model of man has been the desire of the practical man of Soviet politics to reassure himself that the world is not beyond his powers of control.

Moreover, the activist must have some reluctance to consider fully the unintended consequences of his action. In the Soviet politician's rejection of empirical research must be at least an unconscious fear of discovering the resentment and hostility that his policies have created. Furthermore, having decided on a course of action and being determined to push it through, he does not want to be bothered *too much* by the reasons why his course of action cannot succeed. Logically, there is no reason why a full realization of the complexities of the situation with which one is dealing should paralyze action. Psychologically, however, it seems in practice to do so.

Finally, the focus of empirical social research tends to shift from means to ends. What often starts out to be a purely technical investigation assumes larger proportions as the implications of the data gathered are seen. Problems are pointed up; the advantages and disadvantages of various courses of action are demonstrated; and ultimately the desirability of the goals of society is brought into question. Therefore, the existence of any independent agency of social inquiry is a potential challenge to the desirability of both intermediate and ultimate goals of the Soviet order. Thus, in addition to factors inherent in the Soviet system, the personal situation of the Bolshevik leader leads him to constrict the social application of psychology.

Especially disturbing to Western scientists is the pragmatic approach which Soviet spokesmen take to theory. It is not the adequacy of the theory as a reflection of the events that it purports to describe that is the criterion for evaluating it. Rather it is judged by its practical effects or its ideological correctness. Considering the close relationship between ideology and practice, ideological correctness in the Soviet system is no more than practicality once removed, although the Soviet definition of what is "practical" is considerably broader than ours. When there is a conflict between immediate practicality and ideological correctness, it depends on the concrete circumstances which is given priority. Without a shadow of a doubt this tendency also impedes the development of psychology as a science. Yet, one must not assume that it means the complete obliteration of the usefulness of psychology. As long as Soviet psychology maintains its contact with world psychology, and there is sufficient evidence that it does, it can exist parasitically on the theoretical work of other psychologists.

This raises the immediate question: "Can a theory be useful if it is not true?" Let it first be understood that it would be very difficult to say that the theories of Soviet psychologists are not "true" any more than that many of the theories held by Western psychologists are not true. Virtually all the points of view held by Soviet psychologists can be found in the literature of Western psychology and are held by Western psychologists of importance. What is characteristic of Soviet psychological theory is the extent to which social and political considerations have had an explicit role in its shaping and the limited range of theory that is acceptable. Since it is impossible to say at any period in the development of a discipline which of competing theories is "true" in any ultimate sense, because all may ultimately be rejected, one must grant that a theory does not have to be true to have some limited practical usefulness.

Unquestionably the role of a science such as psychology in the Soviet system is antipathetic to all of our values; yet we should not delude ourselves that its emasculated role is entirely a sign of weakness in the system. One of the functions of Soviet psychology, to reënforce the ideological conception of human nature, is alien to our society and values, yet may be a contribution of importance in a system where ideology is so important. Contributions to education and medicine are obvious, although by our standards they might be greater. The absence of other ranges of application have just been noted. There is no doubt but that the direct contributions of psychology and other social sciences to the Soviet system could be considerably greater. Judged by this criterion, the Soviet system does seem to be inherently incapable of making optimum use of its resources.

The documentation of such a critical point of weakness in the Soviet order should not lead us, however, to the conclusion that the over-all system is lacking in strength and adaptability. First, the fate of the social sciences has been conspicuously worse than that of the other sciences, if we may exclude the relatively recent difficulties of genetics. We must remember that in most natural sciences, Soviet scholars seem to have done consistently first-rate work. Second, societies have survived for centuries entirely without the benefits of social science. Furthermore, it is a moot question whether or not the sacrifice of some of the advantages which would come from applied social science are not offset by certain short-run gains from tighter controls and greater flexibility of action. Certainly one of the strong assets of the Soviet regime seems to be its ability quickly to concentrate a wide range of resources on a given problem. Thus, when the decision was made in the mid-thirties to concentrate on the problem of education, virtually the entire resources of the science of psychology were converted to this purpose.

But this strength becomes, in turn, another source of weakness. By concentrating resources to the extent that they do, the Bolsheviks made the next shift of direction increasingly more difficult. The needs of any social order change in time. In a liberal society, the sciences accommodate to such changing demands spontaneously and relatively easily. Psychology in the United States, for example, has, at any time, trained persons in virtually every field of theory and practice. When a new social need for the services of psychology develops, there ensues a shift in balance of research interests and fields of application, but there is seldom any marked commotion in the field. In fact, such trends frequently pass without attracting any specific attention until some student of the discipline does a historical review and notes a shift of emphasis in the field.

In the Soviet Union, however, a central decision is required that a change in line shall take place. Then the machinery for inaugurating a new line must be set in motion. The old position must be attacked, suitable scapegoats found, and in many instances, a new leadership prepared. Each time the process must become more difficult. In psychology, for example, the more effective is the regime in concentrating the energies of psychologists within a limited range of activities, or in demolishing a previous theoretical position, the more difficult it will be to find persons trained in the skills needed when a new task develops, or to revive the demolished position. It is impossible to pull out of a hat the personnel who were never trained under the old line, and it is difficult to obliterate completely the traces of what one previously has said and written.

Deciding just what is a strong point and what is a weak point of the Soviet (or any other) system is a difficult matter and seems to depend primarily on the time perspective with which one views events. As participants in a competing social system, we tend alternately to become overly encouraged by evidences of strain in the Soviet system, and then overly discouraged at the rapidity and thoroughness with which that system is able to mobilize its resources in counteracting these strains. We must remember that short-run flexibility is bought at the expense of long-run inflexibility. Political interference in science does not destroy completely the usefulness of science to the system, but the continued suppression of freedom of scientific inquiry must ultimately lead to the point where the society cannot solve its own problems effectively.

NOTES

The following abbreviations are used throughout the notes:

BSE   Bol'shaia Sovetskaia Entsiklopediia (Large Soviet Encyclopedia)

JASP Journal of Abnormal and Social Psychology

JGcP Journal of Genetic Psychology

JGlP Journal of General Psychology

KN   Krasnaia Nov' (Red Virgin Soil)

NPNS Na Putiakh k Novoi Shkole (On the Way to a New School)

NS   Nachal'naia Shkola (The Elementary School)

PO   Pedagogicheskoi Obrazovanie (Pedagogical Education)

PPT Psikhotekhnika i Psikhofiziologiia Truda (Psychotechnics and Psychophysiology of Work)

PZM Pod Znamenem Marksizma (Under the Banner of Marxism)

SPed Sovetskaia Pedagogika (Soviet Pedagogy)

SPsi Sovetskaia Psikhotekhnika (Soviet Psychotechnics)

VIVL Voprosy Izucheniia i Vospitaniia Lichnosti (Questions of the Study and Training of Personality)

VKA Vestnik Kommunisticheskoi Akademii (Journal of the Communist Academy)

VSA Vestnik Sotsialisticheskoi Akademii (Journal of the Socialist Academy)

CHAPTER 1: THE RELATIONSHIP OF PSYCHOLOGY TO SOCIETY

1. John Dewey, *Psychology and Philosophic Method* (Berkeley, 1899), p. 3.

2. See Franciska Baumgarten-Tramer, "German Psychologists and Recent Events," trans. by Frederick and Gertrude Wyatt, *JASP*, XLIII (1948), 452–465; S. Diamond, "The Co-ordination of Erich Jaensh," *Science and Society*, I (1936), 106–114; Frederick Wyatt and Hans Lukas Teuber, "German Psychology under the Nazi System," *Psychological Review*, LI (1944), 229–247; Eugene Lerner, "Pathological Nazi Stereotypes Found in Recent German Technical Journals," *The Journal of Psychology*, XIII (1942), 179–192.

3. Bertrand Russell, *Philosophy* (New York, 1927), p. 30.

CHAPTER 2: TWO KINDS OF MARXISM

1. Barrington Moore, Jr., *Soviet Politics—The Dilemma of Power* (Cambridge, Mass.: Harvard University Press, 1950) is the most detailed study of the change in Marxist ideology under the impact of the concrete problems of running a state.

2. This comparison is also made by Maynard and Berman. Each of these authors draws the distinction between Marxism as a scheme of analysis and as a tool of revolution. See Sir John Maynard, *Russia in Flux* (New York: Macmillan, 1948), chap. vii, esp. p. 119, and Harold J. Berman, *Justice in Russia* (Cambridge, Mass.: Harvard University Press, 1950), chap. i.

3. Maynard, *Russia in Flux*, p. 123.

4. Joseph Stalin, *Leninism*, trans. by Eden and Cedar Paul (New York: International Publishers, 1932), p. 98.

5. *Ibid.*, p. 80.

6. Good secondary sources on this problem are available in English: Maurice Dobb, *Soviet Economic Development since 1917* (New York: International Publishers, 1948), chap. xiii, "The Planning System"; A. Yugow, *Russia's Economic Front for War and Peace*, trans. by N. I. and M. Stone (New York: Harper, 1942); Alexander Baykov, *The Development of the Soviet Economic System* (New York: Macmillan, 1947), chap. xi. Julius Hecker, *Moscow Dialogues* (London: Chapman and Hall, 1933), discusses the relationship of the dispute in economics to the controversy in philosophy. Alexander Erlich of the staff of the Russian Research Center, Harvard University, is engaged in a major work on this topic. So far he has published "Preobrazhenski and the Economics of Soviet Industrialization," *Quarterly Journal of Economics*, February 1948, pp. 55–88.

7. Cited in Dobb, *Soviet Economic Development*, pp. 203–204.

8. Yugow, *Russia's Economic Front*, pp. 5–6. Yugow cites Strumlin, Grinko, and others.

9. Perhaps the most basic criticism of Bukharin's concept of equilibrium, which lay behind his economic and social thinking, is A. Martynov, (The Theory of the Dynamic Equilibrium of Society and the Interaction Between Society and the External Milieu), *PZM*, 1930, nos. 2–3, pp. 59–76.

10. Joseph Stalin, *Problems of Leninism* (Moscow, 1940). See pages 306–327 for the comments of Stalin on "equilibrium" and on "spontaneity."

11. K. Amelin, P. Chremnykh, (The Advocates of the Theoretical Basis of Right Opportunism), *PZM*, 1931, no. 1–2, pp. 82–112, p. 83.

12. There are several surprisingly good sources concerning this controversy in English. The most complete is in Hecker's *Moscow*

Dialogues. Hecker was an instructor in philosophy in Moscow during the period of the controversy and seems well informed, as well as perceptive and frank in his discussion. John Somerville, *Soviet Philosophy* (New York: Philosophical Library, 1947), chap. vii, pp. 213–219, gives a less rich version. A. Emery, "Dialectics *vs.* Mechanics, a Communist Debate on Scientific Method," *Philosophy of Science,* II (1935), no. 1, pp. 9–38, presents the systematic issues very well.

13. I. Stepanov, (The Dialectical Conception of Nature Is a Mechanical Conception), *PZM,* 1925, no. 3, pp. 205–238.

14. N. Bukharin, *Historical Materialism* (New York: International Publishers, 1925), p. 75; also N. Bukharin, (The Problems of the Theory of Historical Materialism—Some Running Comments), *VSA,* 1923, no. 3, pp. 3–15.

15. For an account of the training of this cadre of dialectical scientists see Resolutions of the second All-Union Conference of Marxist-Leninist Scientific Institutions, *PZM* 1929, no. 5, p. 9.

16. (At a New Level—The Result of the second All-Union Conference of Marxist-Leninist Scientific Institutions), *PZM,* 1929, no. 5, p. 1.

17. (The Decree of the Central Committee of the All-Union Communist Party Concerning Measures to be Taken to Strengthen Scientific Work in Connection with the Conference of Marxist-Leninist Scientific Institutions), *VKA,* 1929, no. 33/3, pp. 282–283.

18. N. Bukharin, *Teoriia Istoricheskogo Materializma,* p. 76, quoted by Martynov, (The Theory of the Dynamic Equilibrium of Society . . .) p. 60.

19. Martynov, (The Theory of the Dynamic Equilibrium of Society . . .), p. 61. My italics.

20. V. Vandek and S. Turtskii, (Some Questions of the Methodology of the Right Deviation in the Bolshevik Party and of Trotskism), *PZM,* 1930, no. 6, p. 61.

21. K. Amelin and P. Cheremnykh, (The Advocates of the Theorectical Basis of Right Opportunism), *PZM,* 1931, nos. 1–2, p. 85.

22. Hecker, *Moscow Dialogues,* p. 169.

23. Emery, "Dialectics *vs.* Mechanics," p. 33.

24. Amelin and Cheremnykh, (The Advocates of the Theoretical Basis of Right Opportunism), p. 85.

25. B. D. Wolfe, *Three Who Made a Revolution* (New York: Dial, 1948).

CHAPTER 3: THE PATTERN OF SOCIAL CHANGE

1. See Harold J. Berman, *Justice in Russia* (Cambridge, Mass.: Harvard University Press, 1950), chap. i.

2. Vladimir Gsovski, *Soviet Civil Law* (2 vols.; Ann Arbor, Mich., 1948), Vol. I.

3. L. Trotsky, *My Life* (Russian ed., 1930), II, 65, cited in Gsovsky, *Soviet Civil Law*, I.

4. Gsovsky, *Soviet Civil Law*, I, 154.

5. "Order of the People's Commissariat of Justice; Leading Principles of the Criminal Law of the RSFSR, 1919, no. 66, art. 590," trans. by Harold J. Berman (unpublished, Cambridge, 1948).

6. Goikhbarg, *Economic Law* (in Russian, 1924), I, 19, cited in Gsovsky, *Soviet Civil Law*, I, 163.

7. Pashukanis' theories and his position in Soviet law are discussed in Gsovsky, *Soviet Civil Law*, in Berman, *Justice in Russia*, and in Rudolph Schlesinger, *Soviet Legal Theory* (London: Kegan Paul, Trench, Trobner, 1945). However, the most compact presentation is that in John N. Hazard, "Reforming Soviet Criminal Law," *Journal of Criminal Law and Criminology*, XXIX (1938–39), 157–164; and John N. Hazard, "Housecleaning in Soviet Law," *American Quarterly on the Soviet Union*, 1938, no. 1, pp. 5–16. My argument tends, in general, to follow Hazard's.

8. Report on the Central Committee to the Sixteenth Congress, cited in J. Towster, *Political Power in the USSR* (New York: Oxford University Press, 1948), p. 13.

9. For a picture of these early revisions, see Hazard, "Housecleaning in Soviet Law," pp. 5–6, esp. pp. 7–8.

10. Joseph Stalin, "On the Draft Constitution of the USSR," *Leninism* (New York: International Publishers, 1942), p. 402.

11. Cited in Gsovsky, *Soviet Civil Law*, I, 174.

12. For Vyshinsky's earlier views, see Mary S. Callcott, *Russian Justice* (New York: Macmillan, 1935), *passim*.

13. Cited in Gsovsky, *Soviet Civil Law*, I, 174.

14. A. Ia. Vyshinsky, "The Foundations of the Marxist-Leninist Theory of State and Law," *The Law of the Soviet State*, trans. by Hugh Babb (New York: Macmillan, 1948), pp. 5–38. (Russian edition, 1938.)

15. Schlesinger, *Soviet Legal Theory*, p. 75.

16. *Ibid.*, esp. pp. 112 ff.

17. Callcott, *Russian Justice*, Part 3 of the Criminal Code of 1926, Art. 6, reprinted as Appendix.

18. For a discussion of the criticism of Pashukanis' approach to guilt, see Hazard, "Reforming Soviet Criminal Law," pp. 162 ff.

19. For a review of developments in Soviet judicial psychiatry, see Harold J. Berman and Donald H. Hunt, "Criminal Law and Psychiatry: The Soviet Solution," *Stanford Law Review*, II (1949–50), 635–663.

20. Ts. M. Feinberg, (Judicial Psychiatry in the USSR for 25 Years), in Feinberg (ed.), *Problemy Sudebnoi Psikhiatrii* (Problems of Judicial Psychiatry; Moscow, 1944), p. 12.

21. V. Tadevosian, (The Struggle against Juvenile Crime in the USSR), *Sovetskoe Gosudarstvo i Pravo*, 1940, no. 4, pp. 62–80.

22. Harold J. Berman, "Principles of Soviet Criminal Law," *Yale Law Journal* LVI (1947), 822 (Berman's source: All-Union Institute of Juridical Science. Criminal Law). My italics.

23. These and the following data on the status of children before the law are from John N. Hazard, "The Child under Soviet Law," *University of Chicago Law Review*, V (1938), 424–445. See esp. pp. 442–444.

24. Tadevosian, (The Struggle against Juvenile Crime in the USSR), pp. 62–80.

25. Manya Gordon, *Workers before and after Lenin* (New York: Dutton, 1941), p. 309.

26. See Preface for further comment on émigrés as a source.

27. D. Gorvits, (The Struggle against Orphaned and Unsupervised Children in the USSR), *Sovetskoe Gosudarstvo i Pravo*, 1940, nos. 5–6, p. 130.

28. *Sovetskaia Iustitsiia*, 1935, no. 10, cited in N. S. Timasheff, *The Great Retreat* (New York: Dutton, 1946), p. 321.

29. See Hazard, "The Child under Soviet Law," p. 424.

30. The argument runs throughout Vyshinsky's *The Law of the Soviet State*.

31. For a more detailed coverage of this topic, the reader is referred to a number of sources readily available in English. The most complete, although not necessarily the most penetrating source is M. J. Shore, *Soviet Education* (New York: Philosophical Library, 1947). Others are N. Hans and S. Hessen, *Educational Policy in Soviet Russia* (London: P. S. King, 1930); A. P. Pinkevitch, *The New Education in the Soviet Republic* (New York: John Day, 1929), which gives a good account of policy in the late twenties by one of the men who made that policy; Gordon, *Workers before and after Lenin;* Beatrice King, *Changing Man: The Education System of the USSR* (New York: Viking Press, 1937); and *"I Want to Be Like Stalin,"* trans. by G. S. Counts and N. P. Lodge (New York: John Day, 1947), which gives a picture of recent trends in education.

32. Resolution of a conference of teachers in 1918, quoted in Hans and Hessen, *Educational Policy*, p. 18.

33. S. N. Harper, *Civic Training in Soviet Russia* (Chicago: University of Chicago Press, 1929), p. 250.

34. *Direktivy VKP(b) i Postanovleniia Sovetskogo Pravitel'stva o Narodnom Obrazovanii za 1917–1947* (Directives of the Bolshevik

Party and Decrees of the Soviet Government on Popular Education; 2 vols.; Moscow-Leningrad, 1947), I, 120 n.

35. V. N. Shul'gin, *Narodnoe Prosveshchenie* (Popular Education), 1925, nos. 10–11, p. 126, quoted in A. G. Kalashnikov, *Ocherki Marksistskoi Pedagogiki* (Essays in Marxist Pedagogy; Moscow, 1929), I, 367.

36. See Shore, *Soviet Education*, pp. 156–163, for a discussion of the opposition to Shul'gin, notably the positions of Kalashnikov and Freedman.

37. See Molotov's speech in *From the First to the Second Five-Year Plan: A Symposium* (New York: International Publishers, no date), p. 127.

38. Stalin, *Leninism*, pp. 363–364.

39. See especially the speech of Stalin in *From the First to the Second Five-Year Plan*, pp. 1–31. Somewhere in virtually every speech in this book this theme occurs.

40. See the discussion of the hero in Soviet literature in G. Reavey, *Soviet Literature Today* (London: Lindsay Drummond 1946), pp. 62–63.

41. *Problems of Soviet Literature* (Moscow, 1935), p. 22.

42. *Pravda*, November 15, 1938.

CHAPTER 4: THE BEHAVIORAL PSYCHOLOGIES OF THE TWENTIES

1. See M. A. Reisner, (Conditioned Symbols as Social Stimuli), *VKA*, 1924, no. 9, pp. 175–197; Anon., (M. A. Reisner [necrology]), *VKA*, 1928, no. 4, pp. 3–6.

2. S. L. Rubinshtein, *Osnovy Obshchei Psikhologii* (The Foundations of General Psychology; 2d ed.; Moscow, 1946), p. 81.

3. One of the best sources for this early period is K. N. Kornilov, (The Contemporary Condition of Psychology in the USSR), *PZM*, 1927, nos. 10–11, pp. 195–217, esp. pp. 197–199.

4. See A. B. Zalkind, (The Psychoneurological Sciences in the Reconstruction Period), *Pedologiia*, 1929, no. 4, pp. 453–457; I. V. Chuvashev, (Pedological Perversions in Pre-school Education Must Be Completely Eradicated), *PO*, 1936, no. 6, pp. 45–70.

5. K. N. Kornilov, (Contemporary Psychology and Marxism), Part I, *PZM*, 1923, no. 1, pp. 41–50; Part II, *PZM*, 1923, nos. 4–5, pp. 86–114.

6. Al. Luriia, (The Moscow State Institute of Experimental Psychology in the Year 1924), in K. N. Kornilov (ed.), *Problemy Sovremennoi Psikhologii* (Problems of Contemporary Psychology; Leningrad, 1926), pp. 244–252.

7. "Chelpanov, Georgii Ivanovich," *BSE, LXI* (1934), 157–158.

8. Pavlov explains his choice of the salivary reflex in these terms: "I and my collaborators investigate the conditioned reflex almost exclusively on the salivary gland, and, as mentioned before, this is because its activity is immediately directed toward the external world (in the form of food or other substances put into the mouth); it has relatively few inner connections, and it functions alone, independently, and not as every skeletal muscle which operates only in a complicated system" (Ivan Pavlov, *Lectures on Conditioned Reflexes* [New York: International Publishers, 1928], p. 227).

9. G. Razran, "Conditioned Responses in Children," *Archives of Psychology*, 1933, no. 148, pp. 10–11.

10. G. P. Frolov, "The Study of Conditioned Reflexes as a Foundation for Pedagogy" (Moscow, 1928), cited in *Psychological Abstracts*, 1930, Vol. IV, no. 1345.

11. A. B. Zalkind, *Pedologiia v SSSR* (Pedology in the USSR; Moscow, 1929), p. 12.

12. N. K. Krupskaia, (The First Pedological Conference), *NPNS*, 1928, no. 1, pp. 3–5.

13. V. Iurinets, (Freudism and Marxism), *PZM*, 1924, no. 8–9, pp. 51–93.

14. The description of the early history of reflexology is taken from A. L. Schniermann, "Bechterev's Reflexological School," in C. Murchison (ed.), *Psychologies of 1930* (Worchester, Mass.: Clark University Press, 1930), pp. 221–242, pp. 223–224; V. M. Bechterev, *General Principles of Human Reflexology* (London, 1933), pp. 195–207.

15. V. M. Bekhterev, *Psikhologiia, Refleksologiia i Marksizm* (Psychology, Reflexology, and Marxism; Leningrad, 1925), p. 5.

16. See especially *Psikhologiia, Refleksologiia i Marksizm*.

17. *Refleksologiia ili Psikhologiia* (Leningrad, 1929).

18. Rubinshtein, *Osnovy Obshchei Psikhologii* (1946), p. 82.

19. Kornilov, (The Contemporary Condition of Psychology in the USSR), pp. 211–212. Kornilov does not give the precise dates of this event, but they must have taken place after 1923 and before 1927. Kornilov's article was written in 1927.

20. Pinkevitch, *The New Education*, pp. 61 ff.

21. Kornilov's original experimental work was done before the Revolution under the direction of Chelpanov and was published in G. I. Chelpanov (ed.), (Moscow University Division of History and Philology, Memoirs Nos. 43–44; Psychological Investigations Carried out under the Direction of Professor G. L. Chelpanov; Moscow, *circa* 1914). The most extensive account of his position is in K. N. Kornilov, *Uchenie o Reaktsiiakh Cheloveka* (The Study of Human Reactions;

Moscow, 1922). Accounts are repeated in various places, notably the
several editions of his text, *Uchebnik Psikhologii* (Textbook of Psychology; 3d ed.; Moscow, 1928), and in K. N. Kornilov, "Psychology
in the Light of Dialectical Materialism," in Murchison (ed.), *Psychologies of 1930*, pp. 243–278.

22. Kornilov, "Psychology in the Light of Dialectical Materialism,"
p. 273.

23. R. S. Schultz and R. A. McFarland, "Industrial Psychology in
the Soviet Union," *Journal of Applied Psychology*, 1935, no. 3, p. 267.

24. A. R. Luria, *The Nature of Human Conflicts* (New York:
Liveright, 1932).

25. L. S. Vygotskii, (The Problems of the Cultural Development
of the Child), *Pedologiia*, 1928, no. 1, p. 58.

26. L. S. Vygotskii and A. R. Luria, *Etiudy po Istorii Povedeniia*
(Studies in the History of Behavior; Moscow, 1930).

27. I. N. Shpil'rein, (Psychotechnics in the Reconstruction Period),
VKA, 1930, no. 39, pp. 166–198.

28. Kornilov, (The Contemporary Condition of Psychology in the
USSR), pp. 199–200.

29. Chelpanov worked as diligently as the materialists in gather-
ing "Marxist" evidence for his position. He issued a brochure in which
he quoted the founders of Marxism as favoring an "empirical" psychology, which he interpreted as arguing against the claims of the
objectivists. See his *Psikhologiia i Marksizm* (Psychology and Marxism; Moscow, 1925), cited and discussed in K. N. Kornilov, (The
Psychology and Marxism of Professor Chelpanov) in Kornilov (ed.),
Psikhologiia i Marksizm, 1925, pp. 231–242.

30. K. N. Kornilov, (The Dialectical Method in Psychology),
PZM, 1924, no. 1, p. 111.

31. *Ibid.*, p. 113.

32. V. M. Bekhterev and A. V. Dubrovskii, (Dialectical Materialism and Reflexology), *PZM*, 1926, nos. 7–8, p. 85.

33. B. G. Anan'ev, (The Methodological Section of the Brain Institute), *VIVL*, 1929, nos. 5–6, p. 102.

34. B. M. Teplov, *Sovetskaia Psikhologicheskaia Nauka za 30 let*
(Thirty Years of Soviet Psychological Science; Moscow, 1947), p. 16.

35. After Pavlov's death, Mitin, then and still the most authorita-
tive of Soviet philosophers, published a eulogy in which he said that
Pavlov had independently "approached" a dialectical position. What
is most revealing in the article is Mitin's statement that in the midst
of the discussion he asked Pavlov if the great physiologist had heard
of Lenin's article, "An Approach to the Question of Dialectics"—
a very critical methodological statement. Pavlov listened to the summary of Lenin's argument "with great interest," and said that he would

have to read the article. M. Mitin, (In Memory of a Great Materialist Physiologist), *PZM*, 1936, no. 3, p. 41.

36. M. S. Bernshtein, (Questions of Methodology at the First All-Union Pedological Congress), *NPNS*, 1928, no. 1, pp. 37–43.

37. Zalkind, (The Psychoneurological Sciences in the Period of Reconstruction), p. 456.

38. *Ibid.*, p. 456.

39. Shpil'rein, (Psychotechnics in the Reconstruction Period), pp. 166–198.

40. Zalkind, (The Psychoneurological Sciences in the Period of Reconstruction), p. 456.

41. A. Gastev, (The Struggle for a Socialist Attitude toward Labor), *Organizatsiia Truda*, 1937, no. 10, p. 5; A. Gastev, (Let us Learn our Lesson), *Organizatsiia Truda*, 1937, no. 5, pp. 1–5, pp. 1–2.

42. Gastev, (The Struggle for a Socialist Attitude toward Labor), p. 5.

43. Shpil'rein, (Psychotechnics in the Reconstruction Period), p. 171.

44. This shift is discussed in detail by Shultz and MacFarland, "Industrial Psychology in the Soviet Union," pp. 265–308, *passim;* Shpil'rein, (Psychotechnics in the Reconstruction Period), pp. 166–198, *passim.*

45. Shpil'rein, (Psychotechnics in the Reconstruction Period), p. 178.

46. Zalkind, *Pedologiia v SSSR*, p. 60.

47. (The Pedological Congress and the Practical Conclusions to be Drawn from It), in Zalkind, *Pedologiia v SSSR*, pp. 73 ff.

48. Cf. V. M. Borovski, "Psychology in the USSR," *JGIP*, 1929, no. 2, pp. 177–186 ("Some of our junior fellows are showing considerable interest lately in the German Gestalt psychology," p. 184); and V. A. Artemov, (Contemporary German Psychology), *Psikhologiia*, 1928, Vol. I, nos 1 and 2.

CHAPTER 5: THE MECHANISTIC MODEL OF PERSONALITY

1. Ivan Pavlov, *Conditioned Reflexes and Psychiatry* (New York: International Publishers, 1941), II, 126.

2. Bechterev, *General Principles of Human Reflexology*, preface to second ed., p. 20.

3. G. N. Sorokhtin, (The Subject Matter and Method of Reflexology), in *Refleksologiia ili Psikhologiia* (Reflexology or Psychology; Leningrad, 1929), p. 25.

4. Kornilov, (Contemporary Psychology and Marxism), Part I, p. 43.

5. B. M. Teplov dates this error from the first edition of Kornilov's text book in 1926 (Teplov, *Sovetskaia Psikhologicheskaia Nauka za 30 let*, p. 15). This error is also expressed in various other places, notably Kornilov's article, "Psychology in the Light of Dialectical Materialism," in Murchison (ed.), *Psychologies of 1930*, pp. 243–278.

6. A. Zalmanzon, (In Defense of the Objective Trend in Psychology), *VKA*, 1926, no. 18, p. 197.

7. A. L. Schniermann, "Present-Day Tendencies in Russian Psychology," *JGlP*, 1928, p. 400.

8. Kornilov, *Uchebnik Psikhologii*, p. 119.

9. For Ukhtomskii's version of this concept see: Speech of Ukhtomskii at the Second All-Union Psychoneurological Congress, report in G. Daian, (The Second Psychoneurological Congress), *KN*, 1924, no. 3, pp. 223–238; A. Ukhtomskii, (The Dominant), *BSE*, XXIII (1931), 136–140; A. Ukhtomskii, (The Dominant as a Factor in Behavior), *VKA*, 1927, no. 22, pp. 215–242.

10. Ukhtomskii, (The Dominant), *BSE*, XXIII (1931), 137.

11. N. V. Oparina, (Concentration in Children with a Disequilibrium of the Activity of the Central Nervous System), *VIVL*, 1928, no. 1, pp. 20–26; V. M. Bekhterev, (The Role of Concentration as a Dominant in Correlative Reflex Activity), *VIVL*, 1927, nos. 1–2, pp. 3–18; I. Il'inskii, (Concerning Concentration), *VIVL*, 1927, nos. 1–2, pp. 19–32; N. F. Dobrinin, (The Tempo of Attention), in Kornilov (ed.), *Problemy Sovremennoi Psikhologii* (1928), III, 101–131; E. S. Nikitina, (The Will Process in Problem Children and in Normal Children), *VIVL*, 1926, nos. 2–3, pp. 180–197.

12. Kornilov, *Uchebnik Psikhologii*, p. 109.

13. For expressions of the compatibility of the concept of the unconscious with the objective approach to psychology, see Bechterev, *General Principles of Human Reflexology*, p. 44; A. R. Luriia, (Psychoanalysis as a System of Monistic Psychology), in Kornilov (ed.), *Psikhologiia i Marksizm* (Psychology and Marxism; Leningrad, 1925), p. 60.

14. Bechterev, *General Principles of Human Reflexology*, p. 41.

15. Daian, (The Second Psychneurological Congress), *KN*, 1924, no. 2, p. 159.

16. A. B. Zalkind, *Ocherki Kul'tury Revoliutsionnogo Vremeni* (Essays on the Culture of the Revolutionary Period; Moscow, 1924), p. 59.

17. L. S. Vygotskii, (Consciousness as a Problem of the Psychology of Behavior), in Kornilov (ed.), *Psikhologiia i Marksizm*, pp. 175–198.

18. L. S. Vygotskii, (The Problem of Dominant Reactions), in

Kornilov (ed.), *Problemy Sovremennoi Psikhologii* (1926), p. 123.

19. Teplov, *Sovetskaia Psikhologicheskaia Nauka za 30 let*, p. 14.

20. The main statement of this position is in Vygotskii and Luriia, *Etiudy po istorii povedeniia* (Studies in the History of Behavior). Other statements of the method, theory, and findings of these investigations appeared in the various volumes of the memoirs of Kornilov's institute and in the journal *Psikhologiia*. The English reading public will find adequate statements in: L. S. Vygotskii, "II. The Problem of the Cultural Development of the Child," *JGcP*, XXXVI (1929), 415–434; A. R. Luria, "The Problem of the Cultural Behavior of the Child," *JGcP*, XXXV (1928), 493–506; Luria, *The Nature of Human Conflicts;* A. N. Leontiev, "Studies on the Cultural Development of the Child. III. The Development of Voluntary Attention in the Child," *JGcP*, XL (1932), 52–83.

21. L. S. Vygotskii, (Consciousness as a Problem of the Psychology of Behavior), in Kornilov (ed.), *Psikhologiia i Marksizm*, p. 187.

22. Leontiev, "Studies on Cultural Development of the Child . . . ," p. 57.

23. Luria, *The Nature of Human Conflicts*, p. 401.

24. Teplov, *Sovetskaia Psikhologicheskaia Nauka za 30 let*, p. 15.

25. Pavlov, *Lectures on Conditioned Reflexes*, p. 82.

26. Bechterev, *General Principles of Human Reflexology*, pp. 103, 313; Luria, (On a System of Behavioral Psychology), *Psikhologiia*, I, (1928), pp. 53–65, esp. p. 54; V. A. Artemov, *Detskaia Eksperimental'naia Psikhologiia* (Experimental Child Psychology; Moscow-Leningrad, 1929), p. 194; S. G. Gellershtein, *Psikhotekhnika* (Psychotechnics; Moscow, 1926), p. 12; S. S. Molozhavyi, (The Science of the Child: Its Principles and Methods), *Pedologiia*, 1928, no. 1, pp. 27–39, esp. p. 26.

27. Kornilov, "Psychology in the Light of Dialectical Materialism," in Murchison (ed.), *Psychologies of 1930*, p. 257.

28. Kornilov, *Uchebnik Psikhologii*, pp. 139–140.

29. I. P. Pavlov, *Conditioned Reflexes* (Oxford University Press, 1927), pp. 9–11; Bechterev, *General Principles of Human Reflexology*, pp. 161–162.

30. Pavlov, *Lectures on Conditioned Reflexes*, p. 280.

31. Bechterev, *General Principles of Human Reflexology*, p. 140.

32. Kornilov, *Uchebnik Psikhologii*, pp. 135, 140, 151.

33. A compact account of the work of such men as Wagner, Borovskii, and Voitonis—active in this period—is given in N. Iu. Voitonis, (The Problem of "Motives" of Behavior and the Study of this Problem), *Psikhologiia*, II (1924), no. 2, pp. 227–253, esp. p. 232; and G. Z. Roginskii, (Comparative Psychology in the USSR), *Vestnik Leningradskogo Universiteta*, 1947, no. 7, pp. 60–69.

34. G. Iu. Malis, (The Professional Interests of Working Youth), *VIVL*, 1928, no. 2, pp. 72–83; Sh. V. Smirnov, (Vocational Orientation and Interests of Blind School Children), *VIVL*, 1929, nos. 5–6, p. 109 (a report read to the Leningrad Medical-Pedological Society, May 27, 1929); V. Gur-Gurevich, (The Reading Interests of Children of Different Social Groups), *Pedologiia*, 1929, nos. 1–2, pp. 235–238; see also six articles on the opinions and ideology of school children and juvenile delinquents in *Pedologiia*, 1929, no. 4; and S. S. Molozhavyi, (Pedology at the First Congress for the Study of Human Behavior), *Pedologiia*, 1939, no. 3, pp. 329–340.

35. Shpil'rein, (Psychotechnics in the Period of Reconstruction), *VKA*, 1930, no. 39, p. 168.

36. Schultz and McFarland, "Industrial Psychology in the Soviet Union," p. 289.

37. Zalkind, *Ocherki Kul'tury Revoliutsionnogo Vremeni*, p. 73.

38. For reports of these speeches, see *ibid.*, p. 74; Daian, (The Second Psychoneurological Conference), *KN*, 1924, no. 2, pp. 161–162; Zalkind, *Pedologiia v SSSR*, pp. 5–54.

39. Daian, (Second Psychoneurological Conference), p. 161.

40. Zalkind, *Pedologiia v SSSR*, pp. 12–13.

41. (Excerpts from the Speeches of N. K. Krupskaia, N. I. Bukharin, A. V. Lunacharskii, and N. A. Semashko on Fundamental Questions of Pedology), *NPNS*, 1928, no. 1, p. 11.

42. This principle of continual change was generally acknowledged by psychologists whenever they discussed the relationship of their discipline to Marxism. See Bekhterev and Dubrovskii, (Dialectical Materialism and Reflexology), *PZM*, 1926, nos. 7–8, pp. 69–94; Kornilov, (The Dialectical Method in Psychology), *PZM*, 1924, no. 1, p. 107; Iu. Frankfurt, (Plekhanov on Dialectics in Psychology), *VKA*, 1927, no. 22, pp. 186–214.

43. Iu. Frankfurt, (The Struggle for a Marxist Psychology), *KN*, 1927, no. 10, p. 170.

44. For Reisner's activities, see M. A. Reisner (Social Psychology and Marxism), in Kornilov (ed.), *Psikhologiia i Marksizm;* M. A. Reisner, *Problemy Sotsial'noi Psikhologii* (Problems of Social Psychology; Rostov-Don, 1925); (M. A. Reisner [necrology]), *VKA*, 1928, no. 4, pp. 3–6.

45. P. P. Blonskii, (Certain Errors Which Are Encountered in Pedology), *NPNS*, 1931, no. 6, pp. 41–50, esp. pp. 45–46.

46. A. S. Zaluzhnyi, (Against the Two Factor Theory in Pedology and in the Theory of the Children's Collective), *Pedologiia*, 1932, no. 3, p. 18.

47. Blonskii, *Osnovi Pedagogiki*, p. 83.

48. See Zalkind's speech in Daian (The Second Psychoneurological Conference), pp. 161–162.

49. See A. V. Dubrovskii, (Consciousness as a Topic of Reflexology), in *Refleksologiia i Psikhologiia* (Leningrad, 1929), p. 39; and Sorokhtin, (The Subject Matter and Method of Reflexology), in *Refleksologiia i Psikhologiia*, p. 22; and B. G. Anan'ev, (The Social Factor in Human Behavior), *VIVL*, nos. 5–6, 1929, pp. 19–23, esp. p. 23.

50. L. B. Chernikhova, (Child Newspaper Vendors and Their Environment), *Pedologiia*, 1929, nos. 1–2, pp. 167–177.

51. M. Syrkin, (Stability of Social Differences as Indicated by Intelligence Tests), *PPT*, 1929, no. 1, pp. 9–14; M. Ionova, (What Determines Mental Development), *NPNS*, 1925, no. 4, pp. 61–66.

52. A. S. Griboedov, (The Contemporary Problem of Intelligence), *VIVL*, 1928, nos. 3–4, p. 95 (a report read to the Scientific Medical-Pedological Society, November 26, 1928).

53. F. P. Petrov, (An Investigation of the Intellectual Development of Chuvash Children by the Binet-Simon Test, 1928), cited in a review by M. Efimov, *Pedologiia*, 1931, nos. 7–8, pp. 127–128.

54. M. Ionova, (The Correlation between Mental Development and Certain Data on the Living Conditions of School Children), in P. P. Blonskii (ed.), *Pedologiia i Shkola* (Pedology and the School; Moscow, 1929), pp. 69–85.

55. L. S. Vygotskii, (The Question of the Plan for the Investigation of the Work in the Pedology of National Minorities), *Pedologiia*, 1929, no. 3, pp. 367–377.

56. A. B. Zalkind, (The Fundamental Characteristics of the Age of Puberty), *Pedologiia*, 1930, no. 1, pp. 3–25.

57. V. M. Gur-Gurevich, (Suicide among Children and Youth before and after the Revolution), *Pedologiia*, 1930, no. 1, pp. 98–106.

58. Sokolianskii, (On So-Called Lip Reading), *Ukr. Visnik refleksologii tia eksperimentalnoi pedagogiki*, 1926, no. 2, p. 49, cited in A. S. Zaluzhnyi, (Against the Two Factor Theory . . .), *Pedologiia*, 1932, no. 3, p. 18.

59. Bekhterev and Dubrovskii, (Dialectical Materialism and Reflexology), *PZM*, 1926, nos. 7–8, p. 77.

60. For a view of this particularly negative attitude toward the role of the school in education, see the series of articles in Blonskii, *Pedologiia i Shkola*.

61. V. N. Shul'gin, (Achievements and Perspectives), *NPNS*, 1927, no. 10, p. 49. My italics.

62. Cited in F. F. Korolev, (It Is Time for a Decisive Fight against Mechanistic Tendencies in Pedology), *Pedologiia*, 1931, no. 3, p. 21.

63. Molozhavyi, (The Science of the Child: Its Principles and Methods), p. 27.

64. Kornilov, *Uchenie o Reaktsiiakh Cheloveka*, pp. 152–153.

65. Pinkevitch, *The New Education*, p. 70.

66. Artemov, *Detskaia Eksperimental'naia Psikhologiia*, p. 194.

67. *Ibid.*

68. V. M. Gur-Gurevich, ("Leftist" Perversions in Pedagogy and Pedology), *Pedologiia*, 1931, nos. 7–8, p. 45.

69. V. A. Artemov, (Contemporary German Psychology), *Psikhologiia*, I (1928), nos. 1–2, *passim*; Artemov, *Detskaia Eksperimental'naia Psikhologiia*, *passim*.

70. Shpil'rein, (Psychotechnics in the Reconstruction Period), p. 170.

CHAPTER 6: CONSCIOUSNESS COMES TO MAN

1. (The Results of the Discussion on Reactological Psychology), *Psikhologiia*, IV (1931), no. 1, p. 5.

2. *Ibid.*

3. A. Mukovnin, (The Results of the Review of the Department of Pedology and Psychology in the Krupskaia Institute of Communist Education), *Pedologiia*, 1931, no. 4, pp. 79–83.

4. M. P. Feofanov, (The Theory of Cultural Development in Pedology . . .), *Pedologiia*, 1932, nos. 1–2, p. 26.

5. Vedenov cited by Teplov, *Sovetskaia Psikhologicheskaia Nauka za 30 Let*, p. 21.

6. A. B. Zalkind, (The Psychoneurological Sciences and Socialist Development), *Pedologiia*, 1930, no. 3, p. 309.

7. *Ibid.*, p. 318.

8. Shore, *Soviet Education*, p. 191.

9. S. I. Kaplun, (The Present Status of the Physiology of Work and the Most Important Tasks with Which We Are Faced in the Present Period of Socialist Construction), *Na Psikhotekhnicheskom Fronte* (Moscow, 1931), p. 13; I. N. Shpil'rein, (The Position on the Psychotechnical Front), *Na Psikhotekhnicheskom Fronte*, p. 9.

10. Shpil'rein, (The Position on the Psychotechnical Front), p. 5.

11. Morris S. Viteles, "Industrial Psychology in Russia," *Occupational Psychology*, 1938, no. 2, pp. 91–92.

12. Sidney and Beatrice Webb, *Soviet Communism: A New Civilization* (New York: Longmans, Green, 1947), p. 725.

13. Gur-Gurevich, ("Leftist" Perversions in Pedagogy and Pedology), p. 45.

14. Editorial, (Pedology in the Fight for the Realization of the

Decree of the Central Committee on the School), *Pedologiia*, 1931, no. 4, p. 11.

15. M. Ia. Basov, (Certain Tasks Facing the Reconstruction of Pedology), *Pedologiia*, 1931, nos. 5–6, p. 16.

CHAPTER 7: THE TURNING POINT IN APPLIED PSYCHOLOGY

1. The main sources of Lenin's theory of knowledge are *Materialism and Empiriocriticism* and his *Filosofskie Tetradi* (Philosophical Notebooks). Soviet intellectual journals around the turn of the thirties are filled with articles on this topic. An especially good one is P. Kucherov, (Lenin and Plekhanov's Theory of Knowledge), *PZM*, 1930, nos. 10–12, pp. 113–142. Hecker deals with the problem in his *Moscow Dialogues*. However, the bare bones of the argument, as presented in such sources, are no substitute for the study of the way in which this theory is used in practice. Much of what is said in this chapter could be deduced only from the meaning given this theory in practice.

2. M. Kammari, (The Theoretical Roots of M. N. Pokrovskii's Erroneous Views in History), *PZM*, 1936, no. 4, p. 7.

3. The current Soviet version of our Webster's is Ushakov's Explanatory Dictionary of the Russian Language. Under "objectivism" one finds the following citation from Lenin: "The objectivist, demonstrating the necessity for a given series of facts, always runs the risk of becoming an apologist for those facts. The materialist discovers class conflicts, and this determines his point of view. The objectivist speaks of 'insuperable historical tendencies': the materialist speaks of which class 'governs' a given economic order which is in its turn the creator of existing forms of conflict between the various classes. Therefore, the materialist, from one point of view, goes further and deeper than the objectivist; he applies objectivism more fully" D. N. Ushakov, *Tolkovyi Slovar' Russkogo Iazyka* [Moscow, 1938], II, 735).

4. A. S. Zaluzhnyi, (In Opposition to the Two Factor Theory in Pedology and in the Theory of the Children's Collective), *Pedologiia*, 1932, no. 3, p. 17.

5. Alexander Afinogenyev, *Fear*, in Eugene Lyons, *Six Soviet Plays* (Boston; Houghton Mifflin, 1934), pp. 391–469.

6. (From the Editors), *PPT*, 1928, no. 1, p. 3.

7. Schultz and McFarland, "Industrial Psychology in the Soviet Union," pp. 298–299.

8. I. N. Shpil'rein, (The Turning Point in Psychotechnics), *PPT*, 1931, nos. 4–6, pp. 251–252.

9. Anon., (The Conference of the Department of Pedagogy and

Pedology in the Commissariat of Education), *Pedologiia*, 1931, nos. 7–8, pp. 145–146.

10. K. N. Kornilov, (In Response to the Summary of the Psychological Discussions), *Psikhologiia*, IV (1931), no. 1, pp. 44–77.

11. A. B. Zalkind, (The Psychoneurological Front and the Psychological Discussion), *Pedologiia*, 1931, no. 3, p. 5.

12. Apart from passing references in various articles, discussions will be found in N. N. Kostin, (Concerning Pedological Statistics), *Pedologiia*, 1932, no. 4, pp. 13–20; and P. Stanevich, (In Opposition to the Superfluous Emphasis on the Method of Statistical Variability and Its Incorrect Application in Anthropometry and Psychometrics), *Pedologiia*, 1931, no. 3, pp. 67–69.

13. Anon., (Resolutions on the Question of the Status of Things on the Defectological Front), *Pedologiia*, 1931, p. 106.

14. Shpil'rein, (Psychotechnics in the Reconstruction Period), p. 176.

15. Cited in P. Leventuev, (Political Perversion in Pedology), *Pedologiia*, 1931, no. 3, p. 63.

16. G. Gak, (Concerning a Harmful Method), *Kommunisticheskaia Revoliutsiia*, 1931, no. 8, p. 26.

17. *Ibid.*, pp. 19–26, *passim*. Gur-Gurevich, ("Leftist" Perversions in Pedagogy and Pedology), p. 47.

18. G. H. S. Razran, "Psychology in the USSR," *Journal of Philosophy*, XXXII (1935), 23.

19. V. N. Kolbanovskii, (The Primary Tasks of Soviet Psychology), *PO*, 1936, no. 5, p. 12.

20. L. S. Vygotskii, (The Question of the Plan for the Investigation of the Work of the Pedology of National Minorities), *Pedologiia*, 1929, no. 3, pp. 367, 368.

21. P. I. Leventuev, A. Bagautdinov, A. R. Z. Musael'iants, Mangusheva, S. Nugmanov, S. Tillia Khodzhaev, A. A. Usmanov and V. Khalilov, (In Opposition to Great-Power Chauvinism in Pedology), *Pedologiia*, 1932, nos. 1–2, pp. 46–49.

22. V. Gur, (E. Granat and E. Zgorzhel'skaia, "Buriat Children"), *Pedologiia*, 1931, nos. 7–8, p. 130.

23. M. Efimov, (F. P. Petrov, An Investigation of the Intellectual Development of Chuvash Children by the Binet-Simon Test, 1928), *Pedologiia*, 1931, nos. 7–8, p. 128.

24. Shpil'rein, (Psychotechnics in the Reconstruction Period), *VKA*, 1930, no. 39, p. 177.

25. M. Iu. Syrkin, (Class and Nationality Differences in the Tests of Intelligence and their Interpretation), *Na Psikhotekhnicheskom Fronte*, p. 18.

26. N. I. Ozeretskii, (Principles of the Selection and Grouping of

Children for the Auxiliary School), *Pedologiia*, 1931, nos. 7–8, p. 107.
27. *Ibid.*, p. 108.

CHAPTER 8: THE DECREE AGAINST PEDOLOGY

1. P. P. Blonskii, *Pamiat' i Myshlenie* (Memory and Thinking; Moscow-Leningrad, 1935); and P. P. Blonskii, *Razvitie Myshleniia Shkol'nika* (The Development of the Thinking of School Children; Moscow, 1935).

2. The main criticism of the position of these authors on questions of development can be found in E. I. Rudneva, (The Question of Pedological Perversions in the Theory of Instruction), *PO*, 1937, no. 1, pp. 66–67.

3. L. S. Vygotskii, *Myshlenie i Rech'* (Thinking and Speech; Moscow-Leningrad, 1934), p. 213.

4. F. Georgiev, (In Opposition to Behaviorism and Reactology), *PZM*, 1937, no. 1, pp. 163–169.

5. Teplov, *Sovetskaia Psikhologicheskaia Nauka za 30 Let*, p. 22.

6. *Ibid.*

7. S. L. Rubinshtein, (Problems of Psychology in the Works of Karl Marx), *SPsi*, 1934, no. 1, pp. 3–20; S. L. Rubinshtein, *Osnovy Psikhologii* (Foundations of Psychology; Moscow, 1935).

8. S. G. Levit, (Some Results and Prospects of Twin Investigations), *Trud. Med.-Biol. Nauchno-Issled. Inst. Gorkogo*, 1934, no. 3, pp. 5–17, cited in *Psychological Abstracts*, IX, no. 2738. Between the years 1934 and 1936 the *Psychological Abstracts* contain abstracts of fourteen articles in this series.

9. S. G. Levit, "Twin Investigations in the USSR," *Character and Personality*, III (1935), 188–193.

10. The conclusions of this and succeeding sections are based largely on interviews with persons who worked in these areas in the thirties. The reader, however, will find that they can be verified by a careful reading of Soviet journals of this period.

11. Recounted by Sergei Beloussov, formerly with the Children's Theater in Moscow.

12. Told to me by Dr. Bronson Price in private conversation.

13. See the apologetic defenses of Krupskaia and Bubnov in 1934 in T. K. Chuguev, (Concerning the Attacks of the "Planners" on Pedology), *PO*, 1936, no. 6, p. 50.

14. Stalin, *Problems of Leninism*, pp. 435–436.

15. *Ibid.*

16. A. P. Fomichev, (The Tenth Anniversary of the Proclamation of the Central Committee of the Party "Concerning Pedological

Perversions in the System of the Narkom Pros"), *SP*, 1946, no. 7, pp. 11–20.

17. V. Pecherskaia and S. Musatova, (The Decree of the Central Committee of the Party in Action), *Doshkol'noe Vospitanie*, 1937, no. 1, p. 87.

18. L. E. Raskin, (Pedological Perversions on the Question of Repeating), *NS*, 1938, no. 2, p. 44.

CHAPTER 9: THE "NEW MAN" IN SOVIET PSYCHOLOGY

1. P. I. Plotnikov, (Eradicate the Pseudo-Science of Pedology and its Partisans), *SPed*, 1937, no. 1, p. 57.

2. G. F., (The Present State of Psychology in the USSR and the Tasks with which it is Faced), *PZM*, 1936, no. 9, pp. 87–99.

3. For this information about Shpil'rein's fate, I am indebted to Dr. Bronson Price.

4. See series of articles in (Materials for Instruction), *SPed*, 1938, no. 2, pp. 96–115.

5. L. M. Shvarts, (The Projected Program of Psychology for the Teacher's Institutes), *SPed*, 1938, no. 10, pp. 94–96.

6. Anon., (The Program for Psychology in the Teacher's Institute), *SPed*, 1938, no. 10, pp. 98–103.

7. K. N. Kornilov, *et al.*, *Psikhologiia* (Psychology; 1st ed.; Moscow, 1938).

8. *Ibid.*, Introduction.

9. Rubinshtein, *Osnovy Obshchei Psikhologii* (1940).

10. R. A. Bauer, "The Genetics Controversy and the Psychological Sciences in the USSR," *The American Psychologist*, IV, no. 10.

11. V. N. Kolbanovskii, (Concerning Certain Faults of Prof. S. L. Rubinshtein's Book), *SPed*, 1947, no. 6, p. 108.

12. A. A. Smirnov, (The Tasks and Content of Instruction in Psychology in Pedagogical and Teacher's Institute), *SPed*, 1947, no. 12, p. 60.

13. The discussion of the distinction between voluntary and involuntary behavior by Rubinshtein, *Osnovy Obshchei Psikhologii* (1946), chap. xiv on "Will," pp. 506–534, gives this argument in its most complete statement in Soviet literature. Shorter treatments will be found in the chapters on "Will" in B. M. Teplov, *Psikhologiia* (Psychology; 2d ed., Moscow, 1948); K. N. Kornilov, *Psikhologiia* (Psychology; 1946); and Kornilov *et al.*, *Psikhologiia* (Psychology; 1948).

14. Teplov, *Psikhologiia*, p. 144.

15. Rubinshtein, *Osnovy Obshchei Psikhologii* (1946), pp. 508–509.

16. Because of the long-running controversies on this topic, it is impossible to cite a single convenient source to which the reader can turn for an adequate description. Despite criticisms which have recently been directed at Rubinshtein's work, it is my belief that one would get a fairly full picture if one read Rubinshtein's (The Problem of Consciousness in the Light of Dialectical Materialism), *Izvestiia Akademii Nauk SSSR, Seriia Istorii i filosofii*, II (1945), no. 3, pp. 148–158, and relevant parts of his 1946 text, together with one recent criticism, Kolbanovskii, (Some Defects of Professor Rubinshtein's Book), *SPed*, 1947, no. 6, pp. 103–110.

17. Kolbanovskii, (Some Defects of Professor Rubinshtein's Book), p. 105.

18. Rubinshtein, (The Problem of Consciousness in the Light of Dialectical Materialism), p. 155.

19. A. Talankin, (Concerning "The Marxist Psychology of Professor Kornilov"), *Psikhologiia*, IV (1931), no. 1, p. 39.

20. Rubinshtein, (Problems of Psychology in the Works of Karl Marx), *SPsi*, 1934, no. 1, p. 16.

21. Cf. evaluation of Gordon's article in B. G. Anan'ev, (The Present Status of Psychology in the USSR), *SPed*, 1941, no. 5, p. 115. Anan'ev considers the article to be a rather generalized statement and laments the fact that no concrete investigations have been made. According to Anan'ev, a similar statement was made in the same year (1939) by Lezhnev in a volume of papers edited by Kornilov. This article was not obtainable.

22. L. A. Gordon, (Needs and Interests), *SPed*, 1939, nos. 8–9, p. 132.

23. *Ibid.*, p. 133.

24. *Ibid.*

25. *Ibid.*, p. 134.

26. *Ibid.*, p. 135.

27. *Ibid.*, p. 137.

28. *Ibid.*, p. 140.

29. The reader who is acquainted with Western psychology will, when reading Gordon's statement, notice that his conception of needs and interests is very reminiscent of Allport's work. There is, to my knowledge, no reference in Soviet literature to Allport's conception of "functional autonomy," nor to the work of another outstanding need theorist, Henry Murray.

30. V. I. Selivanov, (Concerning the Self-Training of Will and Character), *SPed*, 1949, no. 7, p. 19.

31. Teplov, *Psikhologiia* (2d ed., 1948), p. 152.

32. Kornilov *et al.*, *Psikhologiia*, (3d ed., 1948), p. 406; T. G. Diakonova, (The Training of Interest in Students), *NS*, 1941, no. 4,

216   NOTES TO CHAPTER 9

pp. 7–12; M. F. Beliaev, (The Question of the Dynamics of Interest), *SPed*, 1940, nos. 11–12, p. 152. Also numerous articles in education journals over the last decade.

33. Such statements are common in the Marxist-Leninist classics. They are reënforced, however, in the constant restatements of minor authors. It is particularly important that in 1938 there was a flood of articles on the role of the individual in a socialist society in *PZM*. Typical titles for the year 1938 were: "The Blossoming of the Individual in the USSR," "Socialism and Personality," "Socialism and the Needs of the People." In very recent years the theme has been restated in the public lecture series: M. M. Rozental', *Velikaia Oktiabr'skaia Sotsialisticheskaia Revoliutsiia i Formirovanie Novogo Cheloveka* (The Great October Socialist Revolution and the Formation of the New Man; Moscow, 1947); and Ia. N. Umanskii, *Lichnost' v Sotsialisticheskom Obshchestve* (Personality in a Socialist Society; Moscow, 1947).

34. Gordon, (Needs and Interests), p. 135.
35. For example, *"I Want to be Like Stalin."*
36. K. N. Kornilov, (The Question of Training Will), *SPed*, 1942, nos. 5–6, p. 54.
37. G. S. Kostiuk, (The Role of Inheritance, Environment, and Training in the Psychic Development of the Child), *SPed*, 1940, no. 6, p. 26.
38. A. N. Leont'ev, (The Most Important Problems of Psychology in the Light of the Session of the All-Union Academy of Agricultural Sciences of V. I. Lenin), *SPed*, 1949, no. 1, p. 78.
39. Cf. Bauer, "The Genetics Controversy and the Psychological Sciences in the USSR."
40. Kostiuk, (The Role of Inheritance . . .), p. 21.
41. G. S. Kostiuk, (The Real Question of the Formation of the Child's Personality), *SPed*, 1949, no. 11, pp. 73–101.
42. I. A. Kairov (ed.), *Pedagogika* (Pedagogy; Moscow, 1948), p. 207.
43. Kostiuk, (The Role of Inheritance . . .), p. 34.
44. V. Pecherskaia and S. Musatova, (The Decree of the Central Committee of the Party in Action), *Doshkol'noe Vospitanie*, 1937, no. 1, p. 88.
45. Kostiuk, (The Role of Inheritance . . .), p. 33.
46. Leont'ev, (Soviet Psychology Ten Years after the Decree . . .), p. 23.
47. Rubinshtein, *Osnovy Obshchei Psikhologii* (1946), p. 475.
48. Kornilov, (The Question of Training Will), pp. 56, 57.
49. Kostiuk, (The Role of Inheritance . . .), p. 37.
50. Kornilov, (The Question of Training Will), pp. 56 ff.; and

Selivanov, (Concerning the Self-Training of Will and Character),
pp. 18–29, *passim.*
   51. Rubinshtein, *Osnovy Obshchei Psikhologii* (1946), p. 475.

CHAPTER 10: MODERN SOVIET PSYCHOLOGY

   1. For examples of extremely militant postwar criticism, see
E. Chernakov, (An Addition to the History of Russian Psychology),
Bol'shevik, 1948, no. 12, pp. 55–58; M. N. Maslina, (For Bolshevist
Partisanship in Questions of Psychology), *Voprosy Filosofii*, 1948,
no. 2; P. I. Plotnikov, (Cleanse Soviet Psychology of Homeless Cosmo-
politanism), *SPed*, 1949, no. 4, pp. 11–19; and *Nauchnaia Sessiia
Posviashchennaia Problemam Fiziologicheskogo Ucheniia Akademika
I. P. Pavlova* (The Scientific Session Dedicated to the Problems of
the Physiological Teachings of Academician I. P. Pavlov; Moscow-
Leningrad, 1950).
   2. The major contribution is that of B. G. Anan'ev, *Ocherki Istorii
Russkoi Psikhologii XVIII i XIX Vekov* (Essays in the History of
Russian Psychology of the Eighteenth and Nineteenth Centuries;
Moscow, 1947), p. 166. In addition, there has been a considerable number of articles in *SPed* during the last twelve years.
   3. Rubinshtein, *Osnovy Psikhologii*, pp. 83–84.
   4. *Ibid.*, p. 151 n.
   5. M. Ia. Basov, (The Problems of Functional Psychology in the
System of A. F. Lazurskii), *VIVL*, 1920, no. 2, pp. 219–229.
   6. M. Basov, (The Will as the Subject of Functional Psychology),
VIVL, 1922, nos. 4–5, pp. 805–917.
   7. Perhaps the most compact statement of the Soviet criticism of
"abstract" functionalism is the one made by Shnirman in his review
of the second edition of Kornilov, *et al.* He detected in this text the
faults of the old functional psychology and commented: "In connection with this question it is necessary to introduce some clarity into
the very concept of 'functionalism.' The fact of the matter is that in
recent time certain psychologists have used the slogan of fighting
against functionalism as a pretext for demanding the rejection of any
sort of analysis of the separate psychic processes. Naturally this is not
generally correct. Such a treatment of 'functionalism' and such a
program of combatting it is clearly wrong. The essence of the matter
is not that psychologists identify separate psychic processes and functions, but, first, how these functions are regarded, and, second, whether
all of psychology is to be reduced to the study of these separate
processes. Therefore, overcoming functionalism does not involve the
refusal to consider the separate psychic processes in psychology, but,
rather that one (a) regard these processes as concrete manifestations

of the personality; (b) study not only the separate psychic processes, but also the more broad individual psychological characteristics of the personality; (c) study both the separate psychic processes and the more general individual traits of personality in their development and formation, and in their manifestation in the separate concrete forms of man's activity" (S. L. Shnirman, [The Second Edition of the Teaching Manual "Psychology"], *SPed*, 1941, no. 9, p. 90).

8. This is discussed at some length in Rubinshtein, *Osnovy Obshchei Psikhologii* (1946), pp. 182 ff.

9. S. M. Rives, (The Principles of Soviet Didactics), *SPed*, 1940, no. 1, p. 4.

10. Leont'ev, (Soviet Psychology Ten Years after the Decree of the Central Committee of the Communist Party . . .), pp. 26–28.

11. *Ibid.*, pp. 40–42.

12. Speech by Smirnov in I. A. Kairov, (The Session of the Lenin All-Union Academy of Agricultural Sciences), *SPed*, 1948, no. 11, p. 47.

13. N. A. Rybnikov, (The Themes of Soviet Psychology: 1938–1939), *SPed*, 1940, nos. 4–5, p. 166.

14. The data is compiled from (Directory of Psychological Literature), *SPed*, 1950, no. 12, pp. 96–108.

15. This is in marked contrast to psychology in America, where, in 1938, the most significant trends were the "uninterrupted rise in the use of animal subjects" (J. S. Bruner and G. W. Allport, "Fifty Years of Change in American Psychology," *Psychological Bulletin*, 1940, no. 10, p. 764). This trend has continued in America.

16. The reader who is interested in recent work on conditioned reflexes is referred to: I. D. London, "Contemporary Psychology in the Soviet Union," *Science*, CXIV (1951), 227–233; I. D. London, "Psychology in the USSR," *American Journal of Psychology*, LXIV (1951), 422–428; L. A. Orbeli, (Physiology and Psychology), in B. G. Anan'ev (ed.), *Problemy Psikhologii* (Problems of Psychology; Leningrad, 1948), pp. 7–15; K. M. Bykov, *Novoe v Uchenii Pavlova o Vysshei Nervnoi Deiatel'nosti* (New Developments in the Pavlovian Study of Higher Nervous Activity; Moscow, 1947); and *Nauchnaia Sessiia Posviashchennaia Problemam Fiziologicheskogo Ucheniia Akademika I. P. Pavlova.*

17. For a discussion of work done in Soviet medical psychology, especially during the war, and an elucidation of its relationship to general psychology, see S. L. Rubinshtein, "Soviet Psychology in Wartime," *Philosophy and Phenomenological Research*, 1944, no. 2, pp. 181–198; Joseph Wortis, *Soviet Psychiatry* (Baltimore: Williams and Wilkins, 1950), *passim*, deals with these problems in greater detail. Wortis tends to stress the continuities, whereas I tend to stress the

discontinuities. I believe that in comparison to the situation in the United States and Western Europe, it is the discontinuities that stand out more boldly.

18. Unfortunately very little of this work has been made available to the English reading public. Probably the chapters "Sensation" and "Perception" in Rubinshtein (Foundations of General Psychology) give the most complete presentation of both theory and research in this area. A fair amount of work on problems of sensation has been abstracted in the *Psychological Abstracts* in the last few years.

19. S. V. Ivanov, (The Principle of Conscious Understanding in the Instruction), *SPed*, 1947, no. 10, pp. 49–61.

20. Similar treatments will be found in Rubinshtein (1946), chap. iv, and in the various editions of Kornilov *et al.*, the chapters on "Habit." These chapters, however, were written by Shvarts and are not, therefore, properly to be considered as additional sources. For critiques of behaviorist learning theories, see L. M. Shvarts, (Thorndike's Theoretical Conceptions in Pedagogical Practice), *SPed*, 1937, nos. 5–6, pp. 194–199; and L. M. Shvarts, (A Critical Analysis of Thorndike's Psychological Conceptions), *SPed*, 1937, no. 2, pp. 67–82.

21. Rubinshtein, *Osnovy Obshchei Psikhologii* (1946), p. 128.

22. *Ibid.*, p. 607.

23. See L. I. Bozhovich, (The Psychology and Instruction in Correct Writing), *NS*, 1940, no. 8, pp. 28–31.

24. N. A. Menchinskaia, (Questions of the Psychology of Teaching Arithmetic), *SPed*, 1938, no. 11, pp. 113–124.

25. Rubinshtein, *Osnovy Obshchei Psikhologii*, pp. 298–299.

26. Kornilov *et al.*, p. 429.

27. A. N. Leont'ev, (An Approach to the Theory of the Development of the Psyche of the Child), *SPed*, 1945, no. 4, pp. 34–44; M. V. Sokolov, (The Problem of the Development of the Psyche), *SPed*, 1949, no. 2, pp. 40–48.

28. Rubinshtein, *Osnovy Obshchei Psikhologii* (1946), chap. xvi (Activity), pp. 562–616.

29. For discussions of ability and aptitude, see Rubinshtein (1946), *passim*; B. M. Teplov, (The Problem of Aptitude), *SPed*, 1940, nos. 4–5, pp. 146–155; and Teplov's chapters in the 2d and 3d editions of Kornilov *et al.*; and S. F. Kozlov, (Aptitude and Ability), *SPed*, 1940, no. 6, pp. 92–101.

30. Teplov, *Psikhologiia* (Psychology; 2d ed; Moscow, 1948), p. 151.

31. V. E. Syrkina, (Typical Traits of Character in Various Concrete-Historical Conditions), *SPed*, 1948, no. 4, pp. 63–73.

32. Characteristic expressions of this sort of pressure will be found in V. Kolbanovskii, (For a Marxist Approach to the Problems of

Psychology—About S. L. Rubinshtein's Textbook "Foundations of General Psychology"), *Bol'shevik*, 1947, no. 17, pp. 50–56; and A. A. Smirnov (The Tasks and Content of Instruction in Psychology in Pedagogical and Teacher's Institutes), *SPed*, 1947, no. 12, pp. 60–69.

33. See *Pravda*, June 22 to July 9, 1950. *Nauchnaia Sessiia Posviashchennaia Problemam Fiziologicheskogo Ucheniia Akademika I. P. Pavlova* (The Scientific Session Dedicated to the Problems of the Physiological Teachings of Academician I. P. Pavlov).

34. *Nauchnaia Sessiia . . .*

35. *Pavlovskie Sredy* (Pavlovian Wednesdays; 3 vols.; Moscow-Leningrad, 1949).

36 Cf. S. Petrushevskii, "The Teachings of I. P. Pavlov and the Marxist-Leninist Theory of Reflection," *Meditsinskii Rabotnik*, August 23, 1951, p. 2.

37. See Petrushevskii, "The Teachings of I. P. Pavlov"; E. N. Sokolov, "Perception in the Light of I. P. Pavlov's Doctrine of Temporal Connections," *SPed*, 1951, no. 7, pp. 27–41; N. A. Khromov, "Against Idealism and Metaphysics in the Conception of the Psyche," *Nevropatologiia i Psikhiatriia*, 1951, no. 2, pp. 82–90.

38. E. G. Vatsuro, "The Teachings of I. P. Pavlov and Certain Questions of Psychology," *SPed*, 1951, no. 9, p. 59.

39. S. D. Kaminskii and Iu. G. Shevvhenko, "A Perverted Theory Which Gives Rise to Perversions in Practice," *Nevropatol. i Psikhiatr.*, 1951, no. 1, p. 26.

40. *SPed*, 1951, no. 8, pp. 105–113.

CHAPTER 11: PSYCHOLOGY AND THE SOVIET SYSTEM

1. The Bolsheviks were not the first group to run into the difficulties of fashioning an effective doctrine of social control with the use of a determinist model of human nature. The Calvinists faced this problem several centuries ago with the doctrine of predestination. Supposedly a person would gain eternal salvation independently of how he acted on this earth. This doctrine simultaneously deprived society of any effective supernatural sanction over social behavior, and the individual of any way of reassuring himself of his salvation. Under pressure from the faithful, the leaders announced that they should act in a socially desirable manner in order to reassure themselves that they had grace. Thus moral behavior was defined as a manifestation of grace rather than as a means of gaining grace. In this fashion it was possible indirectly to use supernatural sanction as a means of social control.

The history of this problem in Thomist theology and psychology is so neatly parallel to that of Soviet psychology and ideology that it is worth considering at some length. The first point of similarity is the attitude of Thomists toward determinism and freedom. Thomas Aquinas taught a doctrine of predestination, but held at the same time that man has freedom of will, with the two concepts being so defined as to be contradictory. Much like present-day Marxists, he attempted to reconcile the two positions by an elaborate framework of argument.

"But although Aquinas teaches a doctrine of predestination, he never ceases to emphasize freedom as one of its fundamental doctrines. To bridge the contrast between the doctrine of freedom and that of predestination, he is obliged to use the most complicated constructions; but, although these constructions do not seem to solve the contradictions satisfactorily, he does not retreat from the doctrine of freedom of will and of human effort, as being of avail for man's salvation, even though the will itself may need the support of God's grace" (Erich Fromm, *Escape from Freedom* [New York, 1941], p. 70).

In present-day Thomistic psychology this has ceased to be a considerable problem. The doctrine of determinism has tended to become completely lost and only the emphasis on freedom of will remains. (Cf. Mortimer Adler, *What Man Has Made of Man* [New York, 1937], and R. E. Brennan, *Thomistic Psychology* [New York, 1941], for a modern version of Thomistic psychology.)

Another point of similarity is the Thomistic tendency to stress the pragmatic effects of theory, their insistence that a theory may say one thing, but direct the attention in a direction that negates what it says. Compare Father Brennan's critique of Freud to the Soviet critique: "It is not enough to say that Freud himself had no intention of denying free will, that he had a deep respect for reason which he sought to liberate from the forces of instinct. The fact remains that the very conditions he set for the exercise of human conduct put man's will face to face with a *tour de force*. In practice Freud would say that we are free. Once asked if a man could be held responsible for his dreams, he replied: 'Whom else would you hold responsible?' But this does not rid his system of its deterministic implications . . . I doubt that Freud, with all his profound interest in human nature, really understood the metaphysical meaning of that nature" (R. E. Brennan, *History of Psychology from the Standpoint of a Thomist* [New York, 1945], p. 234).

Finally, Adler argues that if Marxists really understood their philosophy, they would adopt the Thomistic-Aristotelian formulation of holomorphism (or *formal* materialism) as an escape from the limitations of mechanical materialism. The fact that he made this "prediction" seven or more years after Soviet philosophers had reached the same conclusion detracts in no way from the acuity of his insight (Adler, *What Man Has Made of Man*, pp. 166 ff.).

2. During the middle and late twenties this issue was debated in American psychological journals. The question of whether or not behaviorism is consistent with ethics was raised repeatedly. For an especially pertinent interchange, see A. P. Weiss, "Behaviorism and Ethics," *JASP*, 1928, no. 22, pp. 388–397, and W. H. Roberts, "Behaviorism, Ethics, and Professor Weiss," *JASP*, 1929, no. 23, pp. 393–396.

3. These observations are based partially on my own observations, partially on those of a wide variety of Western observers, and to a considerable extent on the statements of members of both the recent Soviet emigration and the older Russian and early Soviet emigration, with whom the new émigrés are contrasted.

4. Shpil'rein's case was mentioned in Chapter IX, p. 128. Professor Vashchenko, a Ukrainian psychologist, has informed me that he was arrested for "Trotskyism" in 1935. Other cases have been reported to me, but less reliably.

5. This point is made very cogently by J. R. Kantor, "Current Trends in Psychological Theory," *Psychological Bulletin*, January 1941, pp. 29–65, *passim*.

6. An amusing illustration of this is an incident which happened to an American sociologist of my acquaintance. He explained to a recent Soviet émigré in some detail what a sociologist is and does. The ex-Soviet citizen listened in puzzlement for a while. Finally his face lit up and he said, "Oh, that sounds like what we call Marxism-Leninism!"

7. Cf. Bauer, "The Genetics Controversy and the Psychological Sciences in the USSR."

INDEX

Ach, N., 59
Adaptation, 27, 75, 76, 97
Adler, Alfred, 97, 98
Adolescence, 85
Agit-Prop Bureau, 52, 65
Agricultural production, 20, 21; effect of collectivization, 22
Allport, Gordon W., 139
All-Ukrainian Institute of Labor, 113
Animal psychology, 60, 118, 159, 160, 163–164
Anokhin, P. K., 171
Applied psychology, 59, 109, 120, 155, 157, 158, 163
Aptitudes and abilities, 167, 168
Artemov, V. A., 118
Associationism, 88, 173
Attitude studies, 110, 111, 120, 123, 154, 169, 186
Autogenetic movement, 28, 94, 95, 96, 97, 98, 124, 137, 149, 168
Avenarius, Richard, 71

Basov, M. Ia., 60, 71, 155
Behavior, determinants of, 68, 69, 70, 72, 73, 74–75, 79, 96–97, 123
Behaviorism, 51, 52, 53, 59–60, 62, 67, 68, 96, 97, 118, 134, 151, 154, 163
Bekhterev, V. M., 51, 52, 53, 55, 56, 57, 59, 62, 63, 64, 68, 69, 70, 71, 72, 75, 76, 77, 82, 86, 88, 118, 121
Beritashvilii (or Beritov), 171
Beritov, 171
Bernard, Claude, 75

Biogenetic law, 83. *See also* Ontogenetic law.
Biological endowment, *see* Heredity
Biology, 51, 55, 67, 75, 95, 96, 97, 144, 145, 146. *See also* Science
Blonskii, P. P., 52, 59, 71, 82, 83, 97, 117, 128
Boldyrev, V. N., 55
Borovskii, V. M., 60, 118
Bourgeois institutions, *see* Capitalism
Bourgeois morality, 38
Bourgeois racism, 145
Bühler, K., 98
Bukharin, N., 20, 21, 22, 23, 25, 26, 27, 28, 51, 65, 70, 81
Bykov, K. M., 171

Capitalism, 21, 98, 124, 147; analysis of by Marx and Engels, 14; and bourgeois institutions, 15, 19; conflict with needs of individual, 141, 142; function of scientific theories in, 105; function of social institutions in, 14, 50; role of psychotechnics in, 107, 108
Cattel, J. McK., 59
Central Committee (Communist Party), 63, 65; decree on the natural sciences, 26; on education, 64, 93, 100–101, 116, 123
Cerebral cortex, 171
Chance, 94. *See also* Determinism
"Character," 166, 167
Chauvinism, 110, 111